Ramses

The Battle of Kadesh

Also by Christian Jacq

The Son of the Light
The Temple of a Million Years

Ramses

The Battle of Kadesh

Christian Jacq

Translated by Dorothy S. Blair

SIMON & SCHUSTER
A VIACOM COMPANY

First published in Great Britain by Simon & Schuster Ltd, 1998
A Viacom Company

Copyright © Éditions Robert Laffont, S.A., Paris, 1996
English Translation © Dorothy S. Blair, 1997

Simon & Schuster
West Garden Place
Kendal Street
London W2 2AQ

Simon & Schuster Australia
Sydney

Hardback: 0-684-82138-9
Trade paperback: 0-684-82121-4

1 3 5 7 9 10 8 6 4 2

A CIP catalogue record for this book is available
from the British Library.

Printed and bound in Great Britain by
The Bath Press, Bath

MAP OF EGYPT

N

Mediterranean Sea

Rosetta
Alexandria
Damietta
Port Said
Tanta
Zagazig
Cairo
Ismailia
Siwa
Oasis
Giza
Memphis
Saqqara
Suez
SINAI

LIBYAN

Lake Karun
El Faiyum

Bahariya
Oasis
Hermopolis

El Minya
Beni Hasan
Tell el-Amarna

Farafra Oasis

Asyut
ARABIAN
DESERT

Nile

Red

DESERT

Akhmim

Abydos
Dendera
Nag Hammadi
Qena
Dakhla
Oasis
Necropolis of Thebes
Luxor

Kharga Oasis
Esna
Edfu

Sea

Kom Ombo
Elephantine
Aswan
Philae

TROPIC OF CANCER

Abu Simbel

200 km

N U B I A

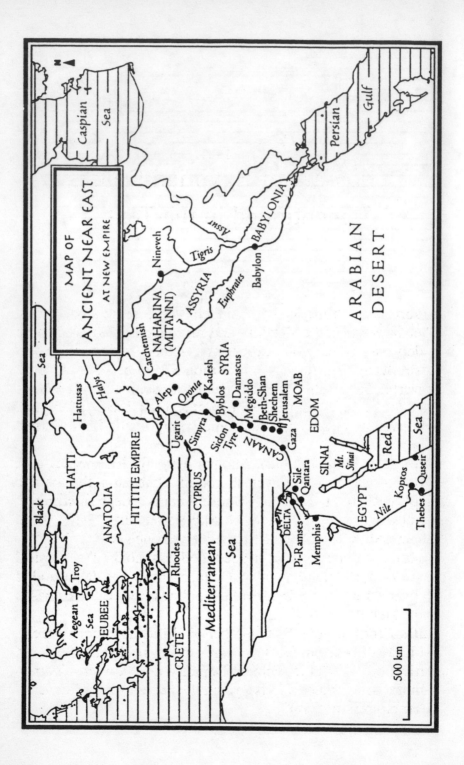

Glossary of Egyptian Deities
mentioned in the Text

Amon (also **Amun**). The 'hidden god', originally a local Theban deity, god of fertility and reproduction, then taken up widely as a war-god, procuring victory to the pharaohs. Assimilated with Ra (q.v.), as Amon-Ra, to become the most powerful god in the Egyptian pantheon, sometimes known as the King of the Gods, with temples at Karnak, Luxor, Memphis. Portrayed as a ram or a handsome young man with a plumed crown.

Aton (also **Aten** or **Adon**). Another name for Ra, the sun-god. Aton was the one, or universal, god of Akhenaton, the 'heretic king', probably the pharaoh whose dreams Joseph interpreted, thereby gaining his favour. Akhenaton may have been influenced by Joseph to adopt the idea of one god.

Bastet (or **Bast**). A cat-headed goddess holding a musical instrument, the guardian of the Delta, of music and dance and of pregnant women. The centre of her cult was the city of Bubastis in the Delta.

Hathor (or **Hather**). Wife/mother of Horus. A major goddess, the Lady of Heaven, Earth and the Underworld, a gentle deity, particularly helpful to women. Depicted as a cow or a woman with the head of a cow. Also given the name of Sekhmet (q.v.) in her aggressive form.

Horus. The son of Osiris (q.v.), the hawk-god and special protector of kings.

Isis. The wife of Osiris; had a reputation as a sorceress, but also represented the rich plains fertilized by the annual flooding of the Nile.

Ma'at. The wife of Thoth (q.v.); goddess of truth and justice, who presided over the judgment of the dead. She was regarded as a moral concept of reason, harmony and the right attitude of individuals to others.

Mut. The goddess-mother, wife of Amon-Ra, depicted as vulture-headed; the centre of her cult was a splendid temple in Thebes.

Osiris. The most widely worshipped of all the Egyptian gods. Identified with the fertile black soil of the Nile Valley, the annual cycle of flooding and new growth corresponding to the cycle of his life, death and rebirth.

Ptah. The local god of Memphis, regarded as the creator of all things, the source of moral order, the Lord of Truth and Justice. The patron of artisans and builders.

Ra. A sky-god, identified with the sun, the oldest and one of the greatest in the Egyptian pantheon. The centre of Ra's cult was Heliopolis (Greek: 'sun-city'). Akhenaton's universal god, Aton, was linked to Ra.

Sekhmet. The wife of Ptah, a lioness-headed goddess of war and healing, associated with Memphis; a figure to be placated. Took the form of a lioness to attack men who turned against Ra.

Set (**Seth**; also **Setekh**). One of the principal gods, sometimes seen as a Satan figure, representing powers of evil and destruction, requiring respect and placating. Storms, thunder, whirlwinds and hail were his instruments.

Thoth. The scribe of the gods, the god of wisdom and patron of science, literature and inventions and of the scribes in the temple. The inventor of writing, language and magic. Depicted as a man with the head of an ibis or as a baboon or dog-headed ape.

D. S. Blair

1

Danio's horse galloped along the scorching track that led to the Abode of the Lion, a little town in southern Syria, not much more than a village, founded by the renowned Pharaoh Seti. Danio, the son of an Egyptian father and a Syrian mother, had entered the honourable profession of courier, and specialized in the delivery of urgent dispatches. The Egyptian government provided him with a horse, food and clothing, accommodation in Sileh, a town on the north-east border, that went with his office, and the possibility of enjoying free lodgings at every staging post. In short, it was a good life, always on the move and with the opportunity to meet Syrian ladies, who were quite uninhibited but who occasionally showed a fancy to wed a government official; in which case he beat a hasty retreat as soon as the affair took too serious a turn.

Danio, whose parents had detected his true nature, thanks to the village astrologer, could not bear to remain enclosed, even in the arms of a saucy mistress. Nothing was more important for him than covering great distances and travelling a dusty road.

Conscientious and well-organized, the courier was well thought of by his superiors. Since the beginning of his career, he had let not a single letter go astray, and he often worked over the official time limit in order to satisfy an urgent customer. It was his sacred mission to deliver the dispatches as quickly as possible.

On Ramses' accession, after the death of Seti, Danio, like many Egyptians, had feared the young Pharaoh might turn out to be a warlord, ready to set forth with his army to conquer Asia, in the hope of restoring an immense empire, with Egypt at its centre. During the first four years of his reign, Ramses, in his youthful enthusiasm, had enlarged the Luxor temple, completed the gigantic Hall of Pillars in the Karnak temple, begun the construction of his Temple of a Million Years on the west bank of Thebes and built a new capital, Pi-Ramses, in the Nile Delta; but he had not modified his father's foreign policy, which consisted of observing a non-aggression pact with the Hittites, the redoubtable warriors of Anatolia. The latter seemed to have abandoned their attacks on Egypt and were respecting her protectorate of southern Syria.

The future would have been bright, had not the number of military dispatches between Pi-Ramses and the fortresses on the Way of Horus increased in unusual proportions. Danio had questioned his superiors and made inquiries among officers; no one knew anything, but there was talk of trouble in northern Syria in the province of Amurru,* which was under Egyptian influence. Evidently, the purpose of the dispatches Danio was carrying was to warn the commanders of the fortresses on the Way of Horus to be alert.

Thanks to Seti's energetic action, Canaan,† Amurru and southern Syria formed a vast buffer zone, protecting Egypt from any sudden attack. It is true they had to keep a constant eye on the princes of these unruly regions and frequently bring them to their senses; Nubian gold quickly allayed the vague tendencies to betrayal which emerged with every new season. The presence of Egyptian troops and the military

* Coinciding more or less with present-day Lebanon.
† Canaan was made up of Palestine and Phoenicia.

2

parades associated with important feasts, such as that of the harvest, were other effective means of preserving a fragile peace.

On several occasions in the past, the gates of the fortresses on the Way of Horus had been closed and foreigners forbidden to cross the border; the Hittites had never attacked them and the fear of bitter fights had vanished. So Danio remained optimistic; the Hittites knew the strength of the Egyptian army, the Egyptians feared the violence and cruelty of the Anatolians. It was in the interests of the two countries, which would both risk being bled white by a direct conflict, to remain ensconced in their positions and be satisfied with verbal challenges. Ramses, busy with his programme of great works, had no intention of provoking a confrontation.

Danio galloped past the stele which marked the limit of the farming region belonging to the Abode of the Lion. Suddenly he reined in his horse and turned back. He had noticed something unusual.

He dismounted in front of the stele. To his indignation he saw that the arch was damaged and several hieroglyphs had been erased. The magic inscription, now illegible, no longer protected the site. The person responsible for this destruction would be severely punished; the penalty for damaging a living stone was death.

The courier was doubtless the first witness of this tragedy. He would hasten to report it to the military governor of the region, who would draw up a detailed statement for Pharaoh.

A brick wall surrounded the town; a stone sphinx was set on either side of the entrance gate. The courier stopped short, aghast: the greater part of the outer wall had been destroyed, the two sphinxes lay on their sides, shattered.

The Abode of the Lion had been attacked.

Not a sound issued from the town. It was usually busy with infantry exercising, cavalry training, discussions in the main square near the fountain, children shouting, donkeys braying . . . The unaccustomed silence gripped the messenger by the throat. He unstoppered his gourd and took a long drink to cool his parched lips.

Curiosity overcame his fear. He could have turned back and warned the nearest garrison, but he wanted to know what had happened. He knew nearly all the inhabitants of the Abode of the Lion, from the governor down to the innkeeper; some of them were his friends.

His horse whinneyed and reared up; Danio patted the animal's neck, calmed it down, but it refused to go on. He entered the silent town on foot.

The corn silos had been ripped open, the oil jars smashed. Nothing remained of the stores of food and drink. The little two-storey houses were in ruins; none had escaped the attackers' destructive fury, which had not even spared the governor's dwelling.

Not one wall of the little temple still stood. The statue of the god had been smashed with a sledgehammer and decapitated.

And still that dense, oppressive silence.

Dead donkeys had been thrown into the well. In the main square, there still smouldered a fire in which furniture and papyrus had been burned.

The smell.

A sickly, acrid, nauseating smell which filled his nostrils and led him towards the butcher's stall at the northern edge of the town, under a wide portico, sheltered from the sun. That was where the slaughtered oxen were cut up, where the quarters of meat were cooked in a huge cauldron and where poultry was roasted on the spit. A noisy area where the courier liked to eat when he had delivered his dispatches.

What Danio saw next took his breath away.

There they all were: soldiers, merchants, artisans, old men, women, children, infants. All slaughtered, the corpses piled up on one another. The governor had been impaled, the three officers of the detachment hanged from the beam that supported the roof of the butcher's stall.

On a wooden pillar, an inscription in Hittite lettering: '*The army of Muwatallis, the mighty sovereign of Hatti, is victorious. So shall all his enemies perish.*'

The Hittites . . . In their customary fashion they had carried out an extremely violent raid, sparing not one of their opponents; but this time they had left their zone of influence to strike near Egypt's north-eastern border.

The courier was seized with panic. What if the Hittite raiding party was still lurking nearby?

Danio backed away, unable to take his eyes off the awful spectacle. How could anyone be so cruel as to massacre human beings and leave them without burial?

His head on fire, he returned to the gate of the sphinxes. His horse had vanished.

He anxiously scanned the horizon, fearing to see Hittite soldiers appear. There, in the distance, at the foot of a hill, a cloud of dust. Chariots . . . Chariots were approaching!

Mad with terror, Danio ran till his breath gave out.

2

Pi-Ramses, the new capital of Egypt, created by Ramses in the heart of the Delta, already had more than a hundred thousand inhabitants. Situated between two branches of the Nile, that of Ra and that of Avaris, it enjoyed a pleasant climate, even in summer. It was criss-crossed by numerous waterways and offered the pleasures of boating on its lake, while well-stocked ponds provided anglers with abundant catches.

The fertile countryside all around supplied a variety of foods. The exceptionally bright blue glazed tiles which adorned the façades of the houses everywhere had earned Pi-Ramses the name of the 'Turquoise City'.

A strange city, in truth: it was both a fortress, with four huge barracks and an arsenal situated near the palace, and at the same time a place of peace and harmony. For several months workmen had been busy night and day, manu-facturing chariots, armour, spears, shields and arrowheads. In the centre of the arsenal, there was a vast foundry with a section specializing in bronze work.

A war chariot, both sturdy and light, had just been completed. It was standing at the top of the ramp leading down to the main portico-ed courtyard, in which vehicles of the same type were stored, when the foreman tapped the joiner, who was checking the finish, on the shoulder.

'There, at the bottom of the ramp. It's him!'

'Him?'

The man looked.

It was indeed him, Pharaoh, the Lord of Upper and Lower Egypt, the Son of the Light, Ramses.

Now aged twenty-six, Seti's successor had been on the throne for four years and enjoyed the love and admiration of his people. Of athletic build, nearly six foot tall, with a long face crowned by a magnificent head of red-gold hair, a broad forehead, arching, bushy eyebrows, a long, thin, slightly hooked nose, bright, deep-set eyes, round ears with delicate rims, fleshy lips, firm chin, Ramses possessed a strength that some had no hesitation in calling supernatural.

For long trained to exercise power by a father who had initiated him into the duties of king by many harsh trials, Ramses had inherited the widespread authority of Seti, his glorious predecessor. Even when not wearing his ritual garments, his very presence commanded respect.

The king climbed up the ramp and examined the chariot. Petrified, the foreman and the joiner awaited his opinion with trepidation. For Pharaoh to come in person to inspect this factory without warning was proof of the interest he took in the quality of the weapons produced there.

Ramses was not satisfied with a superficial examination. He scrutinized each piece of wood, tested the strength of the shaft and assured himself of the quality of the wheels.

'Fine workmanship,' he judged, 'but the chariot's strength must be tried out on the ground.'

'That we intend to do, Majesty,' the foreman assured him. 'If there is any problem, the charioteer points out the weakness and we fix it immediately.'

'Are there many problems?'

'No, Majesty, and the workshop takes advantage of them to rectify mistakes and improve the material.'

'Do not relax your efforts.'

'Majesty, may I ask you something?'

'I am listening.'

'The war . . . is it imminent?'

'Would you be afraid, if it were?'

'We manufacture weapons, but we fear a conflict. How many Egyptians will die, how many women will be widowed, how many children will be left fatherless? May the gods grant that we avoid such a conflict!'

'May they hear your prayer! But what would be our duty if Egypt were threatened?'

The foreman lowered his eyes.

'Egypt is our mother, our past and our future,' Ramses reminded him. 'She gives without calculating, at every moment she offers us her bounty. Shall we answer her with ingratitude, selfishness and cowardice?'

'We want to live, Majesty!'

'If need be, Pharaoh himself will lay down his life in order that Egypt may live. Continue your work in peace, foreman.'

How bright and cheerful the capital was! Pi-Ramses was the realization of a dream, a moment of happiness that grew greater day by day. The former site of Avaris, a city cursed by the invaders from Asia, had been transformed into a delightful, elegant city, where acacias and sycamores bestowed their shade on rich and humble alike.

The king used to take pleasure in strolling in the country, with its lush pastures, flower-lined paths and waterways where it was good to bathe; he liked to sample an apple sweet as honey, or a mild onion, to wander through the vast olive grove, whose oil was as abundant as the sands on the river bank, and to breathe the sweet scents wafted from the gardens. He would end his walk at the inland port, which was increasingly busy, surrounded by warehouses in which the wealth of the city was stored – precious metals, rare woods, stocks of corn.

But in recent weeks Ramses had no longer strolled through the countryside, nor through the streets of his Turquoise City, but spent most of his time in the barracks, in the company of high-ranking officers, charioteers and infantrymen, who were very appreciative of their billets in the new premises.

The members of the professional army, which included many mercenaries, were delighted with their pay and the quality of the food. But many complained of the intensive training and regretted having joined up a few years previously at a time when peace seemed quite settled. The prospect of going from even the most rigorous exercises to fighting against the Hittites pleased no one, not even the most seasoned professionals. All feared the cruelty of the Anatolian warriors, who had never yet been defeated.

Ramses had sensed the fear gradually creeping into their minds, and tried to fight against the evil by visiting each barracks in turn and being present at the manoeuvres performed by the different brigades. The king had to appear calm and to maintain the confidence of his troops, even though his heart was tormented.

How could he be happy in this town from which Moses, his childhood friend, had fled, after overseeing the teams of Hebrew brickmakers who had erected palaces, villas and dwellings? True, Moses had been accused of slaying an Egyptian, Sary, the king's brother-in-law, but Ramses still had his doubts about this, since Sary, his former tutor, had plotted against him and had treated the workmen under him abominably. Had Moses fallen into a trap?

When he was not thinking of his friend, who had disappeared and could still not be found, the king spent long hours in the company of his elder brother, Shaanar, the minister for foreign affairs, and Ahsha, the head of intelligence. Shaanar had made every effort to prevent his younger brother from becoming Pharaoh, but his failure seemed to have brought him wisdom and he took his office seriously. As for Ahsha, a brilliantly clever diplomat, he had been a fellow student of Ramses and Moses at the Royal Academy of Memphis, and enjoyed the king's full confidence.

Every day the three men examined the messages from southern Syria and tried to judge the situation clearly.

How far could Egypt tolerate the Hittite advance? Ramses obsessively studied the huge map of the Middle East and Asia, hanging in his study. To the north, the kingdom of Hatti,* with its capital, Hattusa, in the heart of the Anatolian plateau. Further to the south, the immense land of Syria, along the shores of the Mediterranean, watered by the River Orontes. The principal fortified place in the land, Kadesh, was controlled by the Hittites. In the south, the province of Amurru and the ports of Byblos, Tyre and Sidon owed allegiance to Egypt; then Canaan, whose princes were loyal to Pharaoh.

Five hundred miles separated Pi-Ramses, the Egyptian capital, from Hattusa, the residence of Muwatallis, the Hittite sovereign. A glacis extending from the north-eastern border as far as central Syria seemed to protect both countries against any attempt at invasion.

But the Hittites were not satisfied with the state of affairs imposed by Seti. The Anatolian warriors had sallied forth from their territory and made a breakthrough in the direction of Damascus, Syria's principal city.

That, at any rate, was what Ahsha's spies had given him to believe. But Ramses needed to be certain before placing himself at the head of his army, with the firm intention of driving the enemy back towards the north. Neither Shaanar nor Ahsha could allow himself to express a categorical opinion. It was up to Pharaoh, and Pharaoh alone, to weigh his decision and to act.

Ramses' first impulse had been to counterattack as soon as

* Present-day Turkey.

he heard of the Hittites' machinations; but it was taking several weeks, if not months, to prepare his troops, of which the main body had been transferred from Memphis to Pi-Ramses. This delay, which the king bore impatiently, had perhaps allowed them to avoid a useless conflict: for over a week no alarming news had come from central Syria.

Ramses made his way to the palace aviary, where humming-birds, jays, tits, hoopoes, lapwings and a great many other varieties of bird flitted in the shade of the sycamores and skimmed the water in the pools where blue water-lilies grew.

He was sure to find her there, strumming an ancient air on her lute.

Nefertari, the Great Royal Wife, his sweet love, the only woman to fill his heart. Although not of noble birth, she was more beautiful than all the palace beauties and her voice, sweet as honey, never uttered a vain word.

At a time when the young Nefertari was destined to a life of meditation, a priestess, living the life of a recluse in a provincial temple, Prince Ramses had fallen madly in love with her. Neither of them had expected their union to lead to their becoming the royal couple, in charge of the destinies of Egypt.

Nefertari, with her glossy black hair and blue-green eyes, with her love of silence and meditation, had won over the whole court. Discreet and capable, she assisted Ramses and accomplished the miracle of combining the role of queen with that of wife.

Meritamon, the daughter she had borne to the king, resembled her. Nefertari could have no more children, but this suffering weighed no more heavily on her than a breeze in springtime. She felt her love for Ramses, which had been growing for nine years, to be one of the sources of her people's happiness.

Ramses stood watching her, unseen. The queen was

talking to a hoopoe which flitted around her, piping a few delighted notes, and then settled on her arm.

'You are near me, aren't you?'

He came forward. As usual, she had sensed his presence and what he was thinking.

'The birds are nervous today,' the queen remarked. 'A storm is brewing.'

'What are people talking about in the palace?'

'They try to forget their worries, joking about the enemy's cowardice, boasting of the strength of our weapons, announcing forthcoming marriages, watching out for possible appointments.'

'And what do they say about the king?'

'That he more and more resembles his father, and that he will be able to protect his country from misfortune.'

'If only the courtiers could speak the truth . . . '

Ramses took Nefertari in his arms; she laid her head on his shoulder.

'Bad news?'

'Everything seems calm.'

'Have the Hittite incursions stopped?'

'Ahsha has received no alarming message.'

'Are we ready to fight?'

'None of the soldiers is ready to confront the Anatolian warriors. The old campaigners think we stand no chance of defeating them.'

'What do *you* think?'

'To undertake a war on this scale requires experience I do not possess. My father himself abandoned such a risky venture.'

'If the Hittites have modified their attitude, it's because they believe victory to be within their grasp. In the past, the queens of Egypt fought with all their might to preserve the independence of their country. Although I abhor violence, I shall be at your side if conflict is the only solution.'

12

Suddenly the aviary was the scene of noisy agitation. The hoopoe flew up to the highest branch of a sycamore and the birds scattered in every direction.

Ramses and Nefertari looked up and caught sight of a carrier pigeon, flying with difficulty; it seemed exhausted and was trying in vain to reach its destination. The king stretched out his arms to welcome it. The pigeon alighted in front of him.

A little roll of papyrus, a few inches long, was fastened to its right claw. The text, written in minute but legible hieroglyphs, was signed by one of the army's scribes.

As he read it, Ramses felt as if a sword were piercing his flesh.

'You were right,' he said to Nefertari. 'A storm was brewing. And it has just broken.'

3

The great audience chamber in Pi-Ramses was one of the wonders of Egypt. It was reached by a monumental staircase, adorned with statues of slain enemies. They personified the forces of evil, which were endlessly reborn, and which Pharaoh alone could subject to Ma'at, the law of harmony, of which the queen was the living embodiment.

Around the entrance, the monarch's coronation names were painted in blue on a white ground and placed in cartouches, ovals symbolizing the cosmos, the kingdom of Pharaoh, son of the creator and his representative on earth. Anyone crossing the threshold of Ramses' domain would be aware of its serene beauty.

The floor was covered with glazed, painted terracotta tiles depicting fountains and flower gardens. There, a duck could be seen swimming on a blue-green pond, here a *boulti* fish threading its way among white water-lilies, On the walls, birds flitted merrily in an enchanting marshland scene all pale greens, deep reds, light blue, golden-yellow and off-white, while the eye was beguiled by floral friezes representing water-lilies, poppies, marguerites and cornflowers.

For many, the outstanding artistic achievement of the whole chamber, itself a hymn to the perfection of nature tamed, was the face of a young woman deep in meditation before a clump of hollyhocks. The resemblance to Nefertari was so striking that no one doubted the tribute thus paid by the sovereign to his spouse.

As he climbed the steps to his golden throne – on the top step was carved a lion closing its jaws on an enemy emerging from the shadows – Ramses glanced briefly at the roses, imported from the Egyptian protectorate of southern Syria, whose thorns pierced his heart.

The whole assembled court fell silent.

Those present included the ministers with their deputies, the ritualists, royal scribes, magicians and their experts in sacred lore, the officials in charge of the daily offerings, the keepers of the secrets, great ladies who occupied official posts and all the men and women whom Remet, the jovial, conscientious palace steward, had admitted.

It was rare for Ramses to summon such a large audience, who would then immediately repeat his discourse, allowing its tenor to reverberate rapidly throughout the land. All held their breath, fearing the announcement of a disaster.

The king was wearing the double crown – which combined the Red Crown of Lower Egypt and the White Crown of Upper Egypt – the symbol of the essential unity of the country. On his chest, the power-sceptre, the *sekhem*, which indicated Pharaoh's mastery over the elements and the life-giving forces.

'A Hittite raiding party has destroyed the Abode of the Lion, a village founded by my father. The barbarians have massacred all the inhabitants, including women, children and infants in arms.'

A murmur of anger arose. No soldier of any army had the right to act like that.

'A courier discovered this shameful deed,' the king continued. 'He was brought back, crazed with terror, by one of our patrols, who reported this to me. To this slaughter, the Hittites added the destruction of the local sanctuary and the profanation of Seti's stele.'

15

Greatly distressed, the head keeper of secrets, a handsome old man in charge of the palace archives, left the crowd of courtiers and bowed before Pharaoh. 'Majesty, have we proof that the Hittites are really the authors of this crime?'

'They left their signature: "The army of Muwatallis, the mighty sovereign of Hatti, is victorious. So shall all his enemies perish." I can also tell you that the princes of Amurru and Palestine have pledged allegiance to the Hittites. Some Egyptian residents there have been killed and the survivors have taken refuge in our fortresses.'

'Then, Majesty, it is—'

'War.'

Ramses' office was spacious, light and airy; the windows, whose frames were covered with blue and white glazed tiles, allowed the king to enjoy the perfection of each season and the intoxicating scent of a thousand and one flowers. Bunches of lilies were scattered on small gilded tables and papyrus scrolls lay open on a long acacia-wood table. In one corner of the room stood a diorite statue of Seti seated on his throne, looking up towards the heavens.

Ramses had summoned a small council, restricted to his friend and loyal private secretary, Ahmeni, his elder brother, Shaanar, and Ahsha.

Ahmeni was small, thin, pale and almost bald at twenty-four; his long, delicate hands, slight build and weak back made him unfit for any sport and he had dedicated his life to serving Ramses. He was a tireless worker, at his desk day and night, sleeping little and able in one hour to absorb more dossiers than his team of experienced scribes could manage in a week. Sandal-bearer to Ramses, Ahmeni could have claimed any ministerial post, but he preferred to remain in Pharaoh's shadow.

'The magicians have done what is necessary,' he stated. 'They made wax statuettes in the form of Asiatics and Hittites

16

and threw them into the fire. They also inscribed the enemies'
names on vases and terracotta dishes which they then
smashed. I have recommended them to perform the same rites
every day until our army sets out.'

Shaanar shrugged. Ramses' elder brother, stocky and
running to fat, had a round moon face and podgy cheeks. His
lips were thick and greedy-looking; he had small brown eyes
and an unctuous, hesitating voice; he had shaved off the beard
he had grown during the mourning period for his father, Seti.

'We must not depend on magic,' he recommended. 'I, as
minister for foreign affairs, propose to recall our ambassadors
from Syria, Amurru and Palestine. They are toadies who can't
see the spider's webs the Hittites have woven in our
protectorates.'

'That has already been done,' Ahmeni said.

'I should have been told,' Shaanar replied with irritation.

'It has been done, that's the main thing.'

Indifferent to this verbal sparring, Ramses placed his
finger on a particular spot on the large map unrolled on the
acacia-wood table. 'Are the garrisons on the north-west
frontier in a state of alert?'

'Yes, Majesty,' replied Ahsha. 'No Libyan can cross it.'

The only son of a wealthy, noble family, Ahsha was every
inch the aristocrat, elegant, refined, an arbiter of fashion, with
a long, fine-boned face, bright eyes and a slightly disdainful
look. He spoke several foreign languages and was passionate
about international relations.

'Our patrols control the Libyan border strip and the desert
zone to the west of the Delta. Our fortresses are on full alert
and will have no difficulty in containing any attack – though
an attack seems unlikely: no warrior is able, at the present
time, to unite the Libyan tribes.'

'Is that conjecture or certainty?'

'Certainty.'

'At last some reassuring information!'

17

'That is all there is, Majesty. My agents have just let me know of appeals for help from the mayors of Meggido, where caravans arrive, of Damascus and of the Phoenician ports, the destination of many merchant ships. Hittite raids and the destabilization of the region are already upsetting commerce. Unless we intervene quickly, the Hittites will isolate us from our allies and then annihilate them. The world that Seti and his ancestors built will be destroyed.'

'Do you think, Ahsha, that I'm not aware of that?'

'Can one ever be sufficiently aware of a threat of death, Majesty?'

'Have all the resources of diplomacy really been used?' inquired Ahmeni.

'The population of a village has been massacred,' Ramses reminded him. 'After such a grisly deed, what diplomacy can we use?'

'War will cause thousands of deaths.'

'Is Ahmeni suggesting that we capitulate?' asked Shaanar slyly.

The king's private secretary clenched his fists. 'Withdraw your question, Shaanar!'

'Are you finally prepared to fight, Ahmeni?'

'Enough,' interrupted Ramses. 'Keep your energy for defending Egypt. Shaanar, are you in favour of immediate, direct armed intervention?'

'I'm not sure . . . Wouldn't it be better to wait till we've strengthened our defences?'

'The supply corps isn't ready,' Ahmeni made clear. 'To set out on a campaign with only those means already available would lead to disaster.'

'The longer we temporize,' Ahsha ventured, 'the more the rebellion in Canaan will spread. It must be put down rapidly so as to restore a buffer zone between us and the Hittites. Otherwise, they will have an advance base from which to prepare an invasion.'

'Pharaoh must not risk his life rashly,' said Ahmeni, annoyed.

'Are you accusing me of irresponsibility?' asked Ahsha icily.

'You do not know the real state of our troops! Their equipment is still inadequate, even with the arsenals working flat out.'

'Whatever the difficulties, we must restore order in our protectorates without delay. Egypt's survival is at stake.'

Shaanar was careful not to intervene in the argument between the two friends. Ramses, who had equal confidence in Ahmeni and Ahsha, had listened attentively to them both.

'Leave me,' he commanded.

When he was alone, the king gazed at the sun, the creator of light from which he came.

As the Son of the Light, he was able to look straight into the sun without scorching his eyes.

'Value the radiance and genius of every being,' Seti had recommended. 'Seek in everyone that which is irreplaceable. But you will be the only one to make decisions. Love Egypt more than yourself, and the way will become clear.'

Ramses thought of what each of the three men had said. Shaanar, hesitant, had above all not wanted to displease; Ahmeni wished to preserve the country as a sanctuary and rejected the reality beyond its borders; Ahsha had a global view of the situation and did not seek to hide its seriousness.

Other cares troubled the king: had Moses been caught up in the turmoil? Ahsha, charged with finding him, had been unable to discover any trace of him. His informers remained silent. If the Hebrew had managed to leave Egypt, he would have made his way either towards Libya, or towards the principalities of Edom and Moab, or possibly towards Canaan or Syria. In a time of calm, an informer would eventually have tracked him down. At present, if Moses was still alive, only chance would reveal where he was hiding.

Ramses

Ramses left the palace and made his way to his generals'
residence. His only care must be to speed up his army's
preparations.

4

Shaanar, the minister for foreign affairs, slid the two wooden bolts that secured the door of his office, then looked out of the windows to make sure there was no one in the inner courtyard. He had taken the precaution of ordering the guard on duty in the antechamber to take up his position at the far end of the corridor.

'No one can overhear us,' he told Ahsha.

'Would it not have been wiser to go somewhere else to review the situation?'

'We have to give the impression of working day and night to secure the country's safety. Ramses has ordered all officials who are absent without valid reason to be recalled immediately. We are at war, my dear Ahsha!'

'Not yet.'

'It's obvious the king has made up his mind. You convinced him.'

'I hope so, but we must be circumspect. Ramses is often unpredictable.'

'Our little game succeeded perfectly. My brother believes that I am undecided and don't dare commit myself, for fear of displeasing him. You, on the other hand, with your forcefulness and incisiveness, accentuated my weakness. How could Ramses suspect we are in collusion?'

Shaanar contentedly filled two goblets with white wine

from the city of Imau, famed for its vineyards.

The office of the minister for foreign affairs, unlike that of the king, was not a model of restraint. The panels of the chairs were decorated with water-lilies, there were richly coloured cushions, little tables on bronze pedestals; the walls were covered with painted scenes of marsh-bird shooting and, best of all, there was a profusion of exotic vases from Libya, Babylon, Crete, Rhodes, Greece and Asia. Shaanar adored them. He had paid high prices for most of these unique specimens, but his passion was insatiable and he was filling his villas in Thebes, Memphis and Pi-Ramses with these marvels.

The creation of the new capital, which he had felt to be an intolerable victory for Ramses, turned out to be a stroke of good fortune. Here, he was nearer to the Hittites, who had decided to put him in power, and also to the centre of manufacture of these incomparable vases. To see them, caress them, recall their provenance, filled him with indescribable pleasure.

'I'm not happy about Ahmeni,' Ahsha admitted. 'He does not lack intuition and—'

'Ahmeni is a fool and a weakling, who stagnates in Ramses' shade. His servility prevents him seeing and hearing anything.'

'Nevertheless, he criticized my attitude.'

'That little scribe thinks that Egypt is the whole world, that she can shelter behind her fortresses, close her borders and so prevent any enemy from invading. He's so fanatically anti-war that he's convinced the only chance of peace is to withdraw. So it was inevitable that he would clash with you, but he will help us.'

'Ahmeni is Ramses' closest adviser,' Ahsha objected.

'In times of peace, certainly; but the Hittites have declared war, and your words were quite convincing. And you're forgetting the Queen Mother, Tuya, and the Great Royal

Wife, Nefertari.'

'Do you think they love war?'

'They hate it, but the queens of Egypt have always fought till their last breath to safeguard the Two Lands, and often took remarkable initiatives. It was the great ladies of Thebes who reorganized the army and encouraged it to drive the Hyskos invaders out of the Delta. Tuya, my revered mother, and Nefertari, this enchantress who has the court in her power, will be no exception to the rule. They'll urge Ramses to attack.'

'I hope your optimism is justified.'

Ahsha sipped the strong, fruity wine. Shaanar greedily drained his goblet. Even when dressed in costly tunics and shirts, he never managed to look as elegant as the diplomat.

'It is, dear friend, it is! Are you not head of our spy network, one of Ramses' childhood friends and the only man he listens to in matters of foreign politics?'

Ahsha nodded.

'We are nearing our goal,' Shaanar continued excitedly. 'Ramses will be either killed in battle or defeated; if he is dishonoured, he will be forced to relinquish power. In either case, I shall appear as the only one able to negotiate with the Hittites and save Egypt from disaster.'

'There will be a price to pay for this peace,' Ahsha made clear.

'I have not forgotten our plan. I shall lavish gold on the princes of Canaan and Amurru, I shall offer fabulous gifts to the Hittite emperor and pour out a stream of no less fabulous promises! Egypt may be impoverished for some time, but I shall reign. And Ramses will quickly be forgotten. The weapon I shall use is the stupidity and sheeplike character of the people, who detest today what they will adore tomorrow.'

'Have you abandoned the idea of a vast empire, reaching from the heart of Africa to the plateaux of Anatolia?'

Shaanar looked thoughtful. 'It is true I did mention this to you, but with an eye to trade. When peace is restored we shall create new commercial ports, develop the caravan routes and form ecomomic links with the Hittites. Then Egypt will be too small for me.'

'And suppose your empire were also to be . . . political?'

'I don't follow you.'

'Muwatallis rules the Hittites with an iron fist, but there is much intrigue at the court in Hattusa. Two people are thought to be his possible successors: the one, Uri-Teshup, much in evidence, and the other, more discreet, Hattusilis, the priest of the goddess Ishtar. If Muwatallis died in battle, one of them would seize power. Now, these two men detest each other and their supporters are ready to be at one another's throats.'

Shaanar stroked his chin. 'Are you saying that there's more to this than mere palace feuds?'

'Much more. The Hittite kingdom risks falling apart.'

'If it broke into several pieces, a saviour could reunite them under his banner and join those territories to the Egyptian provinces. What an empire, Ahsha, what a vast empire! Babylon, Assyria, Cyprus, Rhodes, Greece and the northern lands would be my future protectorates!'

The young diplomat smiled. 'The pharaohs lacked ambition because the only thing they cared about was their people's happiness and Egypt's prosperity. You, Shaanar, are different. That is why Ramses must be eliminated, by one means or another.'

Shaanar did not feel like a traitor. If illness had not weakened Seti's mind, the dead pharaoh would have offered the throne to him, his elder son. The victim of injustice, Shaanar would fight to regain what belonged to him by right.

He gazed at Ahsha inquisitively. 'Naturally you haven't told Ramses everything.'

'Naturally, but the king has access at all times to all the messages I receive through my agents. They are registered and filed in this secretariat. None can be spirited away or destroyed without attracting attention and laying me open to suspicion of malpractice.'

'Has Ramses made an inspection yet?'

'Not yet, but we are on the eve of war. So I must take every precaution and not lay myself open to any unexpected checks by him.'

'What measures will you take?'

'I've told you: no report is missing, every one is complete.'

'In which case, Ramses knows everything!'

Ahsha gently ran his finger round the rim of his alabaster goblet. 'Spying is a difficult art, Shaanar; the raw fact is important, its interpretation even more so. My role consists of forming a synthesis of the facts and giving the king an interpretation to trigger his action. In the present situation, he cannot reproach me with either weakness or indecision; I insisted on his organizing a counteroffensive as quickly as possible.'

'You're playing his game, not that of the Hittites!'

'You're only considering the raw facts,' Ahsha retorted. 'That will also be Ramses' reaction. Who will reproach him for it?'

'What do you mean?'

'The transfer of troops from Memphis to Pi-Ramses has posed a number of problems of supply which are far from being solved. By encouraging Ramses to hurry we shall gain our first advantage: an insurmountable obstacle for our soldiers, whose equipment is inadequate in quality and quantity.'

'And what are the other advantages?'

'The terrain itself and the extent of the defection among our allies. While not hiding this from Ramses, I did not stress the extent of the inferno. The savagery of the Hittite raids and the massacre at the Abode of the Lion have terrorized the princes of Canaan and Amurru and the governors of the coastal ports. Seti respected the Hittite warriors; Ramses

25

doesn't. All the local potentates, afraid of being annihilated in their turn, will prefer to place themselves under the protection of Muwatallis.'

'So they are convinced that Ramses won't come to their assistance and have decided to be the first to attack Egypt, so as to satisfy their new master, the Emperor of Hatti. Is that it?'

'That is one interpretation of the facts.'

'And is it yours?'

'Mine includes a few supplementary details. Does the silence of certain of our fortified places mean that the enemy has occupied them? If so, Ramses will meet a much bitterer resistance than was foreseen. What is more, the Hittites have probably delivered a large quantity of arms to the rebels.'

Shaanar opened his mouth, as if eager for a tasty morsel. 'Fine surprises in store for the Egyptian battalions! Ramses could be defeated at the first battle, even before confronting the Hittites!'

'Such a hypothesis is not to be ignored,' ventured Ahsha.

5

Tuya, the Queen Mother, was resting in the palace garden at the end of a trying day. She had celebrated the dawn ritual in a shrine dedicated to the goddess Hathor, the Lady of the Sun, then dealt with some problems of protocol, listened to some courtiers' complaints, and had an interview with the minister for agriculture at Ramses' request and then a talk with Nefertari, the Great Royal Wife.

Tuya, an undisputed moral authority, was slender, with huge almond eyes that were stern and piercing, a straight and delicately formed nose and an almost square chin. The coiled locks of her wig covered her ears and the back of her neck; she wore a long linen dress immaculately pleated, round her neck a collar composed of six rows of amethysts, and golden bracelets on her wrists. Whatever the time of day, Tuya was impeccably attired.

Every day she missed Seti more and more. Time made the dead pharaoh's absence more and more cruel, and his widow yearned to make that final journey which would allow her to join her husband.

Yet the royal couple afforded her many joys: Ramses had the makings of a great monarch and Nefertari of a great queen. Just like Seti and herself, they loved their country passionately and would sacrifice their lives for it if fate so demanded.

When Ramses approached her, Tuya knew instantly that her son had just made a grave decision. The king gave his mother his arm and they took a few steps along the sandy path, between two rows of tamarisks in flower. The air was warm and fragrant.

'The summer will be merciless,' she said. 'Fortunately you have chosen a good minister for agriculture; the dykes will be strengthened and the conservation basins for the irrigation waters enlarged. The rise in the water levels should be good and the crops will be abundant.'

'My reign could have been long and happy.'

'Why should it not be so? The gods have favoured you and nature herself offers you her bounty.'

'War is inevitable.'

'I know, my son. You have made the right decision.'

'I needed your approval.'

'No, Ramses; since Nefertari shares your thoughts, the royal couple is entitled to act.'

'My father gave up fighting the Hittites.'

'The Hittites seemed to have given up fighting the Egyptians. If they had broken the truce, Seti would have launched an offensive without delay.'

'Our soldiers are not prepared.'

'They are afraid, aren't they?'

'Who can blame them?'

'You.'

'The old campaigners are spreading terrifying tales about the Hittites.'

'Are they such as to frighten Pharaoh?'

'The time to dissipate mirages—'

'They will only be dissipated on the battlefield, when courage will save the Two Lands.'

Meba, the former minister for foreign affairs, had no love for Pharaoh. Convinced that the king had relieved him of his post without cause, he was only waiting for an opportunity to have his revenge. Like several members of the court, he had counted on the young Pharaoh failing after four years of success, and admitting defeat when finally tested.

The rich and worldly Meba, with his broad face and martial bearing, was chatting idly about the high society of Pi-Ramses with a dozen notables. The food was excellent, the women superb; after all, he had to pass the time somehow while waiting for Shaanar's arrival.

A servant murmured something in Meba's ear.

The diplomat immediately rose to his feet. 'My friends, the king is on his way; he is honouring us with his presence.'

Meba's hands trembled. Ramses was not in the habit of appearing like this at a private reception.

They all bowed simultaneously.

'You do us too much honour, Majesty! Will you sit down with us?'

'There's no point. I come to announce war.'

'War . . . '

'Perhaps, amidst your festivities, you have heard that our enemies are at the gates of Egypt?'

'It is our main concern,' Meba assured him.

'Our soldiers fear that hostilities have become inevitable,' declared an experienced scribe. 'They know they'll have to march in the heat of the sun, heavily laden, and advance along difficult paths. It'll be impossible to quench their thirst fully, as water will be rationed. Even if their legs arc giving way, they'll have to march on, forgetful of their aching backs and empty bellies. Will they be able to rest when they reach camp? Not a hope, with tasks to be undertaken before they can stretch out on their mats. When the alarm sounds, you jump up, your eyes bleary with sleep. Your food is bad, your wounds receive only cursory treatment. And what about the enemy arrows and javelins, the constant danger, death lurking nearby?'

'Fine words by a well-read scribe,' declared Ramses. 'I too know this old text by heart. But today it's not a question of literature.'

'We have confidence in our army's courage, Majesty,' proclaimed Meba, 'and we know that it will be victorious, whatever sufferings it has to endure.'

'Moving words, but they are not enough. I know your courage and that of the nobles present here, and I am proud to receive, this very moment, your promise to enlist as volunteers.'

'Majesty . . . Our professional army should suffice for the task!'

'They need men of quality to train and supervise the young recruits. Is it not up to the nobles and the wealthy citizens to set an example? You are all expected at the main barracks tomorrow morning.'

The Turquoise City was in ferment. Transformed into a military base, a command post for the chariots, an assembly place for the infantry regiments, an anchorage for the war fleets, it also witnessed manoeuvres and training exercises from dawn to dusk. Delegating to Tuya, Nefertari and Ahmeni the conduct of internal affairs of state, Ramses spent his days in the arsenals and barracks.

The king's presence was reassuring and stimulating; he checked the quality of the spears, swords and shields, inspected the new recruits, chatted to high-ranking officers and simple soldiers alike, promising all of them pay proportionate to their bravery. The mercenaries were assured of receiving good rewards if they led Egypt to victory.

Ramses paid great attention to the horses' welfare; the fate of the battle would depend to a large extent on their good physical condition. Gutters ran through the shingle flooring of every stable, in the middle of which stood a tank that served both to water the animals and to keep the premises clean. Every day, he inspected different stalls, examined the horses and severely punished any slovenliness.

The army gathered in Pi-Ramses was beginning to function as one huge body, governed by a head to whom appeal was made in every case. Always available, intervening rapidly, the king left nothing unclarified and decided any dispute on the spot. Solid trust was established. Every soldier felt that orders were given advisedly and that the troops formed a veritable war machine.

To see Pharaoh so close and sometimes to be able to talk to him were privileges which astonished the soldiers, commissioned or not. Many of the courtiers would have liked to have such good fortune. The king's attitude infused the men with unusual energy, new strength. Yet at the same time Ramses remained distant and inaccessible. He remained Pharaoh, that unique being, driven by a different life.

When Ramses saw Ahmeni enter the barracks where he had once saved him from his persecutors, he was truly astonished. His loyal secretary loathed this sort of place.

'Have you come to wield the sword or the spear?'

'Our poet has arrived in Pi-Ramses and wishes to see you.'

'Have you settled him in?'

'In a house identical to the one he had in Memphis.'

Seated beneath a lemon tree, his favourite tree of all, Homer was savouring an aromatic wine, spiced with aniseed and coriander, and smoking a pipeful of sage leaves tamped down into a thick snail shell; his skin was anointed with olive oil. He greeted the king gruffly.

'Don't get up, Homer.'

'I'm still capable of bowing to the Lord of the Two Lands.'

Ramses sat down on a folding stool beside the Greek poet. Hector, the latter's black and white cat, jumped on to the monarch's lap. As soon as it was stroked, it began to purr.

'How do you like my wine, Majesty?'

'It's a bit harsh, but I like its bouquet. How are you?'

'My bones ache, my sight is still failing, but the climate here relieves my pains.'

'Does this house please you?'

'It's perfect. The cook, the chambermaid and the gardener have accompanied me here; they are good folk, who manage to pamper me without getting in my way. Like me, they were curious to get to know your new capital.'

'Would you not have been more peaceful in Memphis?'

'There's nothing happening any more in Memphis! The fate of the world is being played out here. Who is better qualified than a poet to realize that? Listen to this: "Apollo will descend from heaven, full of wrath. He will advance, black as night, and launch his darts. From his silver bow will come a terrifying sound, warriors will be pierced by his arrows. Countless funeral pyres will be lit to consume the dead. Who will be able to flee from death?"'

'Verses from your *Iliad?*'

'Yes indeed, but do they really speak of the past? This Turquoise City, with its gardens and ornamental ponds, is being transformed into a war camp!'

'I have no choice, Homer.'

'War is mankind's shame, proof that man is a degenerate race, manipulated by invisible forces. Every line of the *Iliad* is an exorcism intended to root out violence from men's hearts, but my magic sometimes seems to me a mockery.'

'Nevertheless you must continue to write, and I must govern, even if my kingdom is transformed into a battleground.'

'It will be your first great war, will it not? And it will even be *the* great war . . . '

'It frightens me as much as you, but I have neither the time nor the right to be afraid.'

'Is it inevitable?'

'It is.'

'May Apollo strengthen your arm, Ramses, and may death be your ally!'

6

Raia, the Syrian merchant, of average height, with sharp brown eyes and a little pointed beard, had become the wealthiest trader in Egypt. Long settled in that country, he owned several stores in Thebes, Memphis and Pi-Ramses; he sold high-quality preserved meat and luxury vases imported from Syria and Asia. His clientele was affluent and refined, not hesitating to pay high prices for foreign craftsmen's masterpieces, which they displayed at banquets and receptions to dazzle their guests.

Courteous and discreet, Raia enjoyed an excellent reputation. Thanks to the rapid spread of his trade, he had acquired some dozen vessels and three hundred donkeys which allowed him to transport foodstuffs and objects rapidly from one city to another. Counting many friends in the government, the army and the police, Raia was one of the suppliers to the court and the nobility.

No one suspected that the amiable merchant was a spy in the service of the Hittites, that he received their coded messages hidden inside certain vases marked with a distinctive sign, and that he sent information to them through one of his agents in southern Syria. Thus Pharaoh's chief enemy obtained detailed information about the development of the situation in Egypt, the mood of the population, the economic and military capacity of the Two Lands.

When Raia introduced himself to the head steward of Shaanar's sumptuous residence, the latter seemed embarrassed.

'My master is very busy. He cannot be disturbed.'

'I have an appointment.'

'I'm very sorry.'

'Tell him I'm here, just the same, and tell him I'd like to show him an exceptional vase, a unique piece, from the hands of a most talented craftsman whose career has just ended.'

The steward hesitated. Knowing Shaanar's passion for exotic collector's pieces, he decided to inform him, at the risk of appearing importunate.

A quarter of an hour later, Raia saw a young person leave, a little too heavily made up, her hair hanging loose, with a tattoo on her naked left shoulder. Doubtless one of the ravishing foreign residents of the most sumptuous ale-house in Pi-Ramses.

'My master is ready for you,' said the steward.

Raia crossed a magnificent garden with a large ornamental pond in the middle, under shady palm trees.

Shaanar was taking the air, and looked weary as he rested on a couch. 'A nice kid, but exhausting. Some beer, Raia?'

'With pleasure.'

'The sole wish of quite a few court ladies is to marry me, but that type of foolishness does not tempt me. When I reign, it will be time to find a suitable wife. For the present, I like a variety of pleasures. And you, Raia? Not yet under the thumb of a female?'

'The gods preserve me, my lord! Business leaves me scarcely any free time.'

'You've a splendid find for me, so my steward tells me.'

From a canvas bag stuffed with rags, the merchant slowly withdrew a tiny porphyry vase with a handle in the shape of a deer. On its sides there were hunting scenes.

Shaanar stroked the piece, examined every detail. He rose

34

to his feet and walked round it, fascinated. 'What a marvel. What an incomparable marvel!'

'And its price is reasonable.'

'My steward will pay you.'

Shaanar whispered, 'And what is the message from my Hittite friends worth?'

'Ah, my lord! More than ever they are resolved to support you, and they consider you the successor to Ramses.'

On the one hand, Shaanar was using Ahsha to deceive Ramses; on the other, he was preparing his own future thanks to Raia, the Hittites' agent. Ahsha was ignorant of Raia's true role, Raia of Ahsha's. Shaanar was the true master of the game, moving the pawns at will, and keeping his secret allies separated in water-tight compartments.

The only unknown quantity, but an important one, was the Hittites.

By matching the information received from Ahsha with that which Raia was going to obtain for him, Shaanar would be able to form a firm opinion, without taking any ill-considered risks.

'What is the extent of the offensive, Raia?'

'The Hittite raiders have made murderous forays into central and southern Syria, along the Phoenician coast and into the province of Amurru, in order to terrorize the population. Their finest exploit is the destruction of the Abode of the Lion and the stele of Seti. They have caught people's imagination to the point of causing unexpected reversals of alliances.'

'Are Phoenicia and Palestine under Hittite control?'

'Better still, they have rebelled against Ramses! Their princes have taken up arms and occupied strongholds from which they have driven out the Egyptian soldiers. Pharaoh does not know that he will come up against a succession of defensive barriers which will exhaust his forces. As soon as Ramses' losses are high enough, the Hittite army will pounce on him and destroy him. That will be your opportunity, Shaanar; you will take the throne of Egypt and conclude a permanent alliance with the conqueror.'

Raia's predictions differed considerably from Ahsha's. In both cases, Shaanar would become Pharaoh in place of the dead or defeated Ramses. But in the first case he would be the Hittites' vassal whereas in the second he would get his hands on their empire. All would depend on the extent of Ramses' defeat and the damage inflicted by the Hittite army. True, his room for manoeuvre was limited, but success was possible, with one aim as a priority: the seizure of power in Egypt. Starting from that base, other conquests could be envisaged.

'How are the merchant cities reacting?'

'As usual, they tend to side with the strongest. Aleppo, Damascus, Palmyra and the Phoenician ports have already forgotten Egypt, and pay homage to Muwatallis, the Emperor of Hatti.'

'Doesn't this disrupt the prosperity of the Egyptian economy?'

'On the contrary! The Hittites are the finest fighters in Asia and the East, but wretched traders. They rely on you to reorganize the international exchanges – and to impose the levies due to you. I'm a merchant, don't forget, and I intend to remain in Egypt and get rich here. The Hittites will bring us the stability we need.'

'You shall be my minister for finance, Raia.'

'If it please the gods, we shall make our fortunes. The war won't last long. The main thing is to stay in the background and gather the fruits that fall from the tree.'

The beer was delicious, the shade refreshing.

'I'm not happy with Ramses' attitude,' Shaanar confessed.

The Syrian looked gloomy. 'What's Pharaoh doing?'

'He's constantly present in one or other of his barracks and inspires the soldiers with energy that they ought never to have. If he goes on like this, eventually they'll believe themselves invincible!'

'What else?'

'The manufacture of weapons goes on day and night.'

Raia scratched his pointed beard. 'That's not serious. The Egyptians are far too far behind schedule to be able to catch up with the Hittites. As for Ramses' influence, it will vanish with the first confrontation. When the Egyptians face the Hittites, it will be a rout.'

'Aren't you underestimating our troops?'

'If you'd witnessed a Hittite attack, you wouldn't reproach anyone for dying of fright.'

'One man at least will not feel the slightest fear.'

'Ramses?'

'I'm speaking of the commander of his personal body-guard, a gigantic Sardinian named Serramanna. He's a former pirate who won Ramses' trust.'

'I know his reputation. Why does he worry you?'

'Because Ramses has appointed him head of an elite regiment, composed for the most part of mercenaries. This Serramanna may prove an embarrassing example and inspire acts of heroism.'

'A pirate and a mercenary? He'll be easily bought.'

'As it happens, no! He has become a friend of Ramses and watches over him with a dog-like loyalty. And a dog's love cannot be bought.'

'He can be got rid of.'

'I've thought of that, my dear Raia, but it's better to avoid obvious violence. Serramanna is a tough character, and very suspicious. He'd be quite capable of killing any would-be attackers. And his murder would arouse Ramses' suspicions.'

'What do you want?'

'Some other way of eliminating Serramanna. Neither you nor I must be implicated.'

'I'm a prudent man, your lordship, and I see a solution.'

'I repeat: this Sardinian has the instinct of a wildcat.'

'I'll get rid of him for you.'

'For Ramses that would be a very bitter blow. You shall have a fine reward.'

The Syrian merchant rubbed his hands. 'I have some other good news for you, Lord Shaanar. Do you know how the Egyptian troops stationed abroad communicate with Pi-Ramses?'

'By messengers on horseback, visual signals and carrier pigeons.'

'In the zones infested with rebels, only carrier pigeons can be used. Now, the main breeder of these valuable birds is not like Serramanna. Although he works for the army, he is open to corruption. So it will be easy for me to destroy messages, intercept them or replace them with different ones. A way of upsetting the Egyptian information services without their knowing . . . '

'A magnificent prospect, Raia. But don't forget to find me some more vases like this one.'

7

Serramanna took a dim view of this war. The Sardinian giant, on relinquishing his profession of pirate to become the commander of Ramses' personal bodyguard, had grown fond of Egypt, liking his official residence, and the Egyptian women with whom he spent hours of bliss. Nenophar, his most recent mistress, outshone all the previous ones. At their last amorous encounter she had managed to exhaust him – and he a Sardinian!

A damnable war indeed, which would take him away from so many pleasures, even if watching over Ramses' safety was no sinecure. How often had the monarch scorned his advice to be careful? But the king was a great king and Serramanna admired him. Since it was necessary to kill a few Hittites to save Ramses' reign, he would do so. And he even hoped personally to cut the throat of Muwatallis, whose soldiers called him 'the great chief'. The Sardinian sniggered: a 'great chief' at the head of a gang of barbarians and murderers! Once his mission had been accomplished, Serramanna would curl his moustache, sprinkle it with perfume and take other Nenophars by storm.

When Ramses put him in charge of the elite corps of the Egyptian army, responsible for dangerous missions, Serramanna had felt the sort of pride which restores one's youthful vigour. Since the Lord of the Two Lands honoured him with such trust, the Sardinian would show him, weapons in hand, that his trust was not misplaced. The training he imposed on the men under his command had already eliminated braggarts and the overfed; he would keep only true warriors, able to fight one against ten, and endure many wounds without a groan.

No one knew the date when the troops would set out, but Serramanna's instinct told him it was near. In the barracks, the soldiers were becoming restless. In the palace, the army leaders met regularly. Ramses often saw Ahsha, the head of his intelligence service.

Bad news travelled by word of mouth; rebellion continued to spread, notables loyal to Egypt had been executed in Phoenicia and Palestine. But the messages brought by the carrier pigeons indicated that the fortresses were holding out and withstanding the enemy's assaults.

Pacifying Canaan would not be difficult; Ramses would probably decide to press on to the north, towards Amurru province and Syria. Then would come the inevitable confrontation with the Hittite army, whose raiders, according to the intelligence agents, had withdrawn from southern Syria.

Serramanna was not afraid of the Hittites. In spite of their reputation for butchery, he was even burning to do battle with the barbarians, to kill as many as possible and to see them flee howling.

Before waging any fabulous fights, which would be engraved in Egyptians' memories, the Sardinian had a mission to accomplish.

On leaving the palace, he had only to walk a short distance to reach the craftsmen's district of Pi-Ramses, near the warehouses. Intense activity reigned in the maze of narrow alleyways, lined with carpenters', tailors' and sandal-makers' booths. A little further on, towards the port, were the Hebrew brickmakers' modest dwellings.

The appearance of the giant sowed confusion among the

workmen and their families. When Moses fled, the Hebrews had lost a model leader, who had defended them against any form of authoritarianism and restored their lost pride. The sudden appearance of the Sardinian, whose reputation was well-established, augured no good.

Serramanna grabbed the loincloth of a lad who was running away. 'Stop waving your arms about, youngster! Where does Abner the brickmaker live?'

'I don't know.'

'Don't annoy me.'

The lad took the threat seriously and his words poured out. He even agreed to lead the Sardinian to the house, where Abner was crouching in a corner of the main room, with a veil covering his head.

'Come here,' ordered Serramanna.

'I refuse!'

'What are you afraid of, friend?'

'I've done nothing wrong.'

'Then you've nothing to fear.'

'Leave me alone, I beg you!'

'The king wants to see you.'

As Abner shrank further away, the Sardinian was obliged to lift him up with one hand and put him on the back of a donkey, which made its sure-footed way quietly to the palace.

Abner was terrified. He prostrated himself in front of Ramses, not daring to look up.

'I'm not satisfied with the inquiry into Sary's death,' said the king. 'I want to know what really happened; you know this, Abner.'

'Majesty, I'm only a brickmaker.'

'Moses is accused of killing Sary, my sister's husband. If it is proved that he did indeed commit this crime, he will have to be punished most severely. But why would he have done such a thing?'

Abner had hoped that no one would be interested in his exact part in this affair; but this was to disregard the friendship between Pharaoh and Moses.

'Moses must have gone mad, Majesty.'

'Stop making a fool of me, Abner.'

'Majesty!'

'Sary had no love for you.'

'Gossip, nothing but gossip—'

'No, there are witnesses. Get up.'

The Hebrew hesitated, trembling. He kept his head lowered, unable to look Pharaoh in the eye.

'Are you a coward, Abner?'

'A humble brickmaker whose ambition is to live in peace, Majesty, that's all I am.'

'Wise men do not believe in chance. Why were you mixed up in this tragedy?'

Abner would have continued to lie, but Pharaoh's voice broke down his defences.

'Moses . . . Moses was in charge of the brickmakers. I owed him obedience, just like my colleagues, but Sary resented his authority.'

'Did Sary ill-treat you?'

Abner muttered something incomprehensible.

'Speak up,' the king commanded.

'Sary . . . Sary was not a good man, Majesty.'

'He was even treacherous and cruel, I'm aware of that.'

Ramses' agreement reassured Abner. 'Sary threatened me,' the Hebrew admitted. 'He forced me to hand over part of my wages.'

'Blackmail. Why did you give in to his demands?'

'I was afraid, Majesty, so afraid! Sary would have beaten me, taken everything I had.'

'Why didn't you complain?'

'Sary had many connections among the police. No one dared oppose him.'

'No one except Moses!'

'Unfortunately for him, Majesty, unfortunately for him . . .'
The Hebrew would have liked to sink into the ground, escape
the king's mind, which bored into him like a drill hollowing
out a vase.

'You confided in Moses, didn't you?'

'Moses was brave, and a good man—'

'The truth, Abner!'

'Yes, Majesty, I did confide in him.'

'What was his reaction?'

'He agreed to defend me.'

'How?'

'By ordering Sary not to bother me any more, I suppose –
Moses didn't talk much.'

'The facts, Abner, just the facts.'

'I was resting at home when Sary burst in, in a violent rage.
"Dog of a Hebrew," he screamed, "you dared to talk!" He hit
me, I protected my face with my hands and tried to escape.
Moses came in, he fought with Sary, Sary died . . . If Moses
hadn't intervened, I'd have been the one to die.'

'In other words, it was a case of self-defence! Thanks to
your evidence, Abner, Moses could be tried and acquitted and
resume his place among the Egyptians.'

'I didn't know. I—'

'Why didn't you say anything, Abner?'

'I was afraid!'

'Of whom? Sary is dead. Would another overseer
persecute you?'

'No, no . . . '

'Who are you frightened of?'

'Justice, the police'

'Lying is a serious fault, Abner. But perhaps you do not
know of the existence of the scales in the next world which
will weigh our actions?'

The Hebrew bit his lip.

'You kept silent,' Ramses resumed, 'because you were afraid the investigators would turn their attention to you. You were not interested in helping Moses, who saved your life.'

'Majesty!'

'That's the truth, Abner: you wanted to remain in the shadows because you too are a blackmailer. Serramanna has managed to loosen the tongues of the novice brickmakers whom you exploit so mercilessly.'

The Hebrew knelt down in front of the king. 'I help them find work, Majesty. It's a fair return.'

'You're a crook, Abner, but you're very valuable to me, as you can prove Moses' innocence and justify what he did.'

'You . . . you're pardoning me?'

'Serramanna will take you to a judge who will take down your statement. You will describe the facts under oath, without omitting one single detail. I never want to hear of you again, Abner.'

8

Bald-Pate, a dignitary of the Heliopolis House of Life, was responsible for checking the quality of the foodstuffs the farmers and fishermen brought him. A stickler for detail and quality, he examined every fruit, every vegetable, every fish. The salesmen feared and respected him, as he paid a fair price; but no one could become his regular supplier, as he was not a slave to routine and granted no privileges. The only thing that counted was the perfection of the food, which would be sanctified by the rite and offered to the gods before being distributed to humans.

When he'd made his selection, Bald-Pate sent his purchases to the kitchens, whose name, 'the place of purity', expressed a permanent care for hygiene. The priest did not spare his surprise inspections, sometimes followed by heavy penalties.

On this particular morning, he made his way to the storeroom for dried and salt fish. He was stunned to see that the wooden lock on the door, whose mechanism was known only to himself and the man in charge of the storeroom, had been sawn off.

He pushed the door open.

All was silent as usual in the semi-darkness. He advanced anxiously, but could see nothing unusual. Vaguely reassured, he stopped at every jar; labels gave details of the name and quantity of the preserved fish and the date of the salting.

Near the door, there was a gap. A jar had been stolen.

To belong to the queen's household was an honour of which all the court ladies dreamed. But Nefertari paid more attention to efficiency and trustworthiness than to fortune and rank. Just like Ramses when he formed his government, she had caused many surprises by choosing young women of modest birth as hairdresser, weaver or lady of the bedchamber.

A pretty brunette, born in a poor suburb of Memphis, had been entrusted with the envied post of mistress of the wardrobe to the Great Royal Wife. The work consisted in particular of looking after Nefertari's favourite garments; the queen, in spite of her extensive wardrobe, remained especially attached to some old gowns and an old shawl which she liked to wear at nightfall. Not only did she fear the cool of evening, but she still remembered wrapping herself dreamily in this shawl the night following her first meeting with Prince Ramses, the fiery, sensitive young man whom she had rebuffed for a long time before admitting her own passion.

Like the other employees of the queen's household, the mistress of the wardrobe revered the sovereign. Nefertari knew how to govern with grace, command with a smile; no task seemed to her too humble to be neglected, and she accepted neither unjustified delays nor lies. When there was a problem, she liked to speak herself to the servant in question and to listen to her explanation. A friend and confidante of the Queen Mother, the Great Royal Wife had managed to win everyone's heart.

The mistress of the wardrobe perfumed the fabrics with fine essences from the palace laboratory and was careful not to crease any garments when she put them away in wooden chests and cupboards. As night approached she went to fetch the old shawl which the queen liked to drape over her shoulders while she celebrated the rites for the day.

The blood drained from the young woman's face: the shawl was not in its place.

'Impossible,' she thought. 'I'm looking in the wrong chest.'

She searched in another one, then another, then in the cupboards, but all in vain. She questioned the queen's ladies of the bedchamber, the hairdresser, the laundrywomen . . . None of them could give her the slightest clue.

Nefertari's favourite shawl had been stolen.

The war council was meeting in Pi-Ramses, in the palace audience chamber. The generals at the head of the four armies had been summoned by the king, the supreme commander of the troops. Ahmeni was taking notes and would draw up a report.

The generals were scribes of mature age, fairly well read, owning large estates, which they administered well. Two of them had fought against the Hittites under Seti, but the engagement had been short and its scope limited. In reality, none of these high-ranking officers had any experience of a large-scale conflict whose outcome was uncertain. The nearer they came to all-out war, the more uneasy they became.

'What state are our weapons in?'

'Good, Majesty.'

'And their production?'

'It hasn't slackened. Following your directives, the bonuses paid to the blacksmiths and arrow-makers have been doubled. But we need more swords and daggers for close combat.'

'The chariots?'

'In a few weeks, we shall have enough.'

'The horses?'

'They are well cared for. They will set out in excellent physical condition.'

'How is the men's morale?'

'That's where the trouble lies, Majesty,' admitted the youngest general. 'Your presence is helpful, but a thousand and one ridiculous stories are still circulating about the Hittites' cruelty and invincibility. In spite of our repeated denials, these stupid tales are leaving their mark on the soldiers' minds.'

'Even those of my generals?'

'No, Majesty, certainly not . . . But doubts remain on certain points.'

'What are those?'

'Well, will the enemy outnumber us very greatly?'

'We shall start by restoring order in Canaan.'

'Are the Hittites there already?'

'No, their army hasn't ventured so far from its base. Only some raiding parties, which sowed discord before going back to Anatolia. They have persuaded the local petty kings to betray us, so as to provoke conflicts which will exhaust our forces. There will be no question of that. We shall quickly reconquer our provinces and so give our soldiers the necessary impetus to press on towards the north and win a great victory.'

'Some people are anxious about our fortresses.'

'They need not be. The day before yesterday and yesterday a dozen carrier pigeons arrived at the palace bringing reassuring messages. Not a single fortress has fallen into enemy hands; they have sufficient food and weapons to resist possible assaults until our arrival. Nevertheless, we must hurry; we have delayed too long.'

Ramses' wish was equivalent to a command. The generals bowed and returned to their respective barracks, in order to speed up the preparations for departure.

'An incompetent bunch,' muttered Ahmeni, putting down the sharpened reed with which he had been writing.

'A harsh judgment,' remarked Ramses.

'Look at them: they're frightened, too rich, too fond of the easy life! Up till now, they've spent more time lounging in the gardens of their villas than fighting on a battlefield. How will they behave when they face the Hittites, who live only for war? Your generals might as well already be dead or put to flight.'

'Do you recommend replacing them?'

'It's too late, and what's the use? All the high-ranking officers are cast in the same mould.'

'Do you want Egypt to abstain from military intervention?'

'That would be a fatal mistake. You're right, we must react. But the situation is clear: our ability to win depends on you and you alone.'

Ramses received his friend Ahsha late at night. The king and the head of the intelligence services granted themselves only rare moments of respite; in the capital the tension was increasingly noticeable.

At one of the windows in Pharaoh's office, side by side, the two men gazed at the night sky, whose soul was made up of thousands of stars.

'Any news, Ahsha?'

'It's stalemate: the rebels on one side, our fortresses on the other. Our supporters are waiting for us to intervene.'

'I am seething with impatience, but I have no right to risk my soldiers' lives. Lack of preparation, inadequate supplies . . . For too long we slept in an illusory peace. The awakening has been cruel, but salutary.'

'The gods listen to you.'

'Do you doubt their help?'

'Shall we be able to rise to the occasion?'

'Those who fight under my command will risk their lives in the defence of Egypt. If the Hittites succeeded in their aims, it would bring in the reign of darkness.'

'Have you thought that you might be killed?'

'Nefertari will ensure the regency, and if necessary she will reign.'

'How beautiful this night is. Why do men think of nothing but killing each other?'

'I dreamed of a peaceful reign. Fate has decided otherwise and I shall not shrink from my destiny.'

'Fate might be against you, Ramses.'

'Have you perhaps lost confidence in me?'

'Perhaps I'm afraid, like everyone else.'

'Have you found any trace of Moses?'

'None at all. He seems to have vanished.'

'No, Ahsha.'

'Why are you so certain?'

'Because you haven't begun to look for him.'

The young diplomat remained perfectly calm.

'You refused to send your agents to track Moses down,' Ramses continued, 'because you don't want him to be arrested and condemned to death.'

'Moses is our friend, isn't he? If I bring him back to Egypt, he's sure to be condemned to death.'

'No, Ahsha.'

'You, Pharaoh, cannot flout the law!'

'I have no intention of doing so. Moses will be able to live in Egypt as a free man, since justice will prove him innocent.'

'But . . . He killed Sary, didn't he?'

'In self-defence, according to evidence which has been duly recorded.'

'That's fantastic news!'

'Search for Moses and find him.'

'It won't be easy. Because of the present turmoil, he may be hiding in some inaccessible place.'

'Find him, Ahsha.'

9

Serramanna had a nasty look on his face as he entered the brickmakers' district. Four young Hebrews from Middle Egypt had been quite prepared to accuse Abner of blackmail and extortion. Thanks to him, they had obtained jobs – but at a price!

The way the police had conducted the investigation was disgraceful. Sary was an undesirable character, though an influential one, and Moses was a troublemaker: the death of the former and the disappearance of the latter were all to the good.

Perhaps some valuable clues had been neglected; so the Sardinian had asked many questions here and there, before once again forcing his way into Abner's house.

The brickmaker was consulting a tablet covered with figures, while eating a piece of bread rubbed with garlic. As soon as he saw Serramanna, he sat on the tablet to hide it.

'Well, Abner, doing your accounts?'

'I'm innocent!'

'If you start your little enterprise up again, you'll have me to deal with.'

'The king protects me.'

'Don't count on it.' Serramanna grabbed a mild onion and took a bite. 'Haven't you got anything to drink?'

'Yes, in the chest.'

Serramanna lifted the lid. 'By the god Bes, here's something to celebrate a fine drunken feast with! Amphorae of wine and beer. Your business is doing well.'

'They're . . . presents.'

'It's nice to be popular.'

'What do you want from me? I've given my evidence.'

'I can't help it. I like your company.'

'I've told all I know.'

'I don't believe it. When I was a pirate, I questioned my prisoners personally. Many of them couldn't recall where they'd hidden their loot, but after a bit of persuasion they eventually remembered.'

'I haven't got a fortune!'

'I'm not interested in your nest egg.'

Abner seemed relieved. While the Sardinian was opening an amphora of beer, the Hebrew slipped the tablet under a mat.

'What were you writing on that piece of wood, Abner?'

'Nothing, nothing.'

'The amounts you've extorted from your Hebrew brothers, I bet. Perfect evidence in a court of law!'

Panic-stricken, the brickmaker did not protest.

'We can come to an understanding, my friend; I'm neither a policeman nor a judge.'

'What . . . what do you suggest?'

'I'm interested in Moses, not in you. You knew him well, didn't you?'

'No better than anyone else.'

'Don't lie, Abner. You wanted to get his protection, so you spied on him to find out what sort of a man he was, how he behaved, who he consorted with.'

'He spent all his time working.'

'Who did he meet?'

'The people on the building sites, the workmen, the—'

'And when he'd finished work?'

'He liked to discuss things with the chiefs of the Hebrew tribes.'

'What did they talk about?'

'We are a proud people, quick to take offence. Sometimes we feel a vague yearning for independence. To a minority of hot-heads, Moses seemed like a guide. Once the building of Pi-Ramses was finished, this folly would have soon been forgotten.'

'One of the workmen you "protected" told me about the visit of a strange character with whom Moses had long private conversations in his official residence.'

'That's true. No one knew that man. They said he was an architect from the South, who'd come to give Moses technical advice, but he never appeared on any building site.'

'Describe him.'

'About sixty, tall, thin, with hawk-like features, a large nose, prominent cheekbones, very thin lips, strong chin.'

'How was he dressed?'

'In an everyday tunic. An architect would have been better dressed. You'd have sworn that man didn't want to be noticed. He spoke to no one except Moses.'

'A Hebrew?'

'Definitely not.'

'How many times did he come to Pi-Ramses?'

'At least twice.'

'Since Moses fled, has anyone seen him?'

'No.'

Serramanna thirstily drained an amphora of mild beer. 'I hope you haven't hidden anything from me, Abner. If you had, my nerves would start tingling and I wouldn't be responsible for my actions.'

'I've told you everything I know about that man.'

'I'm not asking you to become an honest man – that would be asking too much – but try at least to see you are forgotten.'

'Would you like . . . some more amphories like the one you've just drunk?'

Serramanna grasped the Hebrew's nose between his thumb and forefinger. 'Suppose I twist it off, to punish you?'

The pain was so great that Abner fainted.

Serramanna shrugged, left the brickmaker's house and made his way back to the palace, deep in thought.

His investigations had taught him a great deal. Moses was plotting something. He intended to put himself at the head of a Hebrew party, probably to demand new advantages for his people, and possibly an independent city in the Delta. And suppose the mysterious individual was a foreigner, come to offer the Hebrews outside help? In that case, Moses might be guilty of high treason.

Ramses would never agree to listen to such theories. Before he mentioned them and put the king on his guard against a man he thought was his friend, Serramanna would have to obtain proof.

He was putting his hand in a fire.

Iset the Fair, Ramses' lesser wife and the mother of his son, Kha, had the use of magnificent apartments in Pi-Ramses, within the palace precincts. Although no shadow clouded her harmonious relationship with Nefertari, she preferred to live in Memphis, enjoying a round of banquets at which she was idolized for her beauty.

Graceful, lively and cheerful, with her green eyes, small, straight nose and delicate lips, Iset the Fair was condemned to a luxurious, empty existence. In spite of her youth, she had only memories to live on. She had been Ramses' first mistress, had been madly in love with him and still loved him with the same passion, but without the desire to struggle to win him back. For one day, one hour, she had hated this king to whom the gods had granted every gift; did he not also possess the gift of captivating her, while his heart belonged to

Nefertari?

If at least the Great Royal Wife had been ugly, stupid, hateful . . . But Iset the Fair had succumbed to her charm and radiance, and recognized her as an exceptional person, a queen worthy of Ramses.

'What a strange fate,' the young woman reflected, 'to see the man one loves in the arms of another and admit that this cruel situation is just and right.'

Should Ramses appear, Iset the Fair would not reproach him. She would give herself to him, as bedazzled by him as when they had first lain together in a reed hut in the depths of the country. Even if he had been a shepherd or a fisherman, she would have been driven to him by an equally intense desire.

Iset had no taste for power; she would have been incapable of taking on the role of Queen of Egypt and coping with the obligations which weighed so heavily on Nefertari. She was a stranger to envy and jealousy. She thanked the celestial powers for having granted her an incomparable happiness: to love Ramses.

This summer day was a happy one. She was playing with the nine-year-old Kha and Nefertari's daughter, Meritamon, who would soon celebrate her fourth birthday. The two children got on perfectly. Kha's passion for reading and writing was unflagging; he was teaching his sister to trace hieroglyphs and unhesitatingly guided the little girl's hand when she faltered. Today the lesson was on drawing birds, which demanded skill and precision.

'Come and swim,' said Iset. 'The water is delightful.'

'I prefer to study,' Kha replied.

'You must also learn to swim.'

'I'm not interested.'

'Perhaps your sister would like a break.'

The daughter of Ramses and Nefertari was as beautiful as her mother. She hesitated, afraid of displeasing either Kha or

Iset. She liked swimming but she did not want to annoy Kha, who knew so many secrets!

'May I go in the water?' she asked him anxiously.

Kha reflected. 'All right, but don't be too long. You must do the drawing of the quail chick again; its head isn't round enough.'

Meritamon ran to Iset, who was happy in the trust Nefertari showed her by allowing her to participate in her daughter's upbringing. The young woman and the child slipped into the clear, cool water of the pool, in the shade of a sycamore.

Yes, that day was indeed a happy one.

10

The heat in Memphis was becoming stifling. The scorching wind blowing from the north parched the throats of men and beasts. Thick tiles had been placed between the roofs of the houses, to shade the alleyways. The water-carriers had their work cut out to satisfy their customers.

In his comfortable villa, the Libyan magus Ofir did not suffer from the heat. Openings at the top of the walls allowed the air to circulate. The place was peaceful and restful, and favoured the meditation essential for the practice of his evil spells.

Ofir felt himself overcome by a kind of rapture; normally he practised his arts coolly, almost with indifference. But he had never undertaken such a difficult task, and its magnitude excited him. He, the son of a Libyan adviser to Akhenaton, was having his revenge.

His illustrious guest, Shaanar, the minister for foreign affairs, arrived in mid-afternoon, at a time when the streets of the city, big and small, were deserted. Shaanar had taken care to travel in a chariot belonging to his ally Meba, driven by a mute.

The magus greeted Shaanar with deference. The latter, as on the occasion of their previous meeting, felt ill at ease; the Libyan, with his hawk-like profile, had an icy gaze. With his dark green eyes, prominent nose and extremely thin lips, he looked more like a demon than a man. Yet his voice and bearing were tinged with gentleness, and one might have thought at times that one was conversing with some aged priest whose words were reassuring.

'Why this summons, Ofir? I don't much care for this sort of conduct.'

'Because I have continued to work for our cause, my lord. You will not be disappointed.'

'I hope so, for your sake.'

'If you will be so good as to follow me . . . The ladies are waiting for us.'

Shaanar had offered this house to the magus so that he could practise his sorcery in peace and so help him win power. Naturally he had taken the precaution of putting the house in the name of his sister, Dolora. So many valuable allies, who could be exploited at will: Ahsha, the king's childhood friend and a conspirator of genius; the Syrian merchant Raia, the most cunning of Hittite spies; and now this Ofir, who had been introduced to him by the gullible Meba, the former minister for foreign affairs, whose place Shaanar had taken while giving him to believe that Ramses had been responsible for ousting him. Ofir embodied a strange and dangerous world, of which Shaanar was suspicious but whose power to harm was not to be scorned.

Ofir claimed to be the brains behind a political plan which consisted of reviving the heresy of Akhenaton, of restoring the worship of the one god Aton as the state religion, and of placing an obscure descendant of the mad king on the throne of Egypt. Shaanar had given Ofir to understand that he approved the spread of his sect, whose message might attract Moses. That was why the sorcerer had contacted the Hebrew, with the aim of proving to him that they pursued a common ideal.

Shaanar thought that an internal opposition, even a minimal one, would be one more obstacle for Ramses. When the moment came, he would get rid of all these embarrassing allies, since a powerful man must have no past.

Alas! Moses had committed a murder and fled. Without the support of the Hebrews, Ofir had no chance of collecting enough supporters of Aton to destabilize Ramses. True, the magus had proved his efficiency by complicating Nefertari's confinement, to the point of endangering her life and that of her daughter, Meritamon. But both were still alive. Although the queen was unable to have another child, the magic of the royal household had defeated that of the Libyan. Ofir was becoming useless, even an embarrassment, so when Shaanar received the message begging him to come urgently to Memphis, he considered getting rid of him.

'Our host has arrived,' Shaanar announced to two women seated in the half-light, holding hands.

The first was Dolora, Shaanar's tall, dark-haired sister, who seemed permanently weary; the other was Lita, a plump little blonde, whom Ofir introduced as Akhenaton's grand-daughter. Shaanar thought she looked mentally retarded, subservient to the sinister magus's will.

'Is my dear sister in good health?'

'I am pleased to see you, Shaanar. Your presence is proof that we are on the right path.'

Dolora and Sary, her husband, had hoped in vain that Ramses would grant them a privileged position at court. In their disappointment they had plotted against the king. It had needed the intervention of Tuya, the Queen Mother, and Nefertari, the Great Royal Wife, for Ramses to show mercy after their intrigues were uncovered. Sary, the former tutor of Ramses, had been demoted to the station of overseer. Embittered and belligerent, he had turned against the Hebrew brickmakers. A a result of his corruption and unjust deeds, he had provoked the wrath of Moses and brought about his own death. As for Dolora, she had fallen under the spell of Ofir and Lita. She now swore only by Aton, the one god, and worked actively for the return of his worship and the fall of Ramses, the ungodly pharaoh.

Dolora's hatred for Ramses benefited Shaanar, who had promised her an important role in the future government; one way or another, he would use this negative force against his brother. When his sister's madness became intolerable, he would send her into exile.

'Have you any news of Moses?' asked Dolora.

'He has disappeared,' Shaanar replied. 'His Hebrew brothers have no doubt murdered him and buried him in the desert.'

'We have lost a valuable ally,' admitted Ofir, 'but the will of the one god will be done. Are we not more and more numerous?'

'Prudence is vital' was Shaanar's opinion.

'Aton will assist us!' declared Dolora, exalted.

'I have not lost sight of my initial plan,' the sorcerer observed, 'namely to weaken Ramses' magical defences, the only real obstacle in our path.'

'Your first attack wasn't exactly crowned with success,' Shaanar reminded him.

'Acknowledge at least that I showed a certain competence.'

'With inadequate results.'

'I agree, Lord Shaanar. That is why I've decided to use a different technique.'

'What is that?'

With his right hand, the Libyan magus pointed to a jar bearing a label. 'Will you read what it says?'

' "Heliopolis, House of Life. Four fish: grey mullets". Preserves?'

'But not any old preserves: food intended as offerings, selected with care and already charged with magic. I also have this piece of material.' Ofir brandished a shawl.

'I'd swear—'

'Yes, Lord Shaanar, it is indeed the favourite shawl of the Great Royal Wife, Nefertari.'

'Did you steal it?'

'My supporters are many, as I told you. These two elements combined, the sacred food and the shawl that has touched the queen's body, were essential for me to proceed. Thanks to them and to your determination, we shall succeed in restoring the worship of Aton. Lita must reign: she will be Queen, you will be Pharaoh.'

Lita raised wondering, trusting eyes to Shaanar. The girl was quite attractive and would make a very suitable mistress.

'There remains Ramses.'

'He's only a man,' Ofir declared, 'and will not withstand repeated violent attacks. To succeed I need help.'

'You already have the promise of mine!' exclaimed Dolora, clasping Lita's hands more tightly, while the latter did not take her bulging eyes off the Libyan.

'What is your plan?' asked Shaanar.

Ofir crossed his arms on his chest. 'I cannot do without your help too, my lord.'

'Mine? But—'

'All four of us wish for the death of the royal couple: the four of us symbolize the four corners of space, the boundaries of time, the entire world. If one of these four forces were lacking, the spell would not work.'

'I am not a sorcerer.'

'Your willingness is sufficient.'

'Do agree,' begged Dolora.

'What shall I have to do?'

'Perform one simple action,' Ofir explained. 'It will contribute to the downfall of Ramses.'

'Let us begin.'

The magus opened the jar and took out the four dried salt fish. As if in a trance, Lita pushed Dolora away and lay down on the floor. Ofir placed Nefertari's shawl across her chest.

'Pick up one of the fish by the tail,' he ordered Dolora.

She obeyed. Ofir took a tiny figurine in the likeness of Ramses out of the pocket of his tunic, and stuffed it into the mullet's mouth.

'The second fish, Dolora.'

The magus repeated the operation.

'Either the king will be killed in the war,' Ofir prophesied, 'or he will fall into the trap we shall lay for him on his return. He will be separated for ever from the queen.'

Ofir went into a small room, followed by Dolora, holding the fish in her outstretched hands, and by Shaanar, whose hope of harming Ramses was stronger than his fear.

There was a brazier in the middle of this room.

'Cast the fish into the fire, my lord; thus your wish will be fulfilled.'

Shaanar did not hesitate.

When the fourth fish had been consumed in the fire, a scream startled them. The trio returned to the reception room. Nefertari's shawl had caught fire spontaneously, burning Lita, who had fainted.

Ofir picked up the piece of material and the flames went out. 'When the shawl has been completely destroyed,' he explained, 'Ramses and Nefertari will become prey to infernal demons.'

'Must Lita continue to suffer?' Dolora asked anxiously.

'Lita agreed to this sacrifice. As long as this experiment lasts, she will have to remain conscious. You will look after her, Dolora. As soon as her burns are healed, we shall begin again, until the shawl is completely consumed. We shall need time, Lord Shaanar, but we shall succeed.'

11

Dr Pariamaku, the most senior physician in the whole of the North and South Lands and chief physician to the palace, was a lively fifty-year-old. His hands were long, slender and well cared for. Wealthy, married to a Memphis woman of noble birth, who had given him three fine children, he could boast of having had a magnificent career and of being generally held in high regard.

Yet, this summer morning, Dr Pariamaku was fuming with anger as he waited for an audience. Not only was Ramses never ill, but he had kept the distinguished physician waiting for more than two hours.

Finally a chamberlain came to fetch him and showed him in to Ramses' office.

'Majesty, I am your humble servant, but—'

'How are you, my dear Doctor?'

'Majesty, I am very worried! There are rumours at court that you are considering appointing me surgeon to the army which is leaving for the North.'

'That would be a great honour, wouldn't it?'

'True, Majesty, true, but would I not be of more use at the palace?'

'Perhaps I should bear that in mind.'

Pariamaku could not hide his distress. 'Majesty, may I know your decision?'

'On due reflection, you are probably right. Your presence in the palace is indispensable.'

The doctor could scarcely suppress a sigh of relief. 'I have great confidence in all my deputies, Majesty; whoever you choose will give satisfaction.'

'I've already made my choice. You know my friend Setau, I believe.'

An aggressive-looking man, square-headed, unshaven, not wearing a wig, clad in an antelope-skin tunic with a number of pockets, approached the physician, who shrank back.

'Pleased to meet you, Doctor. My career isn't exactly brilliant, I agree, but my snakes are my friends. Would you like to stroke the viper I captured yesterday evening?'

The physician took another step back. He stared at the king, stunned. 'Majesty, the qualifications necessary to run a medical service—'

'Be particularly vigilant while I'm away, Doctor. I hold you personally responsible for the health of the royal family.'

Setau dipped his hand into one of his pockets. Fearing he would bring out some reptile, Pariamaku hurriedly took his leave of the monarch and slipped away.

'How long will you be surrounded by such toadies?' asked the snake-charmer.

'Don't be so hard on him; he sometimes manages to cure his patients. By the way, do you agree to be responsible for the army medical services?'

'The job doesn't interest me, but I have no right to let you leave alone.'

A jar of dried fish from the House of Life in Heliopolis and Queen Nefertari's shawl. Two thefts, one culprit. Serramanna was sure he knew who it was: it could only be Remet, the palace steward. The Sardinian had long suspected him. This suspiciously jolly fellow was a traitor and had even attempted to assassinate the king. Ramses had made a bad choice of steward.

Serramanna could not speak to the king of either Moses or Remet without risking triggering a violent reaction which would not bring about the arrest of the villainous steward, any more than it would put an end to the friendship between the sovereign and the Hebrew. Who could he apply to except Ahmeni, Ramses' private secretary? He was clear-headed and distrustful and would be prepared to listen.

He passed between the two soldiers guarding the door leading from the corridor to Ahmeni's office. The indefatigable scribe had twenty senior officials under him, responsible for all the important dossiers. From these Ahmeni extracted the essentials, which he communicated to Ramses.

There was a sound of hurried footsteps behind the Sardinian. He turned. To his astonishment, a dozen foot-soldiers were pointing their spears at him.

'What's come over you?'

'We've got our orders.'

'I'm the one who gives the orders here.'

'You're under arrest.'

'Have you gone mad?'

'We're obeying orders.'

'Get out of my way, or I'll beat your brains out!'

The private secretary's office door opened and Ahmeni appeared on the threshold.

'Tell these idiots to disperse, Ahmeni!'

'I ordered them to arrest you.'

A shipwreck would not have acted more powerfully on the former pirate: for a few seconds he was transfixed. The soldiers took advantage of this to remove his weapons and tie his hands behind his back.

'Tell me what's going on!'

At a sign from Ahmeni, the guards pushed Serramanna into the office.

The secretary consulted a papyrus. 'Do you know a certain Nenuphar?'

'Certainly. She's one of my mistresses. The latest, to be exact.'

'Have you quarrelled?'

'Lovers' tiffs, in the heat of action.'

'Did you rape her?'

Serramanna smiled. 'We've had some rough encounters, but it was a war to see who could get the most pleasure.'

'You've nothing to reproach this girl with?'

'Oh yes! She exhausts me shamelessly.'

Ahmeni remained icy. 'This Nenuphar has made serious accusations against you.'

'But . . . she was willing, I swear it.'

'I'm talking not about your sexual excesses but about your treachery.'

'*Treachery?* Did I hear you right?'

'Nenuphar accuses you of being a spy in the pay of the Hittites.'

'You're having me on, Ahmeni!'

'This girl loves her country. When she discovered some rather peculiar wooden tablets hidden in the linen chest of your bedchamber, she thought she ought to bring them to me. Do you recognize them?'

Ahmeni showed Serramanna the tablets.

'They don't belong to me!'

'They are proof of your crime. According to the rather crudely written text on them, you tell your Hittite correspondent that you'll make sure the elite corps you command is ineffective.'

'That's ridiculous!'

'Your mistress has made a sworn statement before a judge. He read it out in front of witnesses and she confirmed her account.'

'This is a manoeuvre to discredit me and weaken Ramses.'

'According to the dates on the tablets, you've been a traitor for eight months. The Hittite emperor has promised you a fine fortune after Egypt is defeated.'

'I'm loyal to Ramses. Ever since he pardoned me when he could have taken my life, my life belongs to him.'

'Fine words, but they're belied by the facts.'

'You know me, Ahmeni! I've been a pirate, it's true, but I've never betrayed a friend.'

'I thought I knew you but you're just like the rest of the courtiers, whose only master is the lure of rewards. Doesn't a mercenary offer himself to the highest bidder?'

Deeply hurt, Serramanna drew himself up to his full height. 'Pharaoh appointed me commander of his personal bodyguard and of an elite army corps because he trusted me.'

'His trust was misplaced.'

'I deny having committed this crime.'

'Untie his hands.'

Serramanna felt intense relief. Ahmeni had questioned him with his usual rigour, simply to prove his innocence!

The secretary handed the Sardinian a sharpened reed, whose tip had been dipped in black ink, and a piece of limestone with a highly polished surface. 'Write your name and your titles.'

Serramanna nervously did as instructed.

'It's the same writing as on the wooden tablets. This new proof will be added to the dossier. You are guilty, Serramanna.'

The former pirate tried frantically to hurl himself at Ahmeni, but four spears pricked his sides, shedding a few drops of blood.

'A confession of guilt, don't you think?'

'I want to see this girl and make her spit out her lies!'

'You'll see her at your trial.'

'I've been set up, Ahmeni!'

'Prepare your defence well, Serramanna. For traitors like

you, there is only one punishment: death. And don't count on Ramses showing any leniency.'

'Let me speak to the king. I've got some vital information for him.'

'Our army sets off on the campaign tomorrow. Your absence will astonish the Hittites.'

'Let me speak to the king, I beg you.'

'See that he's thrown into prison and guarded well,' ordered Ahmeni.

12

Shaanar's mood was excellent and his appetite voracious. His breakfast, 'the cleansing of the mouth', consisted of barley gruel, two roast quail, goat's cheese and round honey-cakes. On this splendid day, which would see the departure of Ramses and his army for the North, he gave himself a treat, a grilled goose-thigh flavoured with rosemary, cumin and chervil.

With Serramanna arrested and thrown into prison, the Egyptian troops' potential for attack would be significantly reduced.

Shaanar was sipping fresh milk from a goblet when Ramses entered his private apartments.

'May your countenance be protected,' said Shaanar, using the ancient courtesy formula reserved for the morning greetings.

The king was wearing a white kilt and a short-sleeved tunic, with silver bracelets on his wrists.

'My beloved brother doesn't seem ready to set out.'

'But . . . Were you intending to take me with you, Ramses?'

'You haven't got a warrior's heart, it would seem.'

'I have neither your strength nor your courage.'

'Here are my instructions: during my absence, you will collect all information coming from foreign lands and submit it to Nefertari, Tuya and Ahmeni, who will form my regency war council, empowered to make decisions. I shall be in the front line, together with Ahsha.'

'He's going with you?'

'His knowledge of the terrain makes his presence vital.'

'Diplomacy has unfortunately failed . . . '

'I am sorry about that, Shaanar, but the time for shilly-shallying is over.'

'What will your strategy be?'

'To restore order in our subject provinces, then pause before marching on Kadesh and confronting the Hittites directly. When this second part of the expedition begins, I may perhaps summon you to join me.'

'It will be an honour to be associated with the final victory.'

'Once again, Egypt will survive.'

'Be careful, Ramses; our country needs you.'

Ramses sailed across the canal which separated the district of workshops and warehouses from the oldest part of Pi-Ramses, the site of Avaris, the former capital of the Hyskos invaders, the Asiatics of evil memory. There stood the temple of Set, the terrifying god of storms and the fury of the heavens, wielder of the most formidable power at work in the universe and protector of Ramses' father, Seti, the only king of Egypt to have dared bear a similar name.

Ramses had given the order to enlarge and embellish the sanctuary of the terrible Set, whom Seti, while preparing him in secret for the highest office, had made him confront in this very place.

In the young prince's heart, fear and the power to overcome fear had come face to face; at the end of the conflict a fire had been born like to the nature of Set, which Seti had transcribed in an axiom: 'To believe in man's goodness is an error which a pharaoh must never commit.'

70

In the courtyard before the temple a stele of pink granite had been erected.* At the top, a strange beast represented Set: a dog-like creature with red eyes, pricking up two huge ears and with a long, downward-curving muzzle. No man had ever set eyes on such a creature and no man ever would. In the arch of the stele, the same Set was represented in human form. On his head he wore a conical diadem, a solar disc and two horns. In his right hand, he held the key of life; in his left, the sceptre 'Power'.

The inscription was dated the fourth day of the fourth month of the summer of the year 400.† So the emphasis was put on the power of the number four, by which the cosmos is organized. The hieroglyphic text carved on the stele began with an invocation:

> *Greetings to thee, Set, son of the goddess of the sky.*
> *Thou whose power is great in the million-year-old ship.*
> *Thou who art at the helm of the ship of light and dost cast*
>   *down its enemies,*
> *Thou, whose voice is as thunder!*
> *Permit Pharaoh to follow thy Ka.*

Ramses entered the covered temple and stood in meditation before the statue of Set. The god's energy would be essential for him in the battle he was about to wage. Was not Set, who was capable of transforming four years of his reign into the four hundred years inscribed in the stone, the best of allies?

Ahmeni's office was crammed with rolls of papyrus – fitted into leather cases, stuck in jars or piled up in wooden chests – all bearing labels indicating the contents of the documents

---

*Over 7 feet tall by approximately 4ft. 3ins. wide.
†Whence the name, 'Stele of the year 400', that Egyptologists give to this remarkable document.

and the date when they had been recorded. Strict order reigned in this domain, which no one was allowed to tidy up. Ahmeni himself meticulously carried out this task.

'I'd have liked to leave with you,' he admitted to Ramses.

'Your place is here, my friend. Every day, you will talk with the queen and my mother. Whatever Shaanar may hint, grant him no powers of decision.'

'Don't be away too long.'

'I intend to strike rapidly and hard.'

'You'll have to manage without Serramanna.'

'Why?'

Ahmeni recounted the circumstances of the Sardinian's arrest.

Ramses seemed saddened. 'Draw up a clear act of indictment,' he ordered. 'On my return I shall question him; he will give me the reasons for his actions.'

'Once a pirate, always a pirate.'

'His trial and punishment will be exemplary.'

'An arm as valiant as his would have been invaluable to you,' deplored Ahmeni.

'His sword might have stabbed me in the back.'

'Are our troops really ready to fight?'

'They no longer have any choice.'

'Does Your Majesty think we have a real chance of winning?'

'We shall defeat the rebels who are sowing disorder among the protectorates, but after that . . .'

'Before launching the attack on Kadesh, give me the order to join you.'

'No, my friend. It is here, in Pi-Ramses, that you are of most use. If I disappeared, Nefertari would need your help.'

'The war effort will continue,' promised Ahmeni. 'We shall continue to manufacture weapons. I have . . . I have asked Setau and Ahsha to watch over your safety. Without Serramanna, you might well take too many risks.'

'If I didn't march at the head of my army, it would be beaten in advance.'

Her hair was blacker than the black of night, sweeter than the fruit of the fig tree, her teeth whiter than gypsum powder, her two breasts as firm as two love-apples. Nefertari, his wife. Nefertari, the Queen of Egypt, the radiance of whose gaze was the delight of the Two Lands.

'After visiting Set,' Ramses confided to her, 'I went to talk with my mother.'

'What did she say?'

'She spoke to me of Seti, of the long hours he spent in meditation before fighting any battle, of his ability to conserve his energy during the interminable days of travelling.'

'The soul of your father lives on in you. He will fight beside you.'

'I place the kingdom in your hands, Nefertari. Tuya and Ahmeni will be your loyal allies. Serramanna has just been arrested; Shaanar will certainly try to assert himself. Keep firm hold on the tiller of the ship of state.'

'Trust no one but yourself, Ramses.'

The king clasped his wife in his arms, as if he were never to see her again.

From the Blue Crown two wide bands of pleated linen hung down to Ramses' waist. He wore a padded leather garment, both doublet and skirt, forming a sort of stomacher covered with little metal plates, and, over the whole, a loose transparent gown, of incomparable majesty.

When Homer saw Pharaoh appear in this warlike apparel, he stopped smoking and rose to his feet. Hector, the black and white cat, took refuge under a chair.

'So, Majesty, the hour has come.'

'I was anxious to greet you before setting out for the North.'

'Here are the lines I have just been writing: "He harnesses to his chariot his two swift steeds with hooves of bronze and manes of gold. He wears a dazzling tunic; he grasps his whip and straightway urges them into a gallop, so that they fly between heaven and earth."'

'My two horses well deserve this tribute; I have spent many days preparing them for the trials we shall endure together.'

'This departure . . . such a pity . . . I'd just acquired an interesting recipe. By mixing a loaf of barley bread with the juice of dates which I stone myself, and letting this ferment, I obtain a digestive beer. I'd have liked to get you to taste it.'

'That's an old Egyptian recipe, Homer.'

'Prepared by a Greek poet, it must taste completely different.'

'When I return we shall drink this beer together.'

'Although I'm becoming cantankerous in my old age, I hate drinking alone, especially when I've invited a very dear friend to share this pleasure. Courtesy requires you to return as speedily as possible, Majesty.'

'That is precisely what I intend to do. What is more, I should very much like to read your *Iliad*.'

'I shall need many more years before I reach the end; that is why I grow old slowly, so as to deceive time. You, Majesty, you compress time in your fist.'

'We shall meet again soon, Homer.'

Ramses climbed into his chariot, drawn by two of his finest horses, Victory-in-Thebes and The-Goddess-Mut-is-Content. Young, vigorous, intelligent, they were happy to be setting out on this adventure, eager to travel great distances.

The king had entrusted his dog, Wideawake, to Nefertari; Invincible, the huge Nubian lion, ran on the right of his chariot. Of prodigious strength and beauty, the beast too felt the wish to show its prowess as a warrior.

Pharaoh raised his right arm.

The chariot shook, the wheels began to turn, the lion regulated its pace to that of the monarch. And thousands of footsoldiers, with the charioteers on either side, followed Ramses.

13

In spite of the extreme June heat, which was even more intense than usual, the Egyptian army believed that the war would be a stroll in the country. Crossing the north-east region of the Delta was a delight; oblivious of the threat hanging over the Two Lands, peasants armed with sickles were reaping ears of spelt. The crops quivered in the light sea breeze and the fields gleamed with green and gold. Although the king insisted on forced marches, the footsoldiers enjoyed the sight of the fields, over which herons, pelicans and rosy-tinted flamingos wheeled.

The army broke its journey in villages where the troops were well received. While maintaining discipline, they foraged for fresh vegetables and fruit and a light local wine to flavour the water, not to mention draughts of mild beer. How distant was that picture of thirsty, starving soldiers, bowed beneath their heavy equipment!

Ramses took the command as supreme head of his army, which consisted of four regiments, each of five thousand men, placed under the protection of the gods Ra, Amon, Set and Ptah respectively. In addition to these twenty thousand footsoldiers, there were reservists, of whom some remained in Egypt, and the cream of the army, namely the chariot corps. In order to facilitate the management of this cumbersome contingent, the king had formed companies of two hundred men, each placed under a standard-bearer.

The general of the chariot corps, the divisional commanders, the army scribes and the head of the supply corps could take no independent initiative and had to consult Ramses as soon as a problem arose. Fortunately, the king could rely on Ahsha, whom all the senior officers respected, to speak briefly and to the point.

As for Setau, he had needed a chariot to bring all the equipment he considered essential for a man of his position setting out for the disquieting lands of the North: five bronze razors, pots of ointments and salves, a whetstone, a wooden comb, several gourds of fresh water, pestles, a hatchet, sandals, mats, a cloak, tunics, canes, several dozen vessels filled with lead oxide, asphalt, red ochre and alum, jars of honey, packets of cumin, bryony, castor oil and valerian. A second chariot contained drugs, potions and remedies, all under the supervision of Lotus, Setau's wife, the only woman on the expedition. As she was known to be able to handle fearsome reptiles like weapons, no one went near the tall, slender, pretty Nubian.

Setau wore round his neck a string of five garlic cloves to ward off noxious effluvia and protect his teeth. Many soldiers copied him, knowing the virtues of this plant, which, according to legend, had preserved the milk-teeth of the young god Horus when he hid with his mother, Isis, in the swamps of the Delta to escape the wrath of Set, who was determined to do away with Osiris's son and successor.

At the first halt, Ramses retired to his tent, accompanied by Ahsha and Setau.

'Serramanna intended to betray me,' he told them.

'Amazing,' commented Ahsha. 'I can claim to know men well, and I felt that he was loyal to you.'

'Ahmeni has collected hard evidence against him.'

'Most odd,' Setau reckoned.

'You didn't care much for Serramanna,' Ramses reminded him.

'We had our clashes, it's true, but I put him to the test. That pirate is a man of honour, who keeps his word. And he gave you his word.'

'You're forgetting the evidence.'

'Ahmeni could be wrong.'

'He isn't usually.'

'Even Ahmeni isn't infallible. You can be sure Serramanna hasn't betrayed you, and that someone wanted him out of the way to weaken you.'

'What do you think, Ahsha?'

'I don't find Setau's theory implausible.'

'When order is restored in our protectorates,' the king declared, 'and as soon as the Hittite has sued for mercy, we shall sort this matter out. Either Serramanna is a traitor or else someone has fabricated the evidence; either way, I want to know the whole truth.'

'That's an ideal I've abandoned,' admitted Setau. 'Wherever men live, lying flourishes.'

'It is my role to fight it and defeat it,' Ramses said.

'That's why I don't envy you. Snakes don't stab you in the back.'

'Unless you run away,' Ahsha corrected him.

'In which case you deserve the punishment they inflict.'

Ramses was aware of the horrible suspicion crossing the minds of his two friends. They knew his feelings and could have argued for hours to repel the spectre: what if Ahmeni himself had faked the evidence? Ahmeni, the rigorous, the indefatigable, scribe to whom Ramses had entrusted the management of the material affairs of the state, in the certainty that he would not be betrayed. Neither Ahsha nor Setau dared accuse Ahmeni directly, but the king had no right to stop his ears.

'Why would Ahmeni have behaved like that?' he asked.

Setau and Ahsha exchanged glances and remained silent.

'If Serramanna had discovered anything disturbing about

my secretary,' Ramses went on, 'he would have told me.'

'It might have been to prevent him from doing so that Ahmeni arrested him,' suggested Ahsha.

'That's unlikely,' Setau ventured. 'We are reasoning in the dark. When we get back to Pi-Ramses, we can reconsider the matter.'

'That's the wisest path' was Ahsha's opinion.

'I don't like this wind,' said Setau. 'It's not normal for summer. It brings disease and devastation as if the year were going to end before the hour is out. Beware, Ramses; this ill wind bodes no good.'

'Rapid action is our best guarantee of success. No wind can delay our advance.'

Disposed along the north-east border of Egypt, the fortresses forming the King's Wall communicated between themselves by means of optical signals and sent regular reports to the court. In times of peace, it was their job to control immigration. Since the general alert, archers and lookouts kept continual watch on the horizon from the top of the covered way. This great wall had been built many centuries earlier by Sesostris I to prevent the Bedouin from stealing cattle in the Delta and give warning of any attempt at invasion.

'Whoever crosses this border becomes one of Pharaoh's sons,' proclaimed the legislative stele placed in each of these fortresses, which were maintained with care and supplied with armed and well-paid garrisons. The soldiers lived together with the customs officers who exacted the requisite taxes from traders wishing to bring goods into Egypt.

The King's Wall, reinforced over the ages, reassured the Egyptian population. Thanks to this proven defensive system, the country feared neither surprise attack nor a flood of barbarians attracted by the fertile lands of the Delta.

Ramses' army advanced without incident. Some old campaigners began to believe they were simply making a round of inspections of the kind that Pharaoh was obliged to carry out from time to time to show off his military strength.

When they saw the battlements of the first fortress bristling with archers ready to shoot, their optimism was somewhat modified.

But the great entrance gates swung open to let Ramses enter. No sooner had his chariot come to a halt in the centre of the vast sandy courtyard, than a pot-bellied individual, sheltering under a parasol held by a servant, hurried towards him.

'May Your Majesty be praised! Your presence is a gift from the gods.'

Ahsha had given Ramses a detailed report on the governor-general of the King's Wall. He was a wealthy landowner, a former scribe, trained at the Academy of Memphis. A good trencherman and the father of four children, he detested army life and couldn't wait to leave this post, which some coveted but which he found boring, to become a high official in Pi-Ramses in charge of supplies to the barracks. He had never handled a weapon and was afraid of violence, but his accounts could not be faulted and, thanks to his taste for good produce, the garrisons enjoyed excellent food.

The king alighted from his chariot and patted his two horses, which responded with a friendly look.

'I have had a banquet prepared, Majesty. You will lack for nothing here. Your bedchamber will be as comfortable as that in the palace, and I hope you will like it and will stay and rest here.'

'I have no intention of resting. I am here to put down a revolt.'

'Of course, Majesty, of course. But that will only take a few days.'

'What makes you so certain?'

'The reports from our fortified places in Canaan are

reassuring. The rebels are incapable of getting organized and are fighting among themselves.'

'Have our positions been attacked?'

'Not at all, Majesty! Here is the latest message, brought by a carrier pigeon that arrived this morning.'

Ramses read the document, which was written by an untroubled hand. Indeed, it promised to be an easy task to make Canaan see reason.

'See to it that my horses get the best of care,' the king ordered.

'They will be pleased with their quarters here and their fodder,' the governor promised.

'Where is the map room?'

'I'll take you there, Majesty.'

The governor hurried so fast, in his determination not to waste a second of the king's time, that he must have lost some weight; his parasol-bearer had great difficult in keeping up with him.

Ramses summoned Ahsha, Setau and the generals.

'As from tomorrow,' he announced, pointing out their itinerary on a map unrolled on a low table, 'we shall make forced marches due north. We shall pass to the west of Jerusalem, skirt the coast, establish contact with our first fortress and subjugate the rebels in Canaan. Then we shall take up residence in Megiddo before resuming the offensive.'

The generals approved. Ahsha remained silent.

Setau left the map room, looked up at the sky and returned to Ramses' side.

'What's the matter?'

'I don't like this wind. It's treacherous.'

14

They kept up a brisk pace and travelled merrily onward, discipline being relaxed somewhat. When they entered the land of Canaan, which was subject to Pharaoh and paid him tribute, the Egyptian army didn't feel that they were venturing into a foreign land or that they were running even the slightest risk.

Ramses had probably taken a local incident too seriously. The deployment of the Egyptian forces was such that the rebels would hasten to lay down their arms and beg the king for pardon. Just another campaign which, thank goodness, would end without any dead or seriously wounded.

It is true that, as they proceeded along the coast, the soldiers had noticed the destruction of a very small fort which was usually occupied by three men responsible for supervising the migration of the herds, but no one had been worried by this.

Setau continued to look surly. Driving his chariot alone, bare-headed in spite of the blazing sun, he did not even exchange a word with Lotus, who was the hub of attention of all the soldiers lucky enough to march near the fair Nubian's chariot.

The sea breeze tempered the heat, the road was not too hard on the feet, the water-carriers frequently offered the soldiers a refreshing drink. Even if it demanded good physical condition and a pronounced taste for marching, the military life was nothing like the hell described by scribes, always quick to denigrate other careers.

On his master's right trotted Ramses' lion. No one dared approach it, for fear of being mauled, but they were all glad the beast was there; it embodied a supernatural force, which only Pharaoh could control. In Serramanna's absence, the lion was Ramses' best protection.

The first fortress of the land of Canaan came into sight. It was an impressive structure with its double sloping brick walls nearly twenty feet high, its reinforced parapets, thick ramparts, watchtowers and battlements.

'Who is the commander of the garrison?' Ramses asked Ahsha.

'An experienced officer from Jericho. He was brought up in Egypt, underwent extensive training there and was appointed to this post after several tours of inspection in Palestine. I've met him; he is reliable, a trustworthy man.'

'Wasn't it from him that the majority of the messages came, telling us of a rebellion in Canaan?'

'Just so, Majesty. This fortress is a vital strategic point for collecting all the information from the region.'

'Would he make a good governor of Canaan?'

'I'm certain of it.'

'In future we shall avoid these disturbances. This province must be controlled better; it's our task to remove any motive for insurrection.'

'The only way to do that,' commented Ahsha, 'is to suppress the Hittite influence.'

'That's exactly what I intend to do.'

A scout galloped off up to the gate of the fortress. From the top of the ramparts an archer gave him a friendly wave.

The scout returned. A standard-bearer gave the men in the van the order to advance. They were weary, wanting only to drink, eat and sleep.

A shower of arrows pinned them to the ground.

Dozens of archers had appeared on the covered way and shot in quick succession at the close and defenceless targets. Dead or wounded, an arrow in the head, the chest or the belly, the Egyptian footsoldiers fell on top of one another. The standard-bearer commanding the vanguard reacted with pride: he rallied the survivors and advanced in an attempt to seize the fortress.

The accuracy of the archers' aim left the attackers no chance. The standard-bearer fell at the foot of the ramparts with an arrow through his throat. In a few minutes many old campaigners and experienced soldiers had succumbed.

As some hundred footsoldiers, spears in hand, were preparing to avenge their comrades, Ramses intervened.

'Fall back!'

'Majesty,' begged an officer, 'let us exterminate these traitors!'

'If you fling yourselves into a disorganized attack, you will all be killed. Fall back.' The soldiers obeyed.

A volley of arrows fell less than two paces from the king; his senior officers, already close to panic, at once rushed to surround him.

'Let your men encircle the fortress, out of range of their arrows. Put the archers in front, then the footsoldiers, with the chariots behind them.'

The king's coolness had a calming effect. The soldiers recalled the orders given during their training and the troops moved in orderly fashion.

'The wounded must be brought back and treated,' Setau insisted.

'Impossible. The enemy archers would shoot down the rescuers.'

'This wind did indeed bode ill.'

'I don't understand,' lamented Ahsha. 'None of my agents informed me that the rebels had seized this fortress.'

'They must have used trickery,' suggested Setau.

'Even if you're right, the commander would have had time to send off several carrier pigeons, bringing the papyri prepared in advance, to give the alarm.'

'The reality is simple and catastrophic,' Ramses concluded. 'The commander has been killed and his garrison wiped out, and we have received false messages, sent by the rebels. If I had dispersed my troops by sending regiments to the different fortresses in Canaan, we would have suffered heavy losses. The extent of the revolt is considerable. Only the Hittites could have organized a military takeover like this.'

'Do you think they're still in the area?' asked Setau.

'Our most urgent task is to regroup at once.'

'The men occupying this fortress won't hold out for long,' hazarded Ahsha. 'Suggest they surrender. If there are Hittites among them, we will hear what they have to say.'

'Take a squadron, Ahsha, and make the suggestion to them yourself.'

'I'll go with him,' said Setau.

'No, let him demonstrate his skill as a diplomat; at least let him bring back our wounded. You must prepare your remedies and assemble your medical assistants.'

Neither Ahsha nor Setau disputed Ramses' orders. Even the snake-charmer, usually so quick to argue, bowed before Pharaoh's authority.

Five chariots, commanded by Ahsha, drove towards the fortress. A charioteer stood beside the young diplomat, bearing a spear at the tip of which was fastened a strip of white cloth, indicating that the Egyptians wished to parley.

The chariots did not even have time to come to a halt. As soon as they were within range, the Canaanite archers let fly. Two arrows pierced the charioteer's throat and a third grazed Ahsha's arm, leaving a bleeding gash.

'Turn back!' he yelled.

*

'Don't move,' ordered Setau, 'otherwise my honey compress won't be properly applied.'

'You're not the one in pain,' Ahsha protested.

'Are you a softy?'

'I enjoy being wounded and I'd have preferred Lotus to attend to me.'

'In desperate cases, I'm the one to take over. As I used my finest honey, you should get better. The wound will heal quickly without any risk of infection.'

'What savages . . . I couldn't even get a glimpse of their defences.'

'It'll be no good asking Ramses to pardon the rebels; he won't tolerate any attempt to kill his friends, even if they've strayed into the tortuous paths of diplomacy.'

Ahsha winced with pain.

'This is a good excuse not to take part in the attack,' Setau commented ironically.

'Would you have liked the arrow to be more accurate?'

'Stop talking nonsense and rest. If a Hittite falls into our hands, we shall need your talents as interpreter.'

Setau left the vast tent that served as field hospital, where Ahsha was the first patient, and hurried to give Ramses the bad news.

Accompanied by his lion, Ramses had driven round the fortress, his eyes glued to the massive brick structure dominating the plain. Once a symbol of peace and security, it had become a threat that had to be destroyed.

From the ramparts, the Canaanite lookouts kept watch on him. No one shouted any abuse. Their one remaining hope was that the Egyptian army would abandon the idea of taking the stronghold in order to divide up and reconnoitre Canaan, before deciding on their strategy. If they did, the ambushes planned by the Canaanites' Hittite masters would force Ramses' troops to withdraw.

Setau, convinced that he had correctly divined the enemy's thinking, wondered if an overall view of the situation would not be preferable to an attack on a well-defended fortress, which risked costing many lives.

The generals were asking themselves the same question and, after discussing it, intended to suggest to the king that he maintain a contingent to prevent the besieged men from escaping, while the main body of the army continued to advance northwards, so as to obtain a clear picture of the insurrection.

Ramses seemed so absorbed in thought that no one dared approach him until he began to stroke the mane of his lion, which stood motionless and dignified at his side. The man and the beast lived in perfect communion, from which emanated such strength that it filled anyone who approached them with unease.

The oldest of the generals, who had served in Syria under Seti, took the risk of angering the sovereign. 'Majesty, may I speak to you?'

'I'm listening.'

'My opposite numbers and I have discussed the situation at length. We think we should discover the extent of the revolt. Because of the falsified information, we are in the dark about it.'

'What do you suggest we do in order to get a clearer view?'

'Rather than making a desperate attempt to storm this fortress, we should deploy over the whole of Canaan. Then we could strike, being in full command of the situation.'

'An interesting view.'

The old general was relieved. So Ramses was not impervious to the voice of moderation and logic. 'Shall I summon your war council to receive your instructions, Majesty?'

'That's not necessary,' replied the king, 'since they can be summed up in a few words: we attack this fortress immediately.'

15

Ramses bent his acacia-wood bow, strung with a bull's tendon – only he had the necessary strength, which was worthy of the god Set – and shot the first arrow.

The Canaanite lookouts had seen the Egyptian king take up his position more than a hundred paces from the fortresss, and smiled, believing it to be merely a symbolic gesture to encourage the army.

The reed-arrow, tipped with bronze and with nocked butt, described an arc in the clear sky and landed in the first lookout's heart. He gave one stunned glance at the blood gushing from his body and fell headlong into the void. The second lookout felt a violent blow in the middle of his forehead, staggered and followed his comrade. The third, panic-stricken, just had time to call for help, but as he turned he was shot in the back and fell into the outer ward of the fortress. Already, a division of Egyptian bowmen was approaching.

The Canaanite archers tried to deploy along the battlements but they were outnumbered by the Egyptians facing them, who took accurate aim and killed half of them with their first salvo.

The relief force met the same fate. As soon as there were too few enemy archers to defend the approach to the fortress, Ramses ordered his engineers to bring up their scaling-ladders and place them against the walls. Invincible, the enormous lion, watched the scene calmly.

The footsoldiers began to climb the the ladders. Realizing that the Egyptians would give them no quarter, the Canaanites fought till they could fight no more. They threw down rocks from the ramparts and succeeded in dislodging one ladder; several of the attackers fell to the ground with broken bones. But Pharaoh's bowmen made short work of annihilating the rebels. Hundreds of soldiers rapidly scaled the walls and occupied the covered way, while archers shot at the enemy gathered in the outer ward.

Setau and his assistants attended to the wounded, whom they carried back on stretchers to the Egyptian camp. Lotus, the fair Nubian, closed up clean, straight cuts with strips of sticky material arranged in a cross; sometimes she had to stitch more serious gashes. She stopped the bleeding by applying fresh meat to the wound; a few hours later she would apply a dressing of honey, astringent herbs and mouldy bread.* As for Setau, he put his medical supplies to good use; they consisted of various concoctions, lozenges, ointments and potions and pellets of anaesthetizing substances; he relieved pain, anaesthetized the most seriously wounded and settled them as comfortably as possible in his field hospital. Those who were fit to undertake the journey would be sent back to Egypt, together with the dead, not one of whom would be buried in foreign soil. The families of the latter would receive a pension for life.

Inside the fortress, the Canaanites put up only a faint resistance; finally rebels and Egyptians fought hand to hand. Outnumbered ten to one, the former were quickly exterminated. To escape interrogation, which he knew would be merciless, their leader cut his own throat with his dagger.

*

*This mixture possesses the qualities of an antibiotic.

The main gate was thrown open and Pharaoh entered the recaptured fortress.

'Burn the dead,' he ordered, 'and purify the place.'

The soldiers sprinkled the walls with natron and fumigated the living quarters, the food stores and the armoury. Sweet scents filled the conquerors' nostrils. By the time dinner was served in the dining hall of the fortress, all trace of the battle had been wiped out. The generals praised Ramses' spirit of decision and saluted the magnificent outcome of his initiative.

Setau and Lotus had remained with the wounded.

Ahsha seemed anxious.

'Why aren't you rejoicing at this victory, my friend?' asked Setau.

'How many more battles like this shall we have to fight?'

'We shall take the fortresses one by one, and Canaan will be pacified. The surprise factor will no longer be against us, and we shall not risk such serious losses.'

'Fifty dead and a hundred wounded . . .'

'It is a heavy toll, because we were victims of a trap that no one could have foreseen.'

'I should have thought of it,' confessed Ahsha. 'The Hittites aren't content with brute force; with them intrigue is second nature.'

'Were there no Hittites among the dead?'

'Not one.'

'So their raiding parties have withdrawn to the north.'

'Which means we have more traps to fear.'

'We'll cope with them. Go to sleep, Ahsha. Tomorrow we resume our campaign.'

Ramses left behind a strong garrison with the necessary provisions. Several messengers were already on their way to Pi-Ramses, to Ahmeni, bearing orders to send convoys to the recaptured stronghold.

The king, at the head of a hundred chariots, paved the way for his army.

Ten times the same pattern was repeated. Three hundred yards from the rebel-occupied fortress, Ramses sowed panic by killing the archers in position on the ramparts. Under cover of an uninterrupted hail of arrows, which prevented the Canaanites from replying, the Egyptian soldiers put up huge ladders, which they then scaled, protecting themselves with their shields, and they seized the covered ways. They never attempted to force the main gates.

In less than a month, Ramses was once again master of Canaan. As the rebels had massacred the small Egyptian garrisons, including the soldiers' wives and children, not one of them attempted to surrender or beg the king for mercy. Ever since his first victory, Ramses' reputation had terrified the rebels. The capture of the last stronghold, in the north of Canaan, was no more than a formality, since the defenders were simply paralysed by fright.

Galilee, the valley to the north of the River Jordan and the trading routes were once more under Egyptian control. The inhabitants of the region acclaimed Pharaoh, swearing him eternal allegiance.

Not a single Hittite had been captured.

The governor of Gaza, the capital of Canaan, gave a splendid banquet for the Egyptian military staff. With remarkable zeal, his fellow citizens had put themselves at the disposal of Pharaoh's army, offering to attend to and feed horses and donkeys and to supply the soldiers with all their needs. The brief war of reconquest had ended in joy and friendship.

The Canaanite governor made a violent speech denouncing the Hittites, those barbarians from Asia who were trying, unsuccessfully, to break the indestructable ties between his country and Egypt. Enjoying the favour of the gods, Pharaoh had flown to the assistance of his allies, whose loyalty could never be shaken and who knew that the monarch would not abandon them. They mourned, naturally, the tragic deaths of Egyptian citizens. But Ramses had acted according to the law of Ma'at, by combating disorder and restoring order.

'Such hypocrisy sickens me,' the king said to Ahsha.

'Do not hope to change men.'

'I have the power to transfer them.'

Ahsha smiled. 'Replacing that one with another? You can indeed do that. But human nature cannot be changed. As soon as the next governor finds it to his advantage to betray you, he won't hesitate to do so. At least we know the present potentate well: a liar, corrupt, greedy. There will be no problem in handling him.'

'You forget that he agreed to the presence of Hittite raiders in territory controlled by Egypt.'

'Anyone else would have acted the same way.'

'So you advise me to leave this wretch in his place?'

'Threaten to get rid of him at the slightest sign of trouble. The deterrent effect will last for a few months.'

'Is there one single person worthy of your respect, Ahsha?'

'My job means that I meet many powerful men who are ready to do anything to preserve or to increase their power; if I granted them the slightest trust, I'd soon be swept aside.'

'You haven't answered my question.'

'I admire you, Ramses, and to feel admiration is, for me, exceptional. But you, too, are a powerful man, aren't you?'

'I am the servant of the Rule and of my people.'

'But what if, one day, you forgot that?'

'That day, my magic would vanish and my defeat would be irreversible.'

'May the gods see to it that such a misfortune never occurs, Majesty.'

'What are the results of your investigations?'

'The traders in Gaza and some officials have agreed to

confide in me for the usual consideration: it was indeed the Hittite advisers who stirred up the rebellion and taught the Canaanites how to seize the fortresses by trickery.'

'What method did they use?'

'The customary delivery of foodstuffs, with armed men hidden in the carts. All the strongholds were attacked at the same time. To save the lives of women and children taken hostage, the commanders preferred to surrender. A fatal error. The Hittites had assured the Canaanites that Egyptian reprisals would be scattered and ineffectual: by exterminating our garrisons, with which they had been on excellent terms, the rebels thought they would have nothing to fear.'

Ramses did not regret his firmness. The armed might of Egypt had struck against a bunch of cowards.

'Has anyone mentioned Moses?'

'There's no trace of him.'

The war council met in the royal tent. Ramses presided, seated on a folding stool of gilded wood, his lion at his feet. He invited Ahsha and every senior officer to express their views.

The old general spoke first. 'The morale of the army is excellent, as is the condition of the animals and equipment. Your Majesty has just won a remarkable victory which will go down in the annals.'

'Allow me to differ.'

'Majesty, we are proud of having taken part in this battle and—'

'Battle? Keep that word for later; we can use it when we meet real resistance.'

'Pi-Ramses is ready to acclaim you.'

'Pi-Ramses can wait.'

'Since we have restored our authority over Palestine, since the whole of Canaan is pacified, is this not the moment to return home?'

'The most difficult thing remains to be done: the recapture of the province of Amurru.'

'The Hittites may have massed considerable forces there.'

'Are you afraid of fighting, General?'

'We need time to work out our strategy, Majesty.'

'It is worked out: we march straight to the north.'

16

Wearing a short wig bound with a bandeau, whose two loose ends rested on her shoulders, and a long tight-fitting tunic tied at her waist with a red girdle, Nefertari cleansed her hands with water from the sacred lake and entered the inner sanctuary of the temple. In her capacity as wife of the god, the queen could claim the title of Daughter of Light, descended from the creative power which ceaselessly fashioned the universe.

The queen closed the doors of the naos, sealed them, left the temple and followed the ritualists who guided her to the Pi-Ramses House of Light, where, as incarnation of the distant goddess, both Death and Mother, she would attempt to ward off the forces of evil. If she could see with the eye of the Sun she would perpetuate life and ensure the continuity of the cycles of nature; the peaceful happiness of halcyon days depended on her ability to transform into harmony and serenity the destructive forces carried by the perilous winds.

A priest presented a bow to the queen, a priestess four arrows.

Nefertari bent the bow, shot the first arrow to the east, the second to the north, the third to the south and the fourth to the west. Thus she would exterminate the invisible enemies who threatened Ramses.

*

Tuya's steward was waiting for Nefertari. 'The Queen Mother wishes to see you urgently.'

A sedan chair conveyed the Great Royal Wife.

Tuya's slender figure was clad in a long, finely pleated linen gown, tied at the waist with a striped girdle; adorned with gold bracelets and a necklace of six rows of lapis lazuli, Tuya was indeed an elegant sovereign.

'Don't be anxious, Nefertari. A messenger has arrived from Canaan, bringing excellent news. Ramses is now master of the whole of the province, order has been restored.'

'When will he return?'

'He does not say.'

'In other words, the army is pressing on to the north.'

'Probably.'

'Would you have done the same?'

'Unhesitatingly.'

'In the north of Canaan lies the province of Amurru which marks the border between the Egyptian zone of influence and that of the Hittites.'

'Seti wanted it so, in order to avoid war.'

'If the Hittite troops have crossed the border . . . '

'It will mean a confrontation, Nefertari.'

'I have shot the arrows to the four corners of the land.'

'If the rite has been accomplished, what have we to fear?'

Shaanar detested Ahmeni. It was intolerable to be obliged, every morning, to encounter this skinny, pretentious little scribe in order to obtain information about Ramses' expedition! When he, Shaanar, reigned, Ahmeni would be sent to clean out the stables of a provincial regiment and lose the little health he possessed. His only satisfaction was that day after day the secretary's face grew longer and longer and his expression ever more downcast, a sure sign that the Egyptian army was making no progress. The king's elder brother put on a look of distress and promised to pray to the gods for a more favourable fate.

With little to do at the Foreign Affairs secretariat, but letting it be known that he was working unremittingly, Shaanar avoided all contact with the Syrian merchant Raia. In these anxious times it would have been shocking for someone of Shaanar's standing to be concerned with buying vases from foreign lands. So he contented himself with the elliptic messages sent by Raia. Their tenor was quite cheerful: according to Syrian observers in the pay of the Hittites, Ramses had fallen into the trap laid by the Canaanites. Pharaoh had been too self-assured and had followed his hot-headed nature, forgetting his enemies' gift for intrigue.

Shaanar had solved the little riddle that had been worrying the court: who had stolen Nefertari's shawl and the jar of dried fish from the Heliopolis House of Life? The culprit could be none other than the fat and jovial head steward of the royal household, Remet. So, before going to his obligatory appointment with Ahmeni, he had summoned the steward under some trifling pretext.

Pot-bellied, plump-cheeked, burdened with a triple chin, Remet carried out his work to perfection. Slow-moving, a stickler for hygiene and detail, he himself tasted the dishes served to the royal family and treated his staff roughly. Appointed to this difficult post by the monarch himself, he had silenced his critics and imposed his standards on all the palace servants. To disobey him meant summary dismissal.

'What can I do for you, my lord?' Remet asked Shaanar.

'Did my steward not tell you?'

'He mentioned a problem of protocol on the occasion of a banquet, but I can't see—'

'Suppose we talk about the jar of dried fish stolen from the store-room of the Heliopolis House of Light?'

'The jar . . . but I know nothing about it.'

'And Queen Nefertari's shawl?'

'I've been told, naturally, and I deplore the scandal, but—'

'Have you looked for the culprit?'

'It's not my job to undertake the investigation, Lord Shaanar!'

'Nevertheless, you are well placed to do so, Remet.'

'No, I don't think so—'

'Oh, yes. Just think! You are the key man in the palace; no incident should escape you.'

'You overestimate me.'

'Why did you commit these offences?'

'Me? You don't think—'

'I don't think. I'm certain. Who did you give the queen's shawl and the jar of fish to?'

'You're wrong to accuse me!'

'I know men, Remet. And I have proof.'

'*Proof?*'

'Why did you take such risks?'

Remet's haggard expression, the unhealthy flush that flooded his forehead and cheeks, the increased flaccidity of his body were so many revealing signs. Shaanar was not mistaken.

'Either you were well paid, or else you hate Ramses. In either case, it is a serious offence.'

'Lord Shaanar . . . I . . . ' His distress was almost touching.

'Since you are an excellent steward, I am prepared to forget this deplorable incident. But if I need you in future, you must not be ungrateful.'

Ahmeni was drawing up his daily report for Ramses. His hand was sure and quick.

'May I bother you for a few moments?' Shaanar asked amiably.

'You're not bothering me. You and I both obey the king, who requires from us a daily up-to-date report on the situation.' The scribe put his palette down on the ground.

'You look exhausted, Ahmeni.'

'It's only a look.'

'Shouldn't you take more care of your health?'

'I am only concerned with the health of Egypt.'

'Have you had . . . bad news?'

'On the contrary.'

'Can you be more explicit?'

'I was waiting for confirmation before telling you of Ramses' success. As we were deceived by false messages brought by carrier pigeons, I have learned to be prudent.'

'One of the Hittites' ideas?'

'It nearly cost us dear! Our fortresses in Canaan had fallen into rebel hands. If the king had dispersed his forces, our losses would have been disastrous.'

'Fortunately, that didn't happen.'

'The province of Canaan has been subdued once more, and access to the coast is open. The governor has sworn to remain a loyal subject of Pharaoh.'

'A magnificent success! Ramses has performed a great exploit and repelled the Hittite menace. I suppose the army is on its way back?'

'That's a military secret.'

'What do you mean, "a military secret"? I'm minister for foreign affairs and don't you forget it!'

'That's all I know.'

'Impossible!'

'That's the way it is.'

Shaanar withdrew angrily.

Ahmeni was feeling guilty. Not because of his attitude to Shaanar, but he was wondering about the summary way he had handled the Serramanna affair. It's true the accumulated evidence against the Sardinian was overwhelming, but had he perhaps been too credulous? Prey to the excitement that accompanied the army's departure, Ahmeni had not been as scrupulous as usual. He should have confirmed the evidence which had thrown the mercenary into prison. It was probably a useless exercise, but conscientiousness demanded it of him.

Annoyed with himself, Ahmeni went back to the Serramanna dossier.

17

The fortress of Megiddo, the military base guarding the access to Syria, stood at the top of a rise, visible from a great distance. The only hill in the middle of a verdant plain, it seemed impregnable: stone walls, battlements, high, square towers, wooden scaffolding, wide, thick gateways. The garrison consisted of Egyptians and Syrians loyal to Pharaoh, but how could one believe the official messages stating that the fortress had not fallen into rebel hands?

Ramses was discovering an unfamiliar landscape: high, wooded hills, oaks with gnarled trunks, muddy rivers, marshes, sometimes sandy soil. A difficult country, hostile and shut in, very different from the beauty of the Nile and the soft Egyptian countryside.

Twice a herd of wild boars had charged the Egyptian scouts, guilty of disturbing the peace of a sow and her young. Handicapped by the dense, overgrown vegetation, the horse-men had difficulty in advancing through the tangle of bushes and threading their way between the trunks of huge trees growing in serried ranks. However, these drawbacks were made up for by an abundance of waterholes and game.

Ramses gave the order to halt, but not to pitch the tents. Keeping his eyes fixed on the fortress of Megiddo, he awaited the scouts' return.

Setau took advantage of the pause to attend to the wounded

and administer his potions. The seriously wounded having been repatriated, the army now consisted solely of men in good physical condition, with the exception of patients suffering from heat and cold, and gastric upsets. Preparations based on bryony, cumin and castor oil cleared up these minor disorders. As a precaution, the men continued to eat garlic and onions, of which the variety known as 'snake-wood', from the margins of the eastern desert, was the one Setau favoured.

Lotus had just saved a donkey that had been bitten on the leg by a water-snake, which she had managed to capture. This journey into Syria was finally taking an interesting turn: up till then she had only come across known specimens. This one, although not very poisonous, was a novelty.

Two footsoldiers came to call on the Nubian's skills, under the pretext that they too had been the victims of a reptile. Resounding slaps rewarded their lies. When Lotus brought the hissing head of a viper out of a bag, the fellows fled and took refuge among their comrades.

More than two hours had passed. With the king's permission, the cavalry had dismounted, the charioteers alighted and the footsoldiers sat down on the ground, surrounded by several lookouts.

'The scouts have been gone for a long time,' said Ahsha thoughtfully.

'I agree,' said Ramses. 'How's your wound?'

'Healed. That Setau is a real sorcerer.'

'What do you think of this spot?'

'I don't like it. In front of us it's all open ground, but there are marshes. On both sides there are oak forests, bushes, tall grass. Our troops are too scattered.'

'The scouts aren't coming back,' Ramses stated. 'Either they've been killed or they're being held prisoner in the fortress.'

'That means that Megiddo has fallen into the enemy's

hands and has no intention of surrendering.'

'This stronghold is the key to southern Syria,' Ramses reminded him. 'Even if the Hittites have shut themselves up here, it is our duty to recapture it.'

'There will be no question of declaring war,' Ahsha said. 'We shall simply be recovering territory which belongs in our zone of influence. So we can attack at any moment without prior warning. Legally, we remain within the framework of a rebellion which must be put down; that's nothing to do with a confrontation between states.'

In the eyes of the surrounding countries, the young diplomat's analysis would be acceptable.

'Warn the generals to prepare to attack.'

Ahsha had no time to pull on the reins of his horse. A troop of horsemen galloped out of a dense wood to the king's right and hurled themselves on the Egyptian charioteers, who were resting. A number of the unfortunates were pierced by short spears, and several horses were hamstrung or had their throats cut. The survivors defended themselves with their pikes and swords; some managed to climb into their chariots and ride back to a position held by the footsoldiers, sheltering behind their shields.

This violent surprise attack seemed crowned with success. The attackers' bandeaux tied round their thick hair, their pointed beards, their fringed gowns falling to their ankles, their coloured sashes covered with a scarf made them easily recognizable as Syrians.

Ramses remained strangely calm.

Ahsha was alarmed. 'They are going to break through our ranks!'

'They're wrong to be elated about what they've achieved.'

The Syrians' advance was blocked. The Egyptian footsoldiers forced them to fall back towards the archers, whose aim was deadly.

The lion growled.

'Another danger threatens us,' said Ramses. 'Now the outcome of this battle is in the balance.'

From the same wood several hundred Syrians sallied forth, armed with short-handled axes. They had only a short distance to go in order to strike the Egyptian bowmen from the rear.

'On!' the king commanded his horses.

At their master's tone of voice, the two war-horses understood that they had to give of their utmost. The lion bounded forward, and Ahsha and some fifty chariots followed.

The skirmish was of unheard-of violence. Those bold enough to attack Ramses' chariot were mauled in the head and chest by the lion, while the king, aiming arrow after arrow, pierced hearts, throats and foreheads. The chariots rode over the wounded; the footsoldiers rallied to the rescue and put the Syrians to flight.

Ramses caught sight of a strange-looking warrior running towards the wood.

'Catch him,' he ordered the lion.

Invincible finished off two Syrians who had fallen behind, and leapt on the man, hurling him to the ground. Although he had tried to contain his strength, the beast fatally injured his prisoner, who lay on the ground, his back torn to shreds. Ramses examined him. He had long hair and an uncut beard; his long red-and-black striped gown was in tatters.

'Send for Setau,' the king ordered.

The battle was drawing to a close. The Syrians had been slaughtered to the last man and had inflicted only light losses on the Egyptian army.

Setau arrived, panting.

'Save this man,' the king requested. 'He's not a Syrian but a sand-traveller. He must tell us why he is here.'

A Bedouin, who'd usually be busy pillaging caravans, so far from his base in the Sinai area . . . ? Setau was intrigued.

'Your lion has made a mess of him.'

The wounded man's face was covered with sweat, blood ran from his nostrils, the back of his neck was stiff. Setau took his pulse and listened to his heartbeat, which was so weak that diagnosis was not difficult: the sand-traveller was dying.

'Can he speak?' asked the king.

'His jaws have contracted, but there may be a chance.'

Setau managed to slip into the dying man's mouth a wooden tube wrapped round with a rag, and poured down it a liquid made from cypress rhizomes.

'This remedy should relieve the pain. If this fellow is tough, he'll survive for a few hours.'

The sand-traveller caught sight of Pharaoh. Terrified, he tried to raise himself, bit through the wooden tube and waved his arms about like a bird unable to fly.

'Quiet, my friend,' Setau advised him. 'I shall look after you.'

'Ramses . . . '

'It is indeed Egypt's Pharaoh who wishes to speak to you.'

The Bedouin stared at the Blue Crown.

'Do you come from Sinai?' asked the king.

'Yes, that is my country.'

'Why are you fighting on the side of the Syrians?'

'Gold . . . They promised me gold . . . '

'Did you meet any Hittites?'

'They gave us a plan of battle and left.'

'Any other Bedouin with you?'

'They have fled.'

'Have you come across a Hebrew named Moses?'

'Moses?'

Ramses described his friend.

'No, I don't know him.'

'Have you heard of him?'

'No, I don't think so.'

'How many men inside the fortress?'

'I . . . I don't know.'

'Don't lie.'

With unexpected abruptness, the wounded man grabbed his dagger, raised himself up and tried to stab the king. Setau disarmed him with a sharp blow to the wrist. The Bedouin's effort had been too violent. His face contracted, his body arched and he fell back, dead.

'So the Syrians have tried to ally themselves with the Bedouin,' commented Setau. 'How stupid! Those peoples will never understand each other.'

Setau returned to the Egyptian wounded, who were already being treated by Lotus and the medical assistants. The dead had been wrapped in mats and loaded on to chariots. A convoy, protected by an escort, would leave for Egypt, where these unfortunates would enjoy the rites of resurrection.

Ramses patted his horses and his lion; the latter's subdued growls sounded like purring. Soldiers crowded round the sovereign, raised their weapons towards the sky and acclaimed the one who had just led them to victory with the skill of an experienced warrior. The generals managed to push their way through and hastened to congratulate Ramses.

He asked, 'Have you seen any other Syrians in the neighbouring woods?'

'No, Majesty. Will you permit us to pitch camp?'

'We have something better to do: recapture Megiddo.'

18

Reinvigorated by an enormous dish of lentils which would not put an ounce of fat on him, Ahmeni, the king's private secretary, had spent the night at his desk, so as to make progress on the next day's work and find time to study the Serramanna file. When his back ached he touched the brush-holder of gilded wood, in the shape of a pillar surmounted by a lily, given him by Ramses when he had engaged him as his secretary. His energy was immediately restored.

Ever since his adolescence Ahmeni had enjoyed invisible links with Ramses and instinctively knew if the son of Seti was in danger or not. Several times he had felt death brushing the king's shoulder and only the latter's personal magic had allowed him to deflect the danger.

If this barrier, erected round Pharaoh by the gods, were to be shattered, Ramses' fearlessness might bring about his defeat. And if Serramanna was one of the stones in this magic wall, Ahmeni had made a serious mistake in preventing him from doing his duty. Was this remorse justified, though?

The accusation rested for the most part on the evidence of Nenophar, Serramanna's mistress. Ahmeni had told the police to bring her to him so he could question her more thoroughly. If this girl had lied, he would force her to speak the truth.

At seven o'clock the policeman in charge of the inquiry, a

level-headed fifty-year-old, presented himself at Ahmeni's office.

'Nenophar won't be coming,' he declared.

'Did she refuse to accompany you?'

'There's no one at her house.'

'Does she in fact live at the address given?'

'According to the neighbours, yes, but she left several days ago.'

'Without saying where she was going?'

'No one knows anything.'

'Have you searched the place?'

'We found nothing. Even the linen chests were empty, as if this woman wanted to suppress all trace of her existence.'

'What have you found out about her?'

'A very frivolous young person, apparently. Malicious tongues claim that she lived off her charms.'

'So she must have worked in an ale-house.'

'No, she didn't. I've made the necessary inquiries.'

'Did men visit her?'

'According to the neighbours, no; but she was often out, especially at night.'

'She must be found so that she can identify her possible employers.'

'We'll find her.'

'You must hurry.'

When the policeman had gone, Ahmeni reread the wooden tablets on which Serrramanna had written the note to his Hittite accomplice, which proved his guilt. In the quiet of his office, at this early hour when his mind was alert, a new idea dawned on Ahmeni. He would have to wait for Ahsha's return in order to verify it.

The Egyptian army, which had deployed over the plain, was overawed by the fortress of Megiddo, standing high on a rocky spur. Because of the height of the walls, they had to construct huge ladders, which it would not be easy to place against the walls. The assault troops risked being decimated by arrows and stones.

With Ahsha at his side, Ramses drove his chariot at great speed round the stronghold, in such a way as not to offer an easy target to the enemy archers. Not a single arrow was aimed at him, not a single bowman appeared on the battlements.

'They'll stay hidden until the last minute,' Ahsha opined. 'That way, they won't waste any missiles. The best solution would be to starve them out.'

'Megiddo's reserves would allow them to hold out for several months. There's nothing more appalling than an interminable siege.'

'If we make successive attacks, we'll lose many men.'

'Do you think I'm so heartless that all I dream of is a new victory?'

'Does not Egypt's honour come before the fate of men?'

'Every life is precious to me, Ahsha.'

'What do you recommend?'

'We shall deploy our chariots round the fortress, within bowshot, and our archers will wipe out the Syrians who emerge on to the battlements. Three teams of volunteers will raise the ladders, protecting themselves behind their shields.'

'And what if Megiddo is impregnable?'

'Let us first try to take it. If all we think of is failure, we've failed before we've begun.'

The energy emanating from Ramses galvanized the soldiers with renewed vigour. Hosts of volunteers presented themselves; bowmen queued up to clamber into the chariots that encircled the stronghold – that silent, alarming beast.

Carrying the long ladders on their shoulders, columns of footsoldiers marched energetically towards the walls. While they were raising the ladders, Syrian archers appeared on the highest tower and bent their bows. Not one of them had time to take aim: Ramses and the Egyptian bowmen shot them down. They were replaced by a second wave of defenders, with thick hair held by a bandeau, and with pointed beards; the Syrians succeeded in firing a few arrows, but failed to hit a single Egyptian. The king and his elite archers wiped them all out.

'What feeble resistance,' the old general commented to Setau. 'You'd swear these people had never fought before.'

'All the better. I shall have less work and may be able to spend a night with Lotus. These battles exhaust me.'

The footsoldiers were starting to scale the walls when some fifty women appeared. The Egyptian army was not in the habit of slaughtering women and children, who were usually taken back to Egypt as prisoners of war and became servants on great farming estates. After changing their names, they were often integrated into Egyptian society.

The general was filled with dismay. 'I thought I'd seen everything! Those wretched women are mad!'

Two Syrian women hoisted a brazier on to the top of the wall and emptied its contents on to the footsoldiers below, who were climbing up. The burning coals skimmed past the attackers, who flattened themselves against the rungs of the ladders. The Egyptians' arrows pierced the women's eyes and they fell into the void. Those who replaced them with new braziers suffered the same fate.

An excited girl placed burning coals in her sling and hurled them into the distance. One of the glowing embers struck the old general on the thigh. He collapsed, clutching the burn.

'Don't touch it,' Setau advised him. 'Stay still and let me see to it.'

Lifting his loin-cloth, the snake-charmer urinated on the burn. Like him, the general knew that urine, as opposed to well or river water, was a sterile medium and cleansed the sore without risk of infection. Stretcher-bearers conveyed the wounded man to the field hospital.

The footsoldiers reached the ramparts, now cleared of defenders. A few minutes later, the vast gate of Megiddo fortress was thrown open. Inside, only a few women and terrified children remained.

'The Syrians tried to beat us off by concentrating all their forces in a battle outside the fortress,' observed Ahsha.

'The manoeuvre could have succeeded,' commented Ramses.

'They don't know you.'

'Who can boast of knowing me, my friend?'

A dozen soldiers were beginning to pillage the fortress treasure-house, which was filled with vessels of alabaster and silver statuettes. A growl from the lion scattered them.

'See that these men are arrested,' decreed Ramses. 'And let the dwelling places be purified and fumigated.'

The king appointed a governor, responsible for selecting a troop of officers and men who would reside in Megiddo. In the storehouses there was enough food for several weeks. Already a detachment of soldiers was setting out in search of game and herds.

Ramses, Ahsha and the new governor reorganized the economy of the region; the peasants, no longer knowing who their master was, had stopped their work in the fields. In less than a week, the Egyptian presence was once more felt to be a guarantee of security and peace.

Some distance to the north of Megiddo the king had little forts built, each occupied by four lookouts and a few horses. In case of a Hittite attack, the garrison would have time to take shelter.

From the top of the main tower, Ramses gazed out over a landscape which was little to his liking. To live far from the Nile, the palm groves, the verdant countryside and the desert, would be an affliction. At this peaceful hour, Nefertari was celebrating the evening rites. How he missed her!

Ahsha interrupted the king's thoughts. 'I've done as you

asked and talked to the officers and men.'

'What are their feelings?'

'They have total confidence in you, but all they want is to go home.'

'Do you like Syria at all, Ahsha?'

'It is a dangerous country, full of pitfalls. To know it well requires long sojourns there.'

'Is the land of the Hittites like it?'

'It is even wilder and more harsh. In winter, on the heights of Anatolia, the wind is icy.'

'Do you think it would appeal to me?'

'You are Egypt, Ramses. No other land will ever find a place in your heart.'

'The province of Amurru is nearby.'

'So is the enemy.'

'Do you think the Hittite army has invaded Amurru?'

'We've no reliable information.'

'What do you really believe?'

'That is probably where they're waiting for us.'

19

Bordering the sea, between the coastal cities of Tyre and Byblos, the province of Amurru lay to the east of Mount Hermon and the trading city of Damascus. It was the last Egyptian protectorate before the frontier of the zone of Hittite influence.

Now more than two hundred and fifty miles from Egypt, Pharaoh's soldiers advanced with a heavy step. Contrary to his generals' advice, Ramses had avoided the coastal road and followed a mountainous track, testing for animals and men alike. There was no more laughter, no more chatting among themselves. The army was preparing to confront the Hittites, whose reputation for ferocity frightened even the most courageous.

According to Ahsha's assessment of the situation, the recapture of Amurru would not be an act of open war. Yet great numbers were likely to succumb under the blood-red sun! Many had hoped that the king would be satisfied with Megiddo and take the road home again. However, Ramses had granted his army only a brief rest before imposing this new effort on them.

A scout galloped back along the column and came to a sudden halt in front of Ramses. 'They are there, Majesty, at the end of this track, between the cliff and the sea.'

'Many of them?'

'Several hundred, hidden behind bushes and armed with spears and bows. As they are keeping watch on the coast road, we shall approach them from their rear.'

'Are they Hittites?'

'No, Majesty, people from Amurru province.'

Ramses was puzzled. What trap was being laid for the Egyptian army?

'Lead me there.'

The general in charge of the chariot corps intervened. 'Pharaoh must not take such a risk.'

Ramses' eyes flashed. 'I must see, judge and decide for myself.'

The king followed the scout. The two men finished their journey on foot and came to an area of steep ground to which rocks clung precariously.

Ramses halted. The sea, the track running along it, the tangle of bushes, the enemy lying in wait, the cliff . . . nowhere for the massed Hittite forces to lay an ambush. But the horizon was closed in by another cliff. Dozens of Anatolian chariots might be hidden a good distance away, able to intervene speedily. Ramses had in his hands the lives of his soldiers, themselves the guarantees of Egypt's safety.

'We will deploy,' he murmured.

The Prince of Amurru's footsoldiers were dozing. As soon as the first Egyptians arrived from the south by the coast road, they would take them by surprise.

Prince Benteshina was applying the strategy forced on him by his Hittite masters. They were convinced that Ramses, in whose path several traps had been laid, would never get as far as this. Even if he did, his forces would be so weakened that one last trap would easily finish them off.

Benteshina, a well-upholstered fifty-year-old endowed with a fine black moustache, had no liking for the Hittites, but he feared them. Amurru was so close to their zone of influence that it was not in his interest to thwart them. True, he was the vassal of Egypt and paid tribute to Pharaoh; but the Hittites took a different view of the matter, forcing him to rebel and strike the final blow against the exhausted Egyptian army.

Parched with thirst, Prince Benteshina asked his cupbearer to bring him some chilled wine while he waited in the shade of a cave in the cliffs.

The servant had only time to take a few steps. 'My lord, look!'

'Hurry up, I'm thirsty.'

'Look! On the cliff. Hundreds, no, thousands, of Egyptians!'

Benteshina rose to his feet, dumbfounded. The cupbearer was telling the truth.

A tall man, wearing a blue crown and a kilt glinting with gold, was making his way down the path to the coastal plain. On his right walked an enormous lion.

First singly, and then as one man, the Amurrite soldiers turned, to be faced by the same sight as their leader. The sleepers were roughly shaken awake.

'Where are you hiding, Benteshina?' asked Ramses in his grave, strong voice.

Trembling, the Prince of Amurru approached Pharaoh.

'Are you not my vassal?'

'Majesty, I have always served Egypt loyally.'

'Why was your army laying an ambush for me?'

'We thought . . . the safety of our province . . . '

A muffled sound, like that of a distant stampede, filled the air. Ramses looked into the distance towards the cliffs behind which the Hittite chariots might be hiding.

For Pharaoh it was the moment of truth. 'You have betrayed me, Benteshina.'

'No, Majesty! The Hittites forced me to obey them. If I had refused, they would have slaughtered me and all my people.

115

We were waiting for you to arrive and free us from their yoke.'

'Where are they?'

'They have left, convinced that only remnants of your army would get as far as here, if you ever managed to overcome all the many obstacles set up in your path.'

'What is that strange noise?'

'Huge waves arise out of the sea, roll across the rocks and crash against the cliff.'

'Your men were ready to give battle. Mine are resolved to fight.'

Benteshina knelt down. 'How sad it is, Majesty, to descend into the land of silence where death reigns! A man who was once awake sleeps an everlasting sleep, day after day, his senses numbed. The abode of those who dwell down there is so deep, with neither door nor window, that their voices cannot reach us. No ray of sunshine lights up the sombre realm of the dead, no breeze breathes new life into their hearts. No one wishes to travel to that frightful country. I implore Pharaoh's pardon! Let the people of Amurru be spared so that they may continue to serve you.'

Seeing their master so submissive, the Amurrite soldiers threw down their arms.

Ramses raised Benteshina, who bowed low before him, and then cries of joy went up from the throats of the Egyptians and their allies.

When he left Ahmeni's office, Shaanar was shattered. At the end of a military campaign conducted with incredible speed, Ramses had reconquered the province of Amurru, which had come under Hittite influence! How had this young, inexperienced king, leading his army into hostile territory for the first time, managed to foil the enemy's ambushes and win such a dazzling victory?

Shaanar had long ceased to believe in the existence of the

gods, but it was obvious that Ramses enjoyed some magical protection which Seti had bequeathed to him in the course of a secret rite. It was that force which was marking out his path.

Shaanar drew up an official letter to Ahmeni. In his capacity as minister for foreign affairs, he was going in person to Memphis to announce the good news to the notables.

'Where is the magus?' Shaanar asked Dolora.

The stout, languid brunette held tight to a fair-haired young woman – Lita, Akhenaton's heiress, who was clearly terrified of Shaanar's anger.

'He is working.'

'I wish to see him immediately.'

'Be patient for a little while. He is preparing a new session of conjuration using Nefertari's shawl.'

'Much good that has done! Do you know that Ramses has reconquered Amurru, recaptured all the Canaanite fortresses and reimposed his law in our northern protectorates? Our losses are minute, our beloved brother has received not the slightest scratch and he has even become a god to his soldiers!'

'Are you sure?'

'Ahmeni is an excellent source of information. That damned scribe is so cautious that he's probably not even telling us the whole truth. Canaan, Amurru and southern Syria will never return to the Hittite fold. You can count on Ramses to set up a well-fortified base there and a buffer zone that the enemy won't cross again. Instead of destroying my brother, we have reinforced his defensive system – a fine result!'

Lita gazed at Shaanar.

'The prospect of our reigning together grows faint, my dear. Suppose you have duped me, you and your magus?'

Shaanar ripped off the top of the young woman's gown,

tearing the shoulder straps. Her breast bore the traces of deep burns.

Lita burst into sobs and huddled against Dolora.

'Don't torture her, Shaanar. She and Ofir are our most valuable allies.'

'Fine allies, indeed!'

'Do not doubt it, my lord,' said a slow, deliberate voice.

Shaanar turned round. The magus Ofir, with his hawk-like features, once more filled him with awe. The Libyan's dark-green eyes seemed able to cast evil spells that could fell an adversary in a few seconds.

'I am dissatisfied with your services, Ofir.'

'You have seen that neither Lita nor I are sparing our efforts. As I explained to you, we are up against a strong opponent and we need time to act. As long as Nefertari's shawl is not completely destroyed, her magic protection will not be abolished. If we proceed too quickly, we'll kill Lita and have no hope of ousting the usurper.'

'How long will it take, Ofir?'

'Lita is delicate, because she is an excellent medium. Between each session of bewitchment Dolora and I treat her burns, and we have to wait for them to heal completely before using her gifts again.'

'Can't you use another creature like her?'

The magus's expression hardened. 'Lita is not a creature but your future wife and Queen of Egypt. She has been preparing for this ruthless battle for several years and we shall win. No one can replace her.'

'Agreed. But Ramses' fame continues to grow!'

'Misfortune may put an end to it in an instant.'

'My brother is no ordinary man, and he is filled with a strange power.'

'I am aware of that, Lord Shaanar. That is why I call on the most arcane resources of my science. It would be a grave mistake to act precipitously. Nevertheless . . . ' Shaanar hung on Ofir's words ' . . . nevertheless I shall try a selective action against Ramses. A victorious man can become too sure of himself and lower his guard. We shall take advantage of any moment of weakness.'

20

There were festivities throughout the province of Amurru. Prince Benteshina had insisted on magificent celebrations in honour of Ramses and the return of peace. Solemn declarations of allegiance had been inscribed on papyrus and the prince had promised the speedy delivery of trunks of cedar trees which would be erected in front of the pylons of Egyptian temples. The Amurrite soldiers brimmed over with expressions of friendship for their Egyptian counterparts; wine flowed freely; the women used their charms on their protectors.

Setau and Lotus were pleased to take part in the festivities, even if they weren't fooled by this forced rejoicing, and they were delighted to meet an old sorcerer who loved snakes. Although the local species had venom of no great quality and were less aggressive than those in Egypt, the specialists exchanged a few professional secrets.

In spite of his host's attentions, Ramses remained grim. Benteshina put this attitude down to the gravity which Pharaoh, the most powerful man on earth, felt bound to maintain in all circumstances.

Ahsha thought otherwise.

At the end of a banquet attended by all the Egyptian and high-ranking Amurrite officers, Ramses withdrew to a terrace of the princely palace where Benteshina had lodged his illustrious guest, and was staring out towards the north.

'May I interrupt your meditations?'

'What do you want, Ahsha?'

'You don't seem to be enjoying the lavish entertainment offered by the Prince of Amurru.'

'He betrayed us, and he'll betray us again. But I'm following your advice: why replace him since we know his weaknesses?'

'I wasn't thinking of him.'

'Do you perhaps know what's troubling me?'

'Your gaze is fixed on Kadesh.'

'Kadesh, the pride of the Hittites, the symbol of their domination over northern Syria, the permanent danger that threatens Egypt! Yes, I'm thinking about Kadesh.'

'To attack that stronghold means entering the zone of Hittite influence. If you decide to do so, we must make a formal declaration of war, according to the rules.'

'Did they respect the rules when they stirred up rebellions in our protectorates?'

'Those were merely gestures of revolt. To attack Kadesh means crossing the real border between Egypt and the Hittite Empire – in other words, full-scale war, a war liable to last several months and to destroy us.'

'We're ready.'

'No, Ramses. You shouldn't be too euphoric about your successes.'

'Do you think they're unimportant?'

'You have beaten only mediocre troops; those from Amurru surrendered their weapons without striking a blow. That won't happen with the Hittites. What's more, our men are exhausted and they long to go home. To engage now in a large-scale conflict will lead us to disaster.'

'Is our army so weak?'

'They were prepared in body and mind for a campaign of reconquest, not for an attack on an empire whose military capacity is superior to ours.'

'Isn't your caution dangerous?'

'The battle of Kadesh will take place, if such is your wish; but see that you prepare well for it.'

'I shall make my decision tonight.'

The festivities were over. At dawn, word circulated through the barracks: prepare for battle. Two hours later, Ramses rode up in his chariot drawn by his two faithful horses. He was wearing his battle armour.

Many a man felt his heart sink. Was there really any truth in the ridiculous rumour that was circulating? To attack Kadesh, to march against the indestructable Hittite citadel, come face to face with barbarians whose cruelty was unequalled . . . No, the young king could not have conceived such a ridiculous plan! As the heir to his father's wisdom, he would respect the enemy's zone of influence and choose to consolidate the peace.

Ramses reviewed his troops. Faces were tense and anxious; from the youngest soldier to the most experienced campaigner, the men stood stiffly to attention, their muscles almost aching. The rest of their lives depended on the words Pharaoh would utter.

Setau, who detested military parades, lay on his stomach in his chariot, being massaged by Lotus, whose naked breasts brushed his shoulder-blades.

Prince Benteshina was lying low in his palace, unable to swallow the creamy cakes with which he normally liked to stuff himself at breakfast. If Ramses declared war on the Hittites, the province of Amurru would serve as a rear base for the Egyptian army and its inhabitants would be recruited as mercenaries. If Ramses were defeated, the Hittites would put the country to fire and the sword.

Ahsha tried to divine the king's intentions, but his face was unreadable.

When the inspection was over, Ramses turned his chariot round. For one moment the horses seemed about to set off for the north, towards Kadesh. Then Pharaoh turned towards the south, towards Egypt.

Setau shaved with a bronze razor, ran his wooden comb with its uneven teeth through his hair, anointed his face with an insect-repellent ointment, cleaned his sandals and rolled up his mat. He was not as elegant as Ahsha, but insisted on looking smarter than usual, in spite of Lotus's tinkling laughter.

Since the Egyptian army had started on the road home, Setau and Lotus had finally had time to make love in the chariot. The footsoldiers continued to sing of Pharaoh's fame, while the occupants of the chariots, the elite arm, simply hummed along. All the military shared the same conviction: how fine a soldier's life was when he didn't have to fight!

The army made good speed crossing Amurru, Galilee and Palestine, whose inhabitants acclaimed them as they passed, presenting them with fresh fruit and vegetables. Before completing the final stage, which would bring them to the entrance to the Delta, they pitched camp in northern Sinai to the west of the Negev, in a region of scorching heat where the desert police kept watch on the nomads' movements and protected the caravans.

Setau was jubilant. Huge vipers and cobras, with very powerful poison, abounded here. With her usual skill, Lotus had already captured a dozen around the camp; with a smile, she watched the soldiers keep their distance as she passed.

Ramses gazed at the desert. He looked towards the north, towards Kadesh.

'Your decision was perceptive and wise,' declared Ahsha.

'Does wisdom consist of retreating in the face of the enemy?'

'It does not consist of getting slaughtered nor of attempting the impossible.'

'You're wrong, Ahsha; true courage is akin to the impossible.'

'For the first time, Ramses, you frighten me; where do you intend to drag Egypt?'

'Do you believe that the threat of Kadesh will disappear by itself?'

'Diplomacy allows apparently inextricable conflicts to be resolved.'

'Will your diplomacy disarm the Hittites?'

'Why not?'

'Bring me the genuine peace I wish for, Ahsha. Otherwise I shall make that peace myself.'

There were a hundred and fifty of them. One hundred and fifty men, sand-travellers, Bedouin and Hebrews, who for several weeks had been scouring the Negev area in search of caravans which had gone astray. All obeyed a one-eyed man of forty who had managed to escape from a military prison before he could be executed. His name was Vargoz. He had made thirty attacks on caravans and murdered twenty-three Egyptian and foreign merchants. Vargoz was a hero in the eyes of his tribe.

When the Egyptian army appeared on the horizon they thought it was a mirage. Chariots, horsemen, footsoldiers . . . Vargoz and his men took shelter in a cave, determined not to emerge until the enemy had vanished.

During the night, one face had haunted Vargoz's dreams: a hawk-like face, and a soft, persuasive voice, that of the Libyan magus Ofir, whom Vargoz had known well in his youth. In an isolated oasis, between Libya and Egypt, the magus had taught him to read and write and had used him as a medium. Last night, that imperious face had emerged from the past and the soft voice had once again given orders Vargoz could not disobey.

White-lipped and with crazed eyes, the chief of the band

124

had woken his accomplices. 'Our finest exploit,' he explained. 'Follow me.'

As usual, they obeyed. Wherever Vargoz led, there was booty to be had.

When they reached the outskirts of the Egyptian camp, several of the bandits rebelled. 'Who do you intend to rob?'

'The finest tent, over there. It contains treasures.'

'We haven't a chance!'

'There aren't many sentries and they don't expect an attack. Work fast and you'll be rich men.'

'It's Pharaoh's army,' objected one of the nomads. 'Even if we succeed, they'll catch up with us!'

'Idiot, do you think we shall stay in the area? With the gold we steal we shall be richer than princes!'

'Gold . . .'

'Pharaoh never moves without a quantity of gold and precious stones. That's what he uses to win over his vassals.'

'Who told you this?'

'A dream.'

The nomad gazed at Vargoz in astonishment. 'You're joking!'

'Are you going to obey me or not?'

'And risk my life for a dream? Are you out of your mind?'

Vargoz brought his axe down on the sand-traveller's neck, half decapitating him. Then he kicked the dying man repeatedly and finished him off by cutting off his head.

'Anyone else want to argue?'

The hundred and forty-nine men crawled towards Pharaoh's tent.

Vargoz would do as Ofir had ordered: cut off one of Pharaoh's legs and turn him into a cripple.

21

Several sentries were dozing while on watch. Others were dreaming of their homes and families. Only one noticed a strange form crawling towards them, and Vargoz strangled him before he could raise the alarm. The members of the tribe had to admit that their chief was right again. Approaching the royal tent presented hardly any difficulties.

Vargoz had no idea whether Ramses carried any treasure with him and he never thought for a moment that the looters would notice that he'd fooled them. He was guided solely by his obsession: to obey Ofir, and be delivered from his face and voice.

Oblivious of the risks, he rushed at the officer drowsing near the entrance to the big tent. He fell on him so violently that the Egyptian had no time to draw his sword before he was winded by a head-butt from his assailant, who trampled on him, and he lost consciousness.

The way was clear. Even if Pharaoh was a god, he couldn't resist such a furious assailant. With the sharp blade of his axe he ripped open the tent-flap.

Ramses, snatched from sleep, sat up. Vargoz raised his weapon and hurled himself on the king.

An enormous weight pinned him to the ground. Agonizing pain shot through his back as if knives were slashing at his flesh. Turning his head, he caught one brief glimpse of an enormous lion whose jaws were closing on his skull and splitting it open like a ripe fruit.

The terrified screams of the nomad who was following Vargoz raised the alarm. Without their chief, confused, not knowing if they should attack or flee, the robbers were transfixed by arrows. Invincible alone dispatched five of them, then, seeing that the archers were doing their job quite well, he went back to sleep behind his master's bed. The furious Egyptians avenged the sentries' deaths by massacring the whole tribe of brigands.

The pleas of one of the wounded men puzzled an officer, who alerted the king. 'A Hebrew, Majesty.'

The looter had two arrows in his belly and was at death's door.

'Have you lived in Egypt, Hebrew?'

'It hurts . . . '

'Speak if you want to be treated!' demanded the officer.

'No, not in Egypt . . . I've always lived here . . . '

'Did someone by the name of Moses join your tribe?' asked Ramses.

'No . . . '

'What was the aim of this attack?'

The Hebrew muttered some incomprehensible words and died.

Ahsha approached the king. 'Are you hurt?'

'Invincible protected me.'

'Who were these bandits?'

'Bedouin, sand-travellers and at least one Hebrew.'

'Their attack was suicidal.'

'Someone incited them to do this crazy thing.'

'Hittite influence?'

'Perhaps.'

'Do you suspect anyone?'

'The demons of darkness are countless.'

'I couldn't get to sleep,' admitted Ahsha.

'Why not?'

'I was thinking about how the Hittites will react. They won't stay passive.'

'Are you by any chance reproaching me for not having attacked Kadesh?'

'We must consolidate our protectorates' defence systems as quickly as possible.'

'That will be your next mission, Ahsha.'

Out of concern for economy, Ahmeni was cleaning an old wooden tablet in order to write on it again. The officials under him knew that he tolerated no waste and respected his materials.

Ramses' triumph in the protectorates and the excellent inundations of the Nile which Egypt was enjoying had brought joy to Pi-Ramses. Rich and poor were preparing to welcome the king; every day boats delivered food and drink for a gargantuan banquet, in which all the inhabitants of the city were to particpate.

During this period of official holidays, the peasants rested or sailed to visit members of their family near and far. The Nile Delta had become a sea from which rose the islands on which the villages were built. Ramses' capital resembled a ship anchored in the heart of this vast stretch of water.

Only Ahmeni was uneasy. If he had thrown an innocent man into prison – one, moreover, who was a follower of Ramses – this miscarriage of justice would weigh heavily in the judgment scales of the next world. The scribe had not dared visit Serramanna, who continued to proclaim his innocence.

The policeman Ahmeni had made responsible for investigating the principal witness to the accusation, Nenophar, Serramanna's mistress, came to his office late in the evening.

'Have you had any results?'

The policeman said slowly, 'Yes.'

Ahmeni was relieved; at last some light would be shed on this affair.

'Nenophar?'

'I've found her.'

'Why haven't you brought her to me?'

'Because she's dead.'

'An accident?'

'According to the doctor I showed her body to, it's a criminal matter. Nenophar was strangled.'

'A crime . . . So someone wanted to get rid of this witness. But why? Because she lied or because there was a risk she'd say too much?'

'With respect, doesn't this tragedy cast doubt on Serramanna's guilt?'

Ahmeni grew paler than usual. 'I have evidence against him.'

'Evidence . . . You can't argue with that,' the policeman admitted.

'Well, yes, actually you can argue with it! What if Nenophar had been paid to accuse Serramanna and took fright at the idea of appearing before a tribunal and lying under oath when faced with the Rule? The person behind all this would have no choice: he'd have to get rid of her. It's true we still have solid evidence against him, but suppose it's a forgery? Suppose someone imitated Serramanna's writing?'

'That wouldn't be difficult. Every morning he wrote out the duty rota for the king's personal bodyguard, and it was put up on their barracks door.'

'So he was the victim of a plot. That's what you think, isn't it?'

The policeman nodded.

'As soon as Ahsha gets back,' Ahmeni said, 'I may be able to clear Serramanna without waiting for the culprit's arrest. Have you found any clues?'

'Nenophar didn't put up a struggle. She probably knew her killer.'

'Where was she killed?'

'In a little house in the commercial district.'

'Who owns it?'

'It was unoccupied, so the neighbours couldn't tell me.'

'The property register will probably give me some indication. And these neighbours, didn't they notice anything suspicious?'

'A half-blind old woman claims she saw a short man leaving the house in the middle of the night, but she can't describe him.'

'Have you made a list of Nenophar's acquaintances?'

'There's not much hope of making one. Serramanna may have been her first big catch.'

Nefertari was enjoying a long, cool shower. With closed eyes, she thought of the delirium of happiness whose sweet redolence drew nearer by the minute, when Ramses, whose absence was torture, would be back.

The maidservants gently rubbed her with ashes and natron, a mixture of carbonate and bicarbonate of soda which dries and purifies the skin. After a final sprinkling, the queen stretched out on warm tiles and a masseuse rubbed her down with an ointment, made of turpentine, oil and citron, which would scent her body for the whole day.

Dreamily Nefertari put herself in the hands of the pedicurist, the manicurist and the make-up specialist, who drew a pale-green line round her eyes, for both adornment and protection. As Ramses' arrival was imminent, she anointed the queen's hair with a special celebratory perfume whose main components were styrax resin and benzoin. Then she handed Nefertari a mirror of polished bronze, whose handle was carved in the shape of a naked girl, the earthly evocation of Hathor's celestial beauty. There only remained to put on a wig made of human hair, with two wide locks hanging down to her chest and curls at the back. Once again, the test with the mirror was favourable.

'If I may be permitted to say so,' the hairdresser murmured, 'Your Majesty has never been more beautiful.'

The dressers clothed the queen in an immaculate white linen gown which had just been woven in the palace workroom. No sooner had she sat down to check the fullness of the magnificent garment than a powerful, thick-set, golden-yellow dog with drooping ears, curly tail and short muzzle crowned with a black nose, leaped on to her lap. The dog had come in from the recently watered garden and his paws made muddy marks on the royal gown.

Horrified, one of the dressers seized a fly-whisk and made to strike the animal.

'Don't touch him,' ordered Nefertari. 'It's Wideawake, Ramses' dog. He must have a reason to behave like this.'

A soft, moist pink tongue licked the queen's cheeks, removing her make-up. Wideawake's huge, trusting eyes were filled with unspeakable joy.

'Ramses will be here tomorrow, won't he?'

The dog put his front paws on the shoulder straps of the queen's gown and wagged his tail with unmistakable enthusiasm.

22

The lookouts on the fortresses and small surveillance forts had just sent visual signals announcing that Ramses was on his way.

The capital was immediately in a turmoil of excitement. From the district adjoining the Temple of Ra to the workshops near the port, from the villas of the high officials to the dwellings of humble folk, from the palace to the warehouses, everyone hurried to carry out their allocated tasks and be ready for the unique moment when the sovereign would make his entrance into Pi-Ramses.

The steward Remet hid his increasing baldness under a short wig. Not having slept himself for forty-eight hours, he was chivvying his subordinates, all guilty of slackness and blundering. For the royal table alone, hundreds of quarters of roast beef would be needed, several dozen roast geese, two hundred baskets of dried meat and fish, fifty pots of cream, a hundred dishes of fish seasoned with spices, not to mention vegetables and fruit. The wines had to be of irreproachable quality, as did the ceremonial beers. And a thousand banquets had to be organized in the different districts of the city, so that even the most deprived could, that day, share in the king's fame and Egypt's happiness. At the slightest hitch who would be blamed if not him, Remet?

He reread the latest papyrus with the delivery orders: one

thousand loaves of different shapes but of very fine flour, two thousand golden, crusty round loaves, twenty-thousand honey-cakes, flavoured with carob juice and stuffed with figs, three hundred and fifty-two sacks of grapes to be arranged in fruit dishes, one hundred and twelve sacks of pomegranates and as many of figs . . .

'Here he comes!' shouted the cup-bearer.

Standing on the kitchen roof, a scullion was waving wildly.

'It's impossible!'

'Yes, it's him!'

The lad jumped off the roof, the cup-bearer ran off towards the main avenue of the capital.

'Stay here!' yelled Remet.

In less than a minute, the kitchen and the outbuildings of the palace were deserted. Remet collapsed on to a three-legged stool. Who was going to take the grapes out of the sacks and arrange them artistically?

He was spellbinding. He was the sun, the powerful bull, the protector of Egypt and the conqueror of foreign lands, the king who had won outstanding victories, the man whom the Divine Light had chosen.

He was Ramses.

Wearing a crown of gold, silver armour and a kilt bordered with gold, holding a bow in his left hand and a sword in his right hand, he stood erect on the platform of a chariot adorned with lilies, driven by Ahsha. Invincible, the Nubian lion with the flaming mane, walked in step with the horses.

Ramses' beauty combined power with radiance. He was the embodiment of the most perfect expression of a pharaoh.

The crowds swarmed along both sides of the long processional road leading to the Temple of Amon. Their arms full of flowers, perfumed with ceremonial oil, musicians and singers celebrated the king's return in a hymn of welcome.

'The sight of Ramses,' it said, 'fills the heart with joy.' So everyone pushed and shoved as the monarch passed, to try to catch a glimpse of him, even if only for a moment.

On the threshold of the sacred place stood Nefertari, the Great Royal Wife, the sweet love, the one whose voice brought happiness, the Lady of the Two Lands, whose crown with its two tall plumes reached to the heavens, and whose necklace of gold adorned with a scarab of lapis-lazuli, concealed the secret of the afterlife. She held in her hands a cubit, the symbol of Ma'at, the eternal Rule.

When Ramses alighted from his chariot the crowd fell silent.

The king advanced slowly towards the queen. He halted ten feet from her, let fall his bow and sword, clenched his right fist and placed it on his heart.

'Who are you, who dare to gaze on Ma'at?'

'I am the Son of the Light, the heir to the legacy of the gods, he who guarantees justice and does not differentiate between the strong and the weak. It is my duty to protect the whole of Egypt from misfortune, at home and abroad.'

'Have you shown respect for Ma'at, when far from the sacred land?'

'I have practised the Rule and I lay my deeds at her feet to be judged by her. Thus, the whole land will be solidly founded on truth.'

'May the Rule acknowledge you as a righteous person.'

Nefertari raised the golden cubit, which shone in the sun.

For many long minutes the crowd applauded their king. Even Shaanar, subdued, could not help murmuring his brother's name.

The only people admitted to the first great courtyard of the Temple of Amon, which was open to the sky, were the notables of Pi-Ramses, all of them eager to be present at the ceremony of the handing over of the 'gold of valour'. Whom was Ramses going to decorate? Who would be promoted? Several names circulated and wagers had even been made.

When the king and queen showed themselves at the Window of Appearances, all held their breath. The generals strutted about in the front row, stealing glances at one another out of the corners of their eyes.

Two fan-bearers stood ready to lead up to the window those fortunate enough to be chosen. For once the secret had been well kept: even the court gossips weren't sure.

'Let the bravest of my soldiers be the first to be honoured,' declared Ramses, 'the one who never once hesitated to protect the life of Pharaoh. Come forward, Invincible.'

The assembly parted in fright to make way for the lion, who seemed to take some pleasure in seeing all eyes on him. With supple, swaying gait he advanced to the Window of Appearances. Ramses leaned forward, stroked his head and placed a thin gold chain round his neck, marking him out as one of the most important personalities in the court. The lion lay down contentedly in the posture of the sphinx.

The king murmured two names to the standard-bearers. Carefully avoiding Invincible, they by-passed the row of generals, then the high-ranking officers, finally the scribes, and asked Setau and Lotus to follow them. The snake-charmer protested, but his pretty wife took his hand.

Even the most indifferent were delighted to see the Nubian woman, with her golden colouring and slender waist, come past, but Setau, looking the country bumpkin in his antelope-skin jerkin with its many pockets, did not meet with the same approval.

'Let those be honoured who attended to the wounded and saved many lives,' said Ramses. 'Thanks to their knowledge and devotion, brave men have overcome suffering and returned to their homeland.'

Leaning forward again, the king placed several gold bracelets on Setau's and Lotus's wrists. The lovely Nubian was moved; the snake-charmer grumbled.

'I appoint Setau and Lotus to run the palace laboratory,' added Ramses. 'Their mission will be to perfect remedies based on snake venom and see that they are distributed throughout the land.'

'I preferred my home in the desert,' muttered Setau.

'Are you sorry to be nearer to me?' asked Nefertari.

The queen's smile disarmed the grumbler.

'Your Majesty . . . '

'Your presence in the palace will be an honour for the court.'

Setau blushed with embarrassment. 'It shall be as you wish, Your Majesty.'

The generals, somewhat shocked, were careful not to express any criticism. After all, they'd had recourse, at one time or other, to the skill of Setau and Lotus, to relieve indigestion or ease congested breathing. The snake-charmer and his wife had shown during the campaign that they knew their place. Their reward, although excessive in the eyes of the officers, was not undeserved.

It remained to be known which of the generals would be honoured and would rise to the post of commander-in-chief of the Egyptian army, under the direct orders of Pharaoh. Much was at stake, as the name of the one fortunate enough to be selected would reveal Ramses' future policy. To choose the oldest general would indicate withdrawal and suspension of hostilities; to choose the commander of the chariot corps would mean the announcement of imminent war.

The two fan-bearers stood one on each side of Ahsha. Of natural distinction, elegant, quite at ease, the young diplomat looked up respectfully at the royal couple.

'I honour you, my noble and loyal friend,' declared Ramses, 'for your counsels have always been most valuable to me. You did not hesitate to expose yourself to danger and you knew how to persuade me to modify my plans, when the situation demanded. Peace is restored, but it is still fragile. We surprised the rebels by the speed of our intervention; but how will the Hittites, the real authors of these troubles, react? True, we have reorganized the garrisons of our fortresses in Canaan and left troops in the province of Amurru, the one most exposed to the enemy's brutal revenge. But we must coordinate our efforts for the defence of our protectorates, so that no new sedition breaks out. I entrust this mission to Ahsha. From now on, the safety of Egypt rests for the most part on his shoulders.'

Ahsha bowed. Ramses placed three gold necklaces round his neck. The young diplomat was elevated to the status of grandee of Egypt.

The generals were united in their resentment. It was not for an inexperienced dignitary to carry out such a difficult task. The king had just committed a grave mistake; it was unpardonable to show such lack of confidence in the military hierarchy.

Shaanar was losing his deputy in the Foreign Affairs secretariat but gaining a valuable ally with extended powers. By appointing his friend to this post, Ramses was hastening his own destruction. The look of collusion that Ahsha and Shaanar exchanged was, for the latter, the best moment of the ceremony.

Accompanied by his dog and his lion, both happy to be reunited and able to play together, Ramses left the temple and climbed into his chariot to keep a promise.

Homer looked younger. He was seated under his lemon tree, stoning dates, which Hector, the black and white cat, his hunger more than satisfied with fresh meat, looked at with the greatest indifference.

'Sorry not to have been present at the ceremony, Majesty. My old legs have grown lazy: I can't remain standing for hours on end. I'm glad to see you back in perfect health.'

'Will you offer me some of that beer made from the juice of dates which you prepare yourself?'

In the calm of the evening, the two men savoured the delicate beverage.

'You grant me a rare pleasure, Homer, that of believing for one instant that I am a man like other men, able to enjoy a moment of quiet without thinking of the next day. Has your *Iliad* progressed?'

'It is filled, like my memory, with slaughter, corpses, lost friends and divine intervention. But have men any destiny other than their own folly?'

'The great war that my people fear has not broken out; Egypt's protectorates have returned to her guardianship and I hope to create an impassable barrier between us and the Hittites.'

'That is great wisdom from a young monarch driven by such fire! Could it perhaps be that you are the miraculous combination of Priam's caution and Achilles' valour?'

'I am convinced that the Hittites are furious at my victory. This peace is only a respite. Tomorrow the fate of the world will be played out at Kadesh.'

'Why is such a serene evening the harbinger of tomorrow? The gods are cruel.'

'Will you agree to be my guest at tonight's banquet?'

'On condition that I can retire early; at my age sleep is the principal virtue.'

'Have you sometimes dreamed that there will be no more war?'

'In writing the *Iliad,* my aim is to depict it in such horrible colours that men will recoil before their desire to destroy; but will the generals listen to the voice of a poet?'

23

Tuya was beautiful: with huge, piercing, almond-shaped eyes, and dressed in her linen gown of perfect cut, held tightly at the waist by a girdle whose striped ends fell nearly to her ankles. She looked long at Pharaoh and her eyes softened.

'Have you indeed not been wounded?'

'Do you think I could ever hide a wound from you? You look superb!'

'I have deeper wrinkles on my forehead and my neck; the best make-up artists cannot perform miracles.'

'Youth still speaks in you.'

'The strength of Seti, perhaps . . . Youth is a foreign land where only you can dwell. But why give in to nostalgia on this joyful evening? I shall be in my place at the banquet, rest assured.'

The king clasped his mother in his arms. 'You are the soul of Egypt.'

'No, Ramses, I am only her memory, the reflection of the past to which you must remain loyal. You, together with Nefertari, form the soul of Egypt. Have you established a lasting peace?'

'Peace, yes; lasting, no. I have restored my authority over the protectorates, including Amurru, but I fear that the Hittites are likely to react violently.'

'You were thinking of attacking Kadesh, were you not?'

'Ahsha persuaded me not to.'

'He was right. Your father abandoned that war, knowing that the losses would be high.'

'Times have changed. Kadesh is a threat we can no longer tolerate.'

'Our guests await us.'

No false note marred the splendour of the banquet over which Ramses, Nefertari and Tuya presided. Remet ran non-stop from the banqueting hall to the kitchens, and from the kitchens back to the banqueting hall, supervising every dish, tasting every sauce and taking a sip of every wine.

Ahsha, Setau and Lotus occupied the seats of honour. The young diplomat's brilliant conversation won over two cantankerous generals. Lotus enjoyed listening to countless speeches celebrating her beauty, while Setau concentrated on his alabaster dish, which, as soon as he emptied it, was immediately refilled with delicious fare.

The nobility and the military shared an evening of relaxation, with no thought for the anxious future.

At last Ramses and Nefertari were alone in their vast chamber in the palace, heavy with the scent of a dozen bunches of flowers, in which the fragrance of jasmine and sweet sage predominated.

'Is this what royalty means, stealing a few hours to spend with the woman one loves?'

'You were away for so long, so long . . . '

They stretched out side by side on the great bed, holding hands, enjoying the pleasure of being together again.

'It's strange,' she said. 'Your absence was a torment, but it was though you were always here, present, in my mind. Every morning, when I went to celebrate the dawn rites, I saw your image emerge from the walls and guide me.'

'During the worst moments of this campaign, your image

never left me. I felt you all round me, as if it were you who made Isis beat her wings when she gave birth again each morning to Osiris.'

'It was magic which created our union; nothing must destroy it.'

'Who could do that?'

'Sometimes I am aware of a cold shadow . . . It draws nearer, withdraws, draws near again, grows faint.'

'If it exists, I shall destroy it. But in your eyes, I see only a light, soft and fiery at the same time.'

Ramses turned on his side to gaze on Nefertari's perfect body. He loosened her hair, slipped the straps of her gown off her shoulders and undressed her slowly – so slowly that she shivered.

'Are you cold?'

'You are too far from me.'

He lay down on top of her and, with mutual desire, they joined in a passionate embrace.

At six in the morning, after showering and rinsing his mouth with natron, Ahmeni had his breakfast of barley gruel, fermented milk, cream cheese and figs brought to his office. He ate quickly, his eyes glued to a papyrus.

The sound of leather sandals on the tiled floor surprised him. One of his subordinates, so early? Ahmeni wiped his lips with a napkin.

'Ramses?'

'Why didn't you attend the banquet?'

'Just look: I'm snowed under with work! You'd swear these files multiply all by themselves. Besides, I dislike those social events. I was intending to ask you for an audience this morning, to present you with the results of my administration.'

'I'm sure they're excellent.'

A faint smile lit up Ahmeni's serious face. Ramses' trust in him was the thing he valued most in life.

'Tell me, why this visit so early in the morning?'

'Because of Serramanna.'

'That's the first subject I wanted to bring up.'

'We missed him on this campaign. You're the one who charged him with treachery, aren't you?'

'The evidence was overwhelming, but . . . '

'But?'

'But I reopened the inquiry.'

'Why?'

'I had the feeling I was being duped. And the famous evidence against Serramanna seemed less and less convincing. The person who accused him, a woman of doubtful morals named Nenophar, has been murdered. As for the document which shows that he was plotting with the Hittites, I am anxious to submit it to Ahsha's shrewd judgement.'

'Would you like us to wake him?'

Ahsha's suspicion of Ahmeni was misplaced. The king kept that satisfaction to himself.

Ahsha was woken with fresh milk sweetened with honey; he delivered the lady who had shared his bed into the expert hands of his masseur and hairdresser.

'If His Majesty in person were not before me,' he said, 'I wouldn't dare open my eyes.'

'Open your ears too,' recommended Ramses.

'Don't the king and his secretary ever sleep?'

'The fate of a man wrongly imprisoned is worth being woken suddenly,' retorted Ahmeni.

'Who are you talking about?'

'Serramanna.'

'But wasn't it you . . . ?'

'Take a look at these wooden tablets.'

Ahsha rubbed his eyes and read the messages that 'Serramanna' had written for the benefit of his Hittite correspondent, promising not to lead his elite troops against the enemy in the event of war.

'Is this a joke?'

'Why do you say that?'

'Because high dignitaries at the Hittite court are extremely sensitive. They attach exaggerated importance to formalities, even in secret dispatches. For letters like this to reach Hattusa, there is a way of expressing observations and requests that Serramanna wouldn't know.'

'So someone forged Serramanna's writing!'

'Quite easily; it is fairly crude. And I am sure these letters were never sent.'

Ramses, in his turn, examined the tablets. 'Isn't one clue very obvious?'

Ahsha and Ahmeni reflected.

'Former pupils of the Kap, the Royal Academy of Memphis, should be more perceptive.'

'It's too early in the morning,' was Ahsha's excuse. 'Of course! The author of these texts must be a Syrian. He speaks our language well, but two turns of phrase are characteristic of his own.'

'A Syrian,' repeated Ahmeni. 'I'm convinced it's the same man who paid Nenophar to supply false evidence against Serramanna. Then, afraid she'd talk, he thought it necessary to do away with her.'

'To murder a woman?' exclaimed Ahsha. 'That's monstrous!'

'There are thousands of Syrians in Egypt,' reflected Ramses.

'Let's hope he's made one slip, one simple little slip,' put in Ahmeni. 'I'm leading an administrative inquiry and am hopeful of finding key evidence.'

'It's possible this person is more than just a murderer,' suggested Ramses.

'What do you mean?' asked Ahsha.

'A Syrian, linked to the Hittites . . . Could there be a network of spies settled in our land?'

'We've no proof of a direct connection between the man behind Serramanna's false imprisonment and our main enemy.'

Ahmeni's next remark cut Ahsha to the quick. 'You raise this objection, my friend, because you're vexed. You, the head of our intelligence service, have just heard an unpleasant truth.'

'Today is beginning badly,' commented the diplomat, 'and there's a risk that those to come will be stormy.'

'Find this Syrian as quickly as possible,' insisted Ramses.

In his cell, Serramanna was keeping fit in his own way; while continuing to declare his innocence, he hammered his fists on the walls in an attempt to demolish them. On the day of the trial, he would break the heads of his accusers, whoever they were. Terrified of the ex-pirate's fury, his jailers passed him his food through the bars of the wooden door.

When this was finally opened, Serramanna felt like hurling himself at the man who dared to face him.

'Majesty!'

'This unpleasant stay hasn't done you too much harm, Serramanna.'

'I did not betray you, Majesty!'

'You have been the victim of a mistake and I have come to free you.'

'I'm really going to get out of this cage?'

'Would you doubt the word of the king?'

'Do you still trust me?'

'You are the commander of my personal bodyguard.'

'Then, Majesty, I'll tell you everything – everything I've learned, everything I suspect, all the reasons why someone wanted to silence me.'

144

24

Under the watchful eyes of Ramses, Ahmeni and Ahsha, Serramanna ate voraciously. Seated comfortably in the palace dining hall, he wolfed down pigeon pâté, roast ribs of beef, broad beans with goose fat, cucumbers in cream, water melon, goat's cheese. His appetite appeared inexhaustible: he scarcely paused to wash everything down with some draughts of a full-bodied red wine undiluted with water.

Finally sated, he gave Ahmeni a nasty look. 'You, scribe, why did you have me imprisoned?'

'Please accept my apologies. Not only was I deceived but I acted impetuously because the army was leaving for the north. My only intention was to protect the king.'

'Excuses, excuses . . . Just you try going to prison instead of me, and you'll see what it's like! Where's Nenophar?'

'Dead,' replied Ahmeni. 'Murdered.'

'I can't waste any tears on her. Who used her and who tried to get rid of me?'

'We don't know, but we shall.'

'*I* know!' The Sardinian tossed off another goblet of wine and wiped his moustache.

'Speak,' commanded the king.

'Majesty,' Serramanna began sententiously, 'I warned you. When Ahmeni arrested me, I was on my way to reveal to you a certain number of things you probably won't like.'

'We're listening.'

'The man who wanted to get rid of me, Majesty, is Remet, the steward you appointed. When a scorpion was smuggled into your cabin, on the boat, I suspected your friend Setau, and I was wrong. When he attended to me I got to know him. He's an honest man, incapable of lying, cheating or doing harm. Remet, on the other hand, is depraved. Who was better placed than him to steal Nefertari's shawl? And it was he or one of his assistants who stole the jar of dried fish.'

'Why should he have done that?'

'I don't know.'

'Ahmeni thinks I have nothing to fear from Remet.'

'Ahmeni isn't infallible,' Serramanna retorted. 'He was wrong about me, and he's wrong about Remet.'

'I shall question him myself,' announced Ramses. 'Do you still defend Remet, Ahmeni?'

The secretary shook his head.

'Any other revelations, Serramanna?'

'Yes, Majesty.'

'About whom?'

'Your friend Moses. I'm totally convinced about him. As I'm still responsible for your protection, I must be frank.'

The fierce look in Pharaoh's eyes would have frightened many another man.

With the help of another beaker of strong wine, Serramanna unburdened his conscience. 'To me, Moses is a traitor and a conspirator. His aim was to become the leader of the Hebrew people and establish an independent principality in the Delta. He may perhaps feel friendly towards you; but in the long run, if he's still alive, he'll be your most implacable enemy.'

Ahmeni feared a violent reaction from the king, but Ramses remained oddly calm.

'Is that mere supposition or the result of an inquiry?'

'As thorough an inquiry as possible. What's more, I have

learned that Moses had several meetings with a stranger who passed himself off as an architect. This man came to encourage him – indeed, to help him. Your Hebrew friend was at the heart of a plot against Egypt.'

'Did you identify this architect?'

'Ahmeni didn't give me time to.'

'Let's forget this controversy, even if you have suffered for it. We should combine our forces.'

After a long hesitation, Ahmeni and Serramanna embraced somewhat reluctantly. The scribe felt he was suffocating in the Sardinian's bear hug.

'This is the worst possible assumption,' commented the king. 'Moses is stubborn; if you're right, he'll stop at nothing. But today, who really knows what his aim is? Does he know it himself? Before accusing him of high treason, we must listen to what he has to say. And in order to listen to him, we have to find him.'

'This false architect,' Ahsha intervened, intrigued. 'Might he not be a key person in this affair?'

'Before we can say definitely,' concluded Ahmeni, 'we shall have to throw more light on many dark places.'

Ramses put his hand on the Sardinian's shoulder. 'Your frankness is a rare virtue, Serramanna. See that you don't lose it.'

During the week following Ramses' triumphant return, Shaanar, in his capacity as minister for forcign affairs, had nothing but good news for his brother. The Hittites had made no official protest and were not reacting to Ramses' victories. The Egyptian army's demonstration of force and speed of action seemed to have persuaded them to respect the terms of the pact laid down by Seti.

Before Ahsha set out on his tour of inspection in the protectorates, Shaanar organized a banquet at which his former collaborator was the guest of honour. Seated on the right of the host, whose receptions were the delight of Pi-Ramses society, the young diplomat enjoyed the sight of three girls dancing, naked except for a girdle of coloured material which did not hide their jet-black bush. They moved gracefully in time to music, now lively, now languid, played by a group of female musicians, a harpist, three flautists and a reed-pipe player.

'Which one would you like for the night, my dear Ahsha?'

'I'm going to surprise you, Shaanar, but I've spent an exhausting week with an insatiable widow and my one wish is to sleep for twelve hours before setting out for Canaan and Amurru.'

'Under cover of this music and the chattering of my guests, we can talk privately without fear of disturbance.'

'I'm no longer working at the secretariat, but you're not likely to be unhappy about my new mission.'

'We couldn't have hoped for anything better, you and I.'

'On the contrary, Shaanar. Ramses could have been killed, wounded or dishonoured.'

'I never imagined he'd prove a good strategist in addition to his innate strength. On due reflection, his victory is only relative. What has he done, except reconquer our protectorates? The lack of reaction from the Hittites surprises me.'

'They're weighing up the situation. Once they've recovered from their surprise, they'll strike.'

'What do you intend to do, Ahsha?'

'By giving me plenary powers in our protectorates, Ramses has provided me with a decisive weapon. Under cover of reorganizing our system of defences, I shall dismantle them, little by little.'

'Aren't you afraid of being found out?'

'I've already persuaded Ramses to leave the princes of Canaan and Amurru at the head of their provinces. They are devious, corrupt individuals, who will sell to the highest bidder; it will be easy for me to make them go over to the Hittites and the famous protective barrier that Ramses dreams of will be nothing but an illusion.'

'Don't do anything rash, Ahsha. There's a lot at stake.'

'We shan't win the match without taking some risks. The most difficult thing will be to assess the Hittites' strategy; fortunately I have some skill in that field.'

An immense empire, from Nubia to Anatolia, an empire of which he would be the master . . . Shaanar had not dared think of it, but now his dream was gradually being transformed into reality. Ramses was choosing his friends badly: Moses, a murderer and an insurgent; Ahsha, a traitor; Setau, an eccentric with no scope for action. There remained Ahmeni, uncompromising and incorruptible, but with no ambition.

'Ramses must be dragged into a senseless war,' Ahsha resumed. 'He will appear as the man who destroyed Egypt, and you as her saviour. That's the guiding line we must keep to.'

'Has Ramses entrusted you with any other mission?'

'Yes, to find Moses. To the king, friendship is sacred. Even if the Sardinian believes Moses guilty of high treason, Pharaoh won't condemn him without giving him a hearing.'

'Any trace of him?'

'None. Either the Hebrew has died of thirst in the desert, or he's hiding among one of the countless tribes which wander through Sinai and the Negev. If he's gone to earth in Canaan or Amurru, I shall hear of him eventually.'

'If Moses became the leader of a rebel tribe, he could be useful to us.'

'There is one worrying detail,' Ahsha added. 'According to Serramanna, Moses had mysterious contacts with a foreigner.'

'Here, in Pi-Ramses?'

'Yes, indeed.'

'Has he been identified?'

'No. All that's known is that he passed himself off as an architect.'

Shaanar tried to look unconcerned. So Ofir was no longer completely unknown. True, the magus was still only a shadow, but he was becoming a potential threat. No link of any kind must connect him to Shaanar. Practising black magic against Pharaoh was a capital crime.

'Ramses wants this individual identified,' Ahsha pointed out.

'Probably a Hebrew whose papers aren't in order. Perhaps he's the one who led Moses into exile. I'll wager we never see either of them again.'

'Probably. We can count on Ahmeni to try to throw light on this matter, especially after his bad blunder.'

'Do you think Serramanna will forgive him?'

'He seems to me to be pretty resentful.'

'Didn't he fall into some sort of trap?' asked Shaanar.

'A Syrian paid a prostitute to accuse the Sardinian and then strangled her to stop her talking. And it was the same foreigner who forged Serramanna's handwriting so that people would believe he was in the pay of the Hittites. A reasonably skilful fabrication, but too superficial.'

Shaanar had some difficulty in keeping calm. 'And that means . . . '

'That a network of spies flourishes in our lands.'

The Syrian merchant Raia, Shaanar's main ally, was in danger. And it was Ahsha, his other indispensable ally, who was trying to find him and arrest him!

'Would you like my secretariat to undertake an inquiry into this Syrian?'

'Ahmeni and I will see to it. It would be better to act discreetly so as not to alarm the prey.'

Shaanar took a long drink of white Delta wine. Ahsha would never know the immense amount of help he was giving him.

'An important person is going to be in serious trouble,' the young diplomat now revealed.

'Who?'

'Remet, the fat palace steward. Serramanna is having him watched constantly, because he's convinced Remet deserves to be in prison.'

Shaanar's back was aching like that of an exhausted wrestler, but he managed to put a good face on it. He had to act fast – very fast – to dispel the stormclouds that were beginning to gather.

25

It would soon be the end of the season of the Nile inundation. The peasants had repaired or strengthened their ploughs which they would harness to two oxen to dig shallow furrows in the soft silt, and then the seed would be sown. As the flooding had been perfect, neither too high nor too low, the irrigation specialists had the ideal amount of water available to make the crops grow. The gods were favourable to Ramses. This year the granaries would be full once more and Pharaoh's people would have enough to eat.

Although the weather at the end of October was mild, with only occasional cold winds, Remet, the palace steward, was not happy. When he was worried, he put on weight. As he became increasingly aggravated, his growing corpulence sometimes made it hard for him to breathe and forced him to sit down for a few minutes before resuming his burden of work.

Serramanna followed him everywhere, never giving him a moment's respite. When it was not the Sardinian in person, it was one of his henchmen, whose burly form did not go unnoticed either in the palace or in the markets where the steward went himself to purchase the articles intended for the royal kitchens.

Formerly, Remet would have been happy at the thought of preparing a new recipe: a mixture of lotus roots, bitter lupin boiled several times, courgettes, chickpeas, mild garlic, almonds and small pieces of grilled perch. But even this delicious prospect could not make him forget that he was being followed everywhere, all the time.

Since his rehabilitation, that monster Serramanna thought he could get away with anything. But Remet couldn't protest. When your heart is sinking and your conscience isn't clear, how can you be at peace with yourself?

Serramanna had the patience of a pirate. He was permanently watching for his prey, that fat steward with the flabby face and the black heart, to make one slip. His instinct had not deceived him; for several months he had suspected Remet of spinelessness, a defect which could lead to the worst treachery. Although he had obtained an important position, Remet suffered from an incurable disease: greed. He was not satisfied with his position and wished to add private means to the modest power which he wielded.

By having him watched all the time, Serramanna was succeeding in shaking the steward's nerves badly. Remet would eventually make a blunder, perhaps even confess his crimes.

As he had foreseen, the steward dared not lodge a complaint. If he had been innocent, he would not have hesitated to speak to the king. In his daily report to Ramses, the Sardinian did not fail to stress this significant fact.

After several days of this treatment, Serramanna would tell his men to continue shadowing Remet, but without letting themselves be spotted. Believing himself finally freed from constraint, Remet might rush into the arms of a possible accomplice, the one who had paid him for the objects he had stolen.

The Sardinian made his way to Ahmeni's office, long after sunset. The secretary was putting the day's papyri away in a large sycamore-wood chest.

'Any news, Serramanna?'

'Nothing yet. Remet is a harder nut to crack than I'd expected.'

'Do you still bear me a grudge?'

'Well . . . it's not easy to forget what you made me suffer.'

'It's no use repeating my apologies; I've got a better suggestion. Will you come with me to the property-register offices?'

'Are you associating me with your inquiry?'

'Exactly.'

'Then my last traces of resentment may vanish like a bad mood! Yes, I'll come with you.'

The officials at the registry were extremely painstaking, so they had needed several months to become as efficient as their Memphis colleagues. Getting used to a new capital, making an inventory of land and houses, identifying proprietors and tenants, all took a number of checks and cross-checks. That was why they had been a long time finding the answer to Ahmeni's request, although it was classed as urgent.

Serramanna thought the director of the registry, a bald, thin man of some sixty years, even more of a bore than Ahmeni. His pasty face indicated that he was never exposed to the sunshine or the fresh air. He received his visitors with icy courtesy and guided them through a maze of wooden tablets piled on top of one another and papyri arranged in pigeon-holes.

'Thank you for seeing us so late,' said Ahmeni.

'I presumed you would prefer a maximum of discretion.'

'Yes indeed.'

'I must tell you that your request has given us a great deal of extra work, but we have at last managed to identify the owner of the house in question.'

'Who is it?'

'A trader from Memphis, named Renuf.'

'Do you know his main place of residence?'
'He lives in a villa in the south of the old city.'

Passers-by hastily made way as the two-horse chariot driven by Serramanna hurtled past. Ahmeni's heart was in his mouth and he kept his eyes tight shut. The vehicle did not slow down as it was driven on to the bridge recently built across the canal separating the new districts of the capital from the old town of Avaris. The wheels creaked, the bodywork trembled, but the chariot did not overturn.

On the old site, fine villas surrounded by well-kept gardens stood side by side with modest two-storey houses. On this cool autumn evening, those who felt the cold were beginning to burn twigs or dried mud to heat their homes.

'This is the place,' said Serramanna.

Ahmeni was clutching one of the straps of the chariot so tightly that he couldn't let go.

'Everything all right?'

'Yes, yes.'

'Well, let's get going then! If the bird hasn't flown the nest, this matter will soon be cleared up.'

Ahmeni managed to free himself; with trembling legs he followed the Sardinian.

Renuf's doorman was sitting in front of the gate set in the outer wall of unburnt bricks, overgrown with climbing plants. The man was eating bread and cheese.

'We want to see the merchant Renuf,' said Serramanna.

'He's not at home.'

'Where can we find him?'

'He's left for Middle Egypt.'

'When will he be back?'

'I don't know.'

'Does anyone know?'

'I don't think so.'

'Let us know as soon as he returns.'

155

'Why should I?'

Serramanna gave the doorman a nasty look and lifted him up by the armpits. 'Because Pharaoh insists. If you're one hour late, you'll have me to deal with.'

Shaanar was suffering from insomnia and heartburn. As Raia was not in Pi-Ramses, he had to go as quickly as possible to Memphis, both to warn the Syrian merchant of the danger hanging over him and to talk to Ofir. However, as minister for foreign affairs, he had to justify his visits to the former capital; fortunately, he had several administrative matters to discuss with senior government officials in Memphis. So it was in Pharaoh's name that Shaanar boarded a boat – it was far too slow for his liking – ostensibly on official duties.

Either Ofir must find some way of silencing Remet or else Shaanar would be forced to get rid of the magus, even though his experiment in witchcraft wasn't complete.

Shaanar was not sorry that he had kept his allies separate; what had just happened proved the validity of his tactics. Someone as intelligent and dangerous as Ahsha would not have been happy to discover the links Shaanar maintained with a network of pro-Hittite spies which the young diplomat did not control. A wily, cruel individual like Raia, who thought he was exploiting Ramses' elder brother, would not have tolerated his playing a game for his personal benefit in addition to his allegiance to the Hittites. As for Ofir, it was preferable for him to be confined to his formidable powers and his uncontrollable lunacy. Ahsha, Raia, Ofir . . . Three great cats that Shaanar was capable of taming to ensure a favourable future, providing he could remove the threat raised by their carelessness.

On the first day of his stay in Memphis, Shaanar had meetings with the senior government officials whom he had to contact and, in the evening, gave at his villa one of the lavish parties for which he was famous. For the occasion he

had told his steward to send for the merchant Raia, who
would offer him rare vases to adorn the banqueting hall.

When it became too chilly in the garden, the guests went
inside.

'The merchant is here,' Shaanar's steward announced.

If he had believed in the gods, he would have thanked
them. Putting on an air of indifference, he made his way to the
main gate of his villa.

The man who greeted him was not Raia.

'Who are you?'

'The manager of his Memphis store.'

'Ah . . . I am accustomed to dealing with your employer.'

'He has left for Thebes and Elephantine to negotiate for a
cargo of luxury preserves. However, in his absence I have
some fine vases to offer you.'

'Show them to me.'

Shaanar examined the work. 'They're nothing special. All
the same, I'll buy two.'

'The price is very reasonable, my lord.'

Shaanar bargained as a formality, and had his steward pay
for the vases.

It was not easy to smile, chat and spout a stream of
trivialities, but Shaanar managed to rise to the occasion. No
one guessed that the minister for foreign affairs, as charming
and loquacious as ever, was suffering extreme anxiety.

'You are looking beautiful,' he said to his sister, Dolora.

The tall, listless brunette was surrounded by young nobles
who fawned on her with idle chitchat.

'Your reception is magnificent, Shaanar.'

He gave her his arm and dragged her away under a portico
alongside the banqueting hall.

'I shall go and see Ofir tomorrow morning. See that he
doesn't leave his house: he's in danger.'

26

Dolora herself opened the door of the villa.

Shaanar turned round. No one had followed him.

'Come in, Shaanar.'

'Everything quiet?'

'Yes, don't worry. Ofir's experiments are progressing well,' Dolora assured him. 'Lita is behaving admirably, but she's frail and we can't hurry the process. Why are you so anxious?'

'Is the magus awake?'

'I'll go and fetch him.'

'Don't be too devoted to him, little sister.'

'He's a wonderful man, who will restore the reign of the true god. He's convinced you are the instrument of fate.'

'Bring him to me. I'm in a hurry.'

The Libyan magus, dressed in a long black gown, bowed to Shaanar.

'You must get out of here today, Ofir.'

'What is happening, my lord?'

'You were seen speaking to Moses, in Pi-Ramses.'

'Was an exact description of me given?'

'I don't think so, but the investigators know that you passed yourself off as an architect and that you're a foreigner.'

'That's not very much, my lord. I have a gift for going

unnoticed when necessary.'

'You were unwise.'

'It was essential to contact Moses. Tomorrow perhaps we shall congratulate ourselves about that.'

'Ramses returned in perfect health from his expedition in our protectorates. He wants to find Moses and now knows of your existence. If witnesses identify you, you'll be arrested and interrogatcd.'

Ofir's smile made Shaanar's blood run cold. 'Do you think a man like me can be arrested?'

'I think you have made a fatal mistake.'

'What is it?'

'Trusting Remet.'

'What makes you think I trust him?'

'On your orders he stole Nefertari's shawl and also the jar of fish from the Heliopolis House of Light, which you needed for your magic.'

'Remarkable deduction, Lord Shaanar, but there is one incorrect detail: Remet stole the shawl and one of his friends, a delivery man from Memphis, was responsible for the jar.'

'A delivery man? And suppose he talked?'

'The unfortunate fellow died of a heart attack.'

'A death . . . from natural causes?'

'Every death is eventually from a natural cause, Lord Shaanar, when the heart fails.'

'There is still fat Remet. Serramanna is convinced of his guilt and continues to harass him. If Remet talks, he'll denounce you. Magicians who attack the person of the monarch are put to death.'

Ofir was still smiling. 'Let's go into my laboratory.'

The vast room was filled with papyri, pieces of ivory bearing inscriptions, pieces of cord and little dishes containing coloured substances. No clutter, a pleasant smell of incense. The place seemed more like a craftsman's studio or a scribe's neat office than the cave of a practitioner of the evil arts.

Ofir stretched his hands out over a copper mirror placed flat on a tripod. Then he poured some water on to it and asked Shaanar to approach.

Gradually a face formed in the mirror.

'Remet!' exclaimed Shaanar.

'Ramses' steward is a good fellow,' Ofir said, 'but weak, greedy and easily influenced. It isn't necessary to be a great sorcerer to bewitch him. The theft he committed, against his will, is eating away at him like acid.'

'If Ramses interrogates him, he will speak.'

'No, Lord Shaanar.'

With his left hand, Ofir traced a circle above the mirror. The water boiled and the copper cracked.

Shaanar stepped back, impressed. 'Will that magic trick be enough to silence Remet?'

'Consider the problem solved. I don't think it necessary for me to move from this house. Isn't it in your sister's name?'

'Yes.'

'Everyone sees her coming and going. Lita and I are her devoted servants, and have no desire to go for walks in the town. Neither she nor I will leave here until we have destroyed the royal couple's magical protection.'

'And the supporters of Aton?'

'Your sister acts as our go-between. On my orders they are proving models of discretion, while waiting for some great event.'

Shaanar left, half reassured. He couldn't care less about that gang of nostalgic visionaries, and his main worry was not to have got rid of the steward Remet with his own hands. He'd have to hope that the magus wasn't boasting.

An extra precaution was needed.

The Nile was a wonderful river. Thanks to its powerful current, which could propel a fast boat at great speed, Shaanar travelled the distance between Memphis and Pi-Ramses in less than two days.

The king's elder brother went to his ministry, organized a quick meeting with his principal colleagues, perused the dispatches from the protectorates sent by the diplomats posted there. Then, under a grey sky, heavy with rain clouds, he had his litter-bearers convey him to the royal palace.

Pi-Ramses was a fine city, but lacked the patina of Memphis and the charm lent by the past. When he reigned, Shaanar would remove its status as capital, especially since Ramses had left too much of his own imprint on it. Busy people were going happily about their daily occupations, as if the peace was eternal, as if the vast Hittite Empire had disappeared into the bottomless pit of oblivion. For one moment Shaanar let himself be attracted by the mirage of this simple existence governed by the rhythm of the seasons. Should he not, like all the people of Egypt, accept Ramses' sovereignty?

No. He was not a servant.

He had the makings of a king whom history would remember, of a monarch with a vaster vision than that of Ramses and the 'great Hittite chief'. From his plan there would be born a new world, of which he would be the master.

Pharaoh did not keep his brother waiting. He was just finishing a conversation with Ahmeni, whose face Wide-awake had been licking painstakingly. The king's private secretary and Shaanar greeted each other coldly, the yellow dog lay down in a faint ray of sunshine.

'A pleasant journey, Shaanar?'

'Excellent. You will forgive me, but I'm very fond of Memphis.'

'Who can blame you? It's an exceptional city which Pi-Ramses will never be able to equal. If the Hittite menace hadn't become so great, I'd never have needed to create a new capital.'

'The administration of Memphis remains a model of

professional conscientiousness.'

'The different services in Pi-Ramses work efficiently. Isn't your ministry proof of that?'

'I don't spare myself any effort, believe me. There are no worrying messages, either official or unofficial. The Hittites are silent.'

'Not the slightest comment from our diplomats?'

'The Anatolians have been crushed by your intervention. They never imagined the Egyptian army could move so fast and win such victories.'

'Possibly.'

'Why do you doubt this? If the Hittites were certain of their invincibility, they would at least have protested strongly.'

'They respect the border drawn by Seti? I don't believe it.'

'Are you growing pessimistic, Majesty?'

'The Hittite Empire's whole reason for existence is to acquire more territory.'

'Isn't Egypt too big a morsel to swallow, even for a starving enemy?'

'When military rulers want confrontation,' opined Ramses, 'neither reason nor wisdom can dissuade them.'

'Only a sizeable opponent will make the Hittites withdraw.'

'Are you recommending intensive armament, and increasing our military strength?'

'What better solution?'

The sunbeam had disappeared; Wideawake jumped on to the king's lap.

'Isn't that tantamount to a declaration of war?' asked Ramses anxiously.

'The Hittites won't understand any language but that of force. That is really what you are thinking, if I'm not mistaken.'

'I'm also anxious to consolidate our system of defences.'

'Making our protectorates into a buffer zone, I know. A

difficult task for your friend Ahsha, even if he does not lack ambition.'

'Do you think it's too much for him?'

'Ahsha is young, you have just decorated him and made him one of the principal personalities of the state. Such rapid promotion might go to his head. No one doubts his immense qualities, but wouldn't it be advisable to be cautious?'

'I'm well aware that the military hierarchy felt they had not been sufficiently honoured. But Ahsha is the man for the job.'

'There is one detail of minor importance, but it is my duty to mention it to you. You know that the palace staff tend to gossip about everything; nevertheless, something I've been told in confidence is perhaps worthy of interest. According to my steward, who is particularly fond of one of the queen's ladies of the bedchamber, this young woman claims she saw Remet steal Nefertari's shawl.'

'Will she give evidence?'

'Remet scares her. She's afraid he'll ill-treat her if she accuses him.'

'Are we in a land of brigands or a country governed by the Rule of Ma'at?'

'Perhaps you should begin by making Remet confess; then the girl will give evidence.'

By implying criticism of Ahsha and particularly by denouncing Remet, thus precipitating Ramses' intervention, Shaanar was playing a dangerous game. But on the other hand, he was becoming more credible in Pharaoh's eyes.

If Ofir's magic turned out to be ineffective, Shaanar would strangle him with his own hands.

27

Remet had found only one way to relieve the anxiety which was responsible for his overeating: he'd prepare a new marinade which would be called 'Ramses' Delight', for which cooks would hand down the recipe from master to disciple. The steward shut himself up in the vast palace kitchen, where he insisted on being alone. He had personally selected the mild garlic, some finest-quality onions, an oasis red wine of famous vintage, olive oil from Heliopolis, vinegar seasoned with the best salt from the land of Set, several kinds of aromatic herbs, fillets of Nile perch of exceptionally succulent flesh and beef worthy of being offered to the gods. The marinade would give this fare a matchless flavour which would delight the king and make Remet irreplaceable.

In spite of the strict orders he had given, the kitchen door opened. 'I insisted that—Majesty! Majesty, you shouldn't be here!'

'There is no place in the kingdom where I may not go.'

'That's not what I meant. Forgive me, I . . . '

'Have I your permission to taste?'

'The marinade isn't ready yet. I've only just begun preparing it. But it will be a remarkable dish, which will enter the culinary annals of Egypt!'

'Have you a taste for secrets, Remet?'

'No, no . . . But good cooking demands discretion. I am jealous of my inventions, I confess.'

'Is there something else you ought to confess to me?'

Ramses' tall figure towered over Remet, who shrank away, closing his eyes.

'My life holds no mysteries, Majesty; it is spent in the palace to serve you, just to serve you.'

'Are you sure about that? They say every man has his weaknesses. What are yours?'

'I . . . I don't know. Greed, probably.'

'Are you dissatisfied with your salary?'

'No. Certainly not!'

'The position of steward is enviable and envied, but it doesn't make anyone rich.'

'That is not my aim, I assure you!'

'Who could resist a favourable offer, in exchange for some small services?'

'The service of Your Majesty is so much more gratifying that—'

'Don't lie to me any more, Remet. Do you remember the regrettable incident of the scorpion in my cabin?'

'Fortunately it didn't harm you.'

'You were promised it would not kill me and that you would never be accused, is that not so?'

'It's false, Majesty, completely false!'

'You should not have yielded to temptation, Remet. Someone appealed to your spinelessness a second time, insisting you steal the queen's favourite shawl. And you no doubt know something about the theft of the jar of fish.'

'No, Majesty, no!'

'Someone saw you.'

Remet was choking. Beads of sweat ran down his forehead. 'It's impossible . . . '

'Have you an evil heart, Remet, or were you the victim of circumstances?'

The steward felt a violent pain in his chest. He wanted to reveal everything to the king, to purge himself of the remorse which was eating into him. He knelt down, hitting his forehead against the edge of the table on which were laid out the ingredients for the marinade.

'No, Majesty, I'm not wicked. I've been weak, too weak. I beg you to forgive me.'

'On condition you finally tell me the truth, Remet.'

Remet felt faint. In the mist enveloping him, Ofir's face appeared, the face of a vulture with a curved beak which dug into his flesh and devoured his heart.

Remet tried to speak, but Ofir's name would not pass his lips. A clammy fear choked him, fear which enjoined him to slide into oblivion in order to avoid punishment.

Remet looked imploringly up at Ramses. His right hand gripped the dish containing his trial marinade and upset it. The spicy sauce spilled over his face and the steward fell down dead.

'He's very big,' said Kha, looking at Invincible, Ramses' lion.

'Are you afraid of him?' the king asked his son.

At the age of nine, Kha, the son of Ramses and Iset the Fair, was as serious as an old scribe. He was bored by the games suitable for his age; he liked only to read and write, and spent most of his time in the palace library.

'He frightens me a bit.'

'You are right, Kha. Invincible is a very dangerous animal.'

'But you aren't afraid of him, because you are the pharaoh.'

'The lion and I have become friends. When he was quite young he was bitten by a snake in Nubia. I found him. Setau healed him, and we have been inseparable ever since. Invincible, in his turn, has saved my life.'

166

'Is he always nice to you?'

'Always. But only to me.'

'Does he talk to you?'

'Yes, with his eyes, his paws, the sounds he makes. And he understands what I say to him.'

'I should like to touch his mane.'

Lying in the posture of a sphinx, the huge lion watched the man and the child. He uttered a deep, solemn growl and little Kha clutched his father's leg.

'Is he angry?'

'No, he says he'll let you stroke him.'

Reassured by his father's calmness, Kha approached. The small hand touched the magnificent mane, first hesitantly, then growing bolder. The lion purred.

'Can I get on his back?'

'No, Kha. Invincible is a warrior and very proud. He has granted you a great favour, but you mustn't ask him for anything more.'

'I shall write his story and tell it to Meritamon. Fortunately she stayed in the palace garden with the queen. A little girl would have been terrified of such a big lion.'

Ramses gave his son a new scribe's palette and a set of brushes. The gift delighted the little boy, who immediately tried out his implements and became engrossed in his writing. His father did not disturb him, only too happy to enjoy these rare moments after having witnessed the shocking death of the steward Remet, whose face had immediately become as wizened as that of an old man. The thief had died of fright, without revealing the name of the person who had led him to his destruction.

A creature of darkness was fighting against Pharaoh. And that enemy was no less formidable than the Hittites.

Shaanar rejoiced. Remet's sudden death from heart failure cut the trail leading to Ofir. The magus had not been boasting.

His magic had killed the fat steward, who had not been able
to face close questioning. His death surprised no one in the
palace. Obsessed by food, Remet had become more and more
obese and increasingly agitated. Coated with fat, worn out by
his permanent state of tension, his heart had simply given out.

Besides the solution of the delicate problem posed by
Remet's existence, there was another source of satisfaction
for Shaanar: the return to Pi-Ramses of the Syrian merchant
Raia, who had asked to see Shaanar to offer him a remarkable
vase. An appointment had been made for late in the morning
of a mild and sunny November day.

'Did you have a good journey to the South?'

'Very tiring, Lord Shaanar, but very profitable.'

The Syrian's small pointed beard was carefully trimmed;
his lively little brown eyes took in the colonnaded reception
hall, where Shaanar exhibited his masterpieces.

Raia removed the cloth wrappings from a potbellied
bronze vase, decorated with stylized vine leaves and
branches. 'It comes from Crete; I bought it from a wealthy
Theban woman who was tired of it. These days they don't
make any more like this.'

'Admirable! Consider it a deal, my friend.'

'I am pleased, my lord, but . . .'

'Did the noble lady impose conditions?'

'No, but the price is rather high. It is a unique piece, really
unique.'

'Put this phenomenon on a pedestal and come with me into
my office. We shall bring our negotiations to a satisfactory
conclusion, I'm sure.'

The thick sycamore-wood door closed behind them. No
one could hear them.

'One of my assistants let me know that you'd come to
Memphis to buy a vase from me. I cut my journey short and
returned to Pi-Ramses as quickly as possible.'

'It was essential.'

'What is happening?'

'Serramanna has been freed. He enjoys Ramses' trust again.'

'Regrettable.'

'That meddling Ahmeni had doubts about the authenticity of the evidence, and then Ahsha interfered.'

'Be wary of that young diplomat. He's intelligent and he knows Asia well.'

'Fortunately he's no longer working at the ministry. Ramses has decorated him and sent him to the protectorates to reinforce our defence systems.'

'A very delicate task – even an impossible one.'

'Ahsha and Ahmeni have reached some very embarrassing conclusions: someone imitated Serramanna's handwriting to give the impression he was corresponding with the Hittites, and this someone could be a Syrian.'

'That's a great pity,' lamented Raia.

'They found the body of Nenophar, Serramanna's mistress, whom you used to trap the Sardinian.'

'She had to be got rid of. That little fool threatened to talk.'

'I agree, but you were imprudent.'

'How was that?'

'Your choice of place for the murder.'

'I didn't choose it. She was going to tell the whole neighbourhood. I had to act quickly and then run.'

'Ahmeni is looking for the owner of that house to question him.'

'He's a merchant who travels a great deal. I met him in Thebes.'

'Will he give your name?'

'I'm afraid so, as I'm his tenant.'

'It's a disaster, Raia! Ahmeni is convinced that a pro-Hittite network of spies is active in our territory. Although it was he who arrested Serramanna, the two men are reconciled and are helping each other. The search for the person who had

Serramanna falsely accused and murdered his mistress has become a state matter. And several clues lead to you.'

'All is not lost.'

'What is your plan?'

'To intercept the Egyptian merchant.'

'And . . . ?'

'And get rid of him, naturally.'

28

Winter was drawing near. The hours of daylight were growing shorter and the sun was losing its intensity. The king preferred the force of summer and the heat of his protecting day-star, which he alone could look in the face without scorching his eyes. But this delightfully mild autumn day offered him a rare joy: to be able to spend the late afternoon in the palace gardens, in the company of Nefertari, their daughter Meritamon and his son Kha.

Seated on folding chairs beside a lake, the king and queen watched the activities of the two children. Kha was trying to make Meritamon read a difficult text about the need for a scribe to have high moral standards, while she wanted to teach him how to swim on his back. In spite of his determined character, the little boy had given in, while protesting that the water was too cold and he would catch a chill.

'Meritamon is as formidable as her mother,' Ramses said. 'She will charm the whole world.'

'Kha has the making of a magician. Look, he's already dragging her back to the papyrus. She'll have to read the text, whether she likes it or not.'

'Are their tutors satisfied?'

'Kha is an exceptional child. According to Nedjem, the minister for agriculture, who is still overseeing his education, he could already pass the scribes' beginners' examination.'

'Is that what he wants?'

'He thinks of nothing but learning.'

'Let us provide him with the nourishment he demands so that his true nature can flourish. Doubtless he'll have many trials to overcome, since those who are second-rate always attempt to stifle exceptional people. I hope Meritamon has a more peaceful life.'

'She has eyes only for her father.'

'And I give her so little of my time.'

'Egypt comes before our children. That is the Rule.'

The lion and the yellow dog mounted close guard in front of the entrance to the garden. No one would have been able to approach without Wideawake rousing Invincible.

'Come here, Nefertari.'

The young queen loosened her hair and came to sit on Ramses' lap, resting her head on his shoulder.

'You are the fragrance of my life and the source of my happiness. We could be a couple like others, and enjoy countless hours like this . . . '

'It is indeed delightful to sit and dream in this garden; but the gods and your father made you the pharaoh, and you have offered your life to your people. What has been given cannot be taken back.'

'At this moment, the only thing that exists is the scented hair of a woman with whom I am deeply in love, hair that dances in the evening breeze and caresses my cheek.'

Their lips were united in the ardent kiss of young lovers.

Raia had to act alone. That was why he had made his way to the port of Pi-Ramses, which was smaller than that of Memphis but just as busy. The river police maintained order as the boats came alongside and unloaded their cargo.

Raia would invite his colleague Renuf to a hearty lunch at a good inn in the presence of many witnesses who would testify, if necessary, to having seen them joking and feasting.

Thus the excellent nature of their relationship would be established. In the evening, Raia would get into Renuf's villa and strangle him. If a servant intervened, he would suffer the same fate. In the Hittite training camps of northern Syria, the merchant had learned how to kill. Naturally, this new crime would be attributed to Nenophar's murderer. But what did that matter? With Renuf out of the way, Raia would be out of danger.

On the quays petty traders were selling fruit, vegetables, sandals, lengths of cloth, cheap necklaces and bracelets. The purchasers indulged in frantic bartering, the pleasure of the endless haggling being an essential ingredient of a satisfactory acquisition. If Raia had had the time, he would have reorganized all this uncoordinated activity in order to reap more profit from it.

The Syrian addressed one of the port controllers. 'Has Renuf's boat arrived?'

'Wharf number five, next to the barge.'

Raia hurried there.

A seaman was asleep on the deck of Renuf's boat. The Syrian crossed the gangway and woke the guard.

'Where's your employer?'

'Renuf? I don't know.'

'When did you arrive?'

'At dawn today.'

'You travelled through the night?'

'Special permission, on account of the fresh cheese from the big dairy in Memphis. Some nobles here won't have any other.'

'After the unloading formalities, your boss must have gone home.'

'I'd be surprised.'

'Why?'

'Because a Sardinian giant with a big moustache made him get into his chariot. An awkward customer, that one.'

173

For Raia this was a bolt from the blue.

Renuf was a jovial fellow, of comfortable rotundity, father of three children, the heir to a family of boatmen and traders. When Serramanna had hailed him immediately after he arrived in Pi-Ramses, he had been astonished. As the Sardinian seemed in a very nasty mood, the merchant had deemed it wise to follow him in order to clear up as quickly as possible whatever misunderstanding there might be.

Serramanna drove him at full speed to the palace and took him to Ahmeni's office. It was the first time Renuf had met the king's private secretary, whose reputation never ceased to grow. He was praised for his serious nature, his capacity for work and his devotion: a power behind the throne, he administered the affairs of the state with exemplary honesty, indifferent to honours and high society life.

Renuf was struck by Ahmeni's pallor. It was rumoured that the scribe hardly ever left his office.

'This interview is an honour,' said Renuf, 'but I'm hard put to see the reason for it. I confess that I'm surprised at being summoned so abruptly.'

'You must forgive me. We are investigating a serious matter.'

'A matter that concerns me?'

'Possibly.'

'How can I help you?'

'By answering my questions frankly.'

'Ask them.'

'Do you know a certain Nenophar?'

'It's a fairly common name. I know at least a dozen.'

'The one we're talking about is young, very pretty, unmarried, a temptress and lives in Pi-Ramses, where she trades on her charms.'

'A . . . prostitute?'

'In a discreet way.'

'I love my wife, Ahmeni. In spite of my many journeys, I have never deceived her. I can assure you that we get on perfectly. Ask my friends and my neighbours, if you don't believe me.'

'Under oath, and before the Rule of Ma'at, will you swear that you have never met Miss Nenophar?'

'I swear,' Renuf solemnly declared.

The declaration impressed Serramanna, who was present at the interrogation though so far he'd said nothing. The merchant seemed sincere.

'That's strange,' he commented, irritated.

'Why? We merchants don't have a good name but I congratulate myself on being an honest man. My employees earn good wages, my boat is kept in good condition, I feed my family well, my accounts are in order, I pay my taxes, the tax-gatherers have never had anything to reproach me with . . . Is that what strikes you as strange?'

'Men of your quality are rare, Renuf.'

'That is to be regretted.'

'What strikes me as strange is the place where Nenophar's body was found.'

The merchant started. 'Her body? You mean . . . ?'

'She was murdered.'

'How horrible!'

'She may only have been a girl of loose morals, but every murder is a capital crime. The strange thing is that the body was found in a house in Pi-Ramses that belongs to you.'

'Where I live? In my villa?' Renuf felt quite faint.

'Not in your villa,' Serramanna intervened, 'but in that house there.' He pointed to a place on the map of Pi-Ramses that Ahmeni had unrolled in front of him.

'I don't understand. I—'

'Does it belong to you, yes or no?'

'Yes, but it isn't a house.'

Ahmeni and Serramanna exchanged glances. Was Renuf

out of his mind?

'It isn't a house,' he explained, 'it's a warehouse. I thought
I needed somewhere to store my goods, so I bought that place.
But my eyes were bigger than my belly; at my age I've no
wish to increase the size of my business. As soon as possible
I shall retire to the country, near Memphis.'

'Do you intend to resell these premises?'

'I've let them.'

A gleam of hope lit up Ahmeni's eyes. 'Who to?'

'To a colleague named Raia. He's a wealthy man, very
busy. He owns several boats and a great number of stores all
over Egypt.'

'What's his speciality?'

'Importing luxury preserves and rare vases that he sells to
high society.'

'Do you know where he comes from?'

'He's a Syrian, but he's lived in Egypt for many years.'

'Thank you, Renuf; your help has been invaluable.'

'You . . . you don't need me any more?'

'I don't think so, but don't say anything to anyone about
this conversation.'

'You have my word on it.'

Raia, a Syrian . . . If Ahsha had been present, he would
have noted the accuracy of his deductions. Before Ahmeni
had time to get to his feet, the Sardinian was already hurrying
to his chariot.

'Serramanna, wait for me!'

29

In spite of the cold, Uri-Teshup, son of the Hittite emperor, Muwatallis, was clad only in a loincloth of coarse wool, revealing his bare chest covered with an abundant growth of red hair. He galloped full-tilt, forcing the horsemen he commanded to demand the utmost exertion from their mounts. Uri-Teshup, long-haired, big and brawny, was proud of having been appointed commander-in-chief of the army, after the failure of the uprising in the Egyptian protectorates.

The speed and the energy of Ramses' reaction had astonished Muwatallis. If one were to believe Baduk, the former commander-in-chief who had been in charge of preparing that insurrection and responsible for controlling and occupying the territories after the success of the revolt, the operation would present no major difficulty.

The Syrian spy, who had lived in Egypt for many years, had sent less reassuring messages. According to him, Ramses was a great pharaoh, of strong character and inflexible will. Baduk had objected that the Hittites had nothing to fear from an inexperienced king and an army consisting of mercenaries, the faint-hearted and the incompetent. The peace imposed by Seti had suited the land of Hatti, insofar as Muwatallis needed time to strengthen his authority by getting rid of the groups of ambitious individuals who coveted his throne. At present there was no disunity under his rule.

The policy of expansion could be resumed. And if there was one country that the Anatolians wished to seize, in order to become masters of the world, it was surely the Egypt of the pharaohs.

According to General Baduk, the time was ripe. With Amurru and Canaan in Hittite hands, they would only need to press on towards the Delta, dismantle the fortresses forming the King's Wall and invade Lower Egypt. It was a magnificent plan, which had filled the Hittite officers with enthusiasm.

There was just one element he had overlooked: Ramses.

In Hattusa,* the Hittite capital, everyone was wondering what sin the empire had committed against the gods. Uri-Teshup alone found no reason to wonder: he attributed this failure to the stupidity and incompetence of General Baduk. So he was riding through the land of the Hittites not only to inspect its fortresses but also to meet Baduk, who was delaying his return to the capital.

He had expected to find him at Gâvur Kalesi,† a hilltop stronghold in the first foothills on the edge of the Anatolian plateau. Three gigantic statues of armed soldiers demonstrated the warlike character of the Hittite Empire, faced with which its opponents had but two options: submit or be exterminated. Along the roads, on rocks near the rivers, on isolated blocks of stone scattered in open country, sculptors had carved martial reliefs showing footsoldiers on the march, each with a javelin in his right hand, a bow hanging from his shoulder. Everywhere in the land of the Hittites love of war prevailed.

Uri-Teshup had sped over well-watered fertile plains planted with walnut trees. He did not even slow down when

---

*Bogazkoy, about 93 miles to the east of Ankara in present-day Turkey.
†About 37 miles south-west of Ankara.

crossing forests of maples separated by marshlands. Exhausting men and beasts, the emperor's son was determined to reach the fortress of Masat* as rapidly as possible. This was the last place where the general could be taking refuge.

In spite of their powers of endurance and their rigorous training, the Hittite horsemen were exhausted when they arrived in sight of Masat, which was built on a low hill in the middle of an open plain between two mountain ranges. From the top of this promontory it was easy to observe the surrounding country. Day and night, archers were posted on the battlements of the lookout towers. The officers, selected from noble families, maintained ruthless discipline.

Uri-Teshup halted about a hundred yards from the gate of the fortress. A javelin sank deep in the earth immediately in front of his horse.

He leaped to the ground and approached. 'Open up!' he yelled. 'Don't you recognize me?'

The gate of the Masat fortress opened. On the threshold, ten footsoldiers pointed their spears at the new arrival.

Uri-Teshup pushed them aside. 'The emperor's son demands to see the governor.'

The latter rushed down from the ramparts, risking breaking his neck.

'Prince, what an honour!'

The soldiers raised their spears and formed a guard of honour.

'Is General Baduk here?'

'Yes. I have put him up in my living quarters.'

'Take me to him.'

The two men climbed the steep, slippery steps of a stone staircase. At the top of the fortress, the north wind raged. Large, rough-hewn blocks of stone formed the walls of the

*Masat-Höyük, 72 miles north-east of Hattusa.

governor's residence, which was lit by oil lamps that gave off a thick smoke, blackening the ceilings.

As soon as he caught sight of Uri-Teshup, a corpulent man of some fifty years rose to his feet.

'Prince Uri-Teshup . . . '

'Are you in good health, General Baduk?'

'The failure of my plan is inexplicable. If the Egyptian army had not reacted so quickly, the insurgents in Canaan and Amurru would have had time to organize. But all is not lost. The Egyptians' conquests are only apparent. The potentates who declare themselves loyal to Pharaoh dream of placing themselves under our protection.'

'Why didn't you order our troops stationed near Kadesh to attack the enemy when they invaded Amurru?'

General Baduk seemed surprised. 'That would have needed a formal declaration of war – and that was outside my jurisdiction. Only the emperor could have made such a decision.'

Formerly as fiery-natured and masterful as Uri-Teshup, Baduk was now only a worn-out old man, his hair and beard turned grey.

'Have you drawn up a report on your action?'

'That's the reason why I've been staying here for a little while. I'm drawing up a detailed report, sparing no one.'

'May I withdraw?' asked the governor of the fortress, who had no wish to hear military secrets reserved for the high command.

'No,' replied Uri-Teshup.

It distressed the governor to witness the humiliation of General Baduk, a great soldier who was devoted to his country. But obedience to orders was the first Hittite virtue, and no one argued with orders from the emperor's son. Any insubordination was punished immediately by death, since there was no other way of holding together an army kept on a permanent war-footing.

180

'The Caaanite fortresses held out well against the Egyptian attacks,' Baduk pointed out. 'Their garrisons, which were trained by us, refused to surrender.'

'That makes no difference to the end result,' Uri-Teshup said. 'The rebels have been wiped out and Canaan is once more under Egyptian domination. There was a similar failure at Megiddo.'

'Alas, yes! And yet our instructors trained our allies perfectly. They had returned to Kadesh in accordance with the emperor's wishes, so that no trace of Hittite presence in Canaan and Amurru would be found.'

'Amurru. Yes, let's talk about Amurru. How many times did you claim that the prince was eating out of your hand and would no longer submit to Ramses?'

'My biggest mistake,' Baduk conceded. 'The Egyptian army's manoeuvre was remarkable; instead of taking the coast road, which would have led them straight into the trap laid by our new allies, they went via the interior. The Prince of Amurru was taken from the rear, and had no alternative but to surrender.'

'Surrender, surrender!' thundered Uri-Teshup. 'That's all you can talk about! Wasn't your strategy supposed to weaken the Egyptian army, whose infantry and chariot corps should have been destroyed? Instead of that, we saw few losses among Pharaoh's soldiers, his troops confident in their courage and a victory for Ramses!'

'I am aware of my failure and do not attempt to minimize it. I was wrong to trust the Prince of Amurru, who preferred dishonour to fighting.'

'Defeat has no place in the career of a Hittite general.'

'There is no question of my men being defeated, Prince. It was the misapplication of a plan to destabilize the Egyptian protectorates.'

'You were afraid of Ramses, weren't you?'

'His forces were much larger than we had expected, and

181

my mission was to instigate rebellion, not to confront the Egyptians.'

'Sometimes, Baduk, it is necessary to know how to improvise.'

'I am a soldier, Prince, and I must obey orders!'

'Why did you take refuge here instead of returning to Hattusa?'

'I told you, I wanted to stand back from the situation in order to draw up my report. And I have some good news: thanks to our allies in Amurru, the insurrection will be resumed.'

'You are imagining things, Baduk.'

'No, Prince. Give me a little time and I shall succeed.'

'You are no longer in charge of the Hittite army. The emperor has decided: I am replacing you.'

Baduk took a few steps towards the huge fireplace in which oak logs were burning. 'Congratulations, Uri-Teshup. You will lead us to victory.'

'I have another message for you, Baduk.'

The former general stood warming his hands, with his back to the emperor's son.

'I am listening, Prince.'

'You are a coward.' He unsheathed his sword and plunged it into Baduk's back.

The governor stood there, petrified.

'This coward was also a traitor,' declared Uri-Teshup. 'He refused to accept his dismissal and attacked me. You are a witness.'

The governor bowed.

'Pick up the corpse, carry it into the middle of the courtyard and burn it without the rites reserved for warriors. So shall all defeated generals perish.'

While Baduk's corpse was burning, under the eyes of the garrison, Uri-Teshup himself greased with mutton-fat the axles of the chariot that would bear him back to the capital to advocate total war against Egypt.

30

Uri-Teshup could not imagine a more beautiful capital. Built on the central Anatolian plateau, where barren steppes alternated with gorges and ravines, Hattusa, the heart of the Hittite empire, embodied the violence of its burning summers and icy winters. A mountain city, occupying a huge area of extremely hilly terrain, it had demanded miracles on the part of the builders. Hattusa consisted of a lower town and then an upper town dominated by an acropolis on which stood the emperor's palace, and looked, at first glance, like a gigantic collection of stone fortifications clinging to the craggy slopes. Surrounded by compact groups of mountains, which formed barriers inaccessible to any possible attacker, the Hittite capital resembled a citadel perched on rocky outcrops and consisting of enormous blocks of stone set on level foundations. Inside the city, stone had been used everywhere for the under-structure, unburned bricks and wood for the walls.

Hattusa, proud, untamed. Hattusa, warlike and invincible, where the name of Uri-Teshup would soon be acclaimed.

More than five-and-a-half miles of ramparts, bristling with towers and battlements, followed the steep terrain, scaled peaks, towered above deep gorges. The hand of man had subjugated nature, stealing the secret of her strength. This rejoiced a soldier's heart.

There were two gates set in the wall of the lower town,

three in that of the upper town. Scorning the Gate of the Lions and the King's Gate, Uri-Teshup made his way to the highest point of access, the Gate of the Sphinx, whose main feature was a fifty-pace-long tunnel leading into the interior.

True, the lower town was dignified by the imposing temple dedicated to the god of storms and the sun goddess, and the district of the sanctuaries contained no fewer than twenty-one monuments of various sizes, but Uri-Teshup preferred the upper town and the royal palace. From this eyrie he liked to gaze down on the terraces, formed by placing rocks side by side, on which official buildings and residences of notables had been erected, apparently at random, but based in fact on the way the land sloped.

On entering the city, the emperor's son had broken three loaves and poured wine on a block of stone, while uttering the ritual incantation: 'May this rock be eternal'. Here and there were placed vessels filled with oil and honey, destined to appease the demons.

The palace stood imposingly on piles formed by three peaks. High walls, reinforced by tall towers permanently manned by elite soldiers, isolated the imperial residence from the rest of the capital and prevented any attack. Muwatallis, prudent and cunning, was familiar with the upheavals and reversals of Hittite history and the bitter struggles to win power. Arguments had frequently been solved by poison and the sword, while very few great Hittite chiefs had died a natural death. So it was preferable for the 'Great Fortress', as the people called it, to be inaccessible from three sides. One narrow entrance alone, watched over day and night, allowed access to visitors after they had been duly searched.

Uri-Teshup submitted to being examined by the guards who, like the majority of the soldiers, had welcomed the appointment of the emperor's son. Young and courageous, he would not be as indecisive as General Baduk.

Inside the palace enclosure were several large water-tanks,

essential during the summer months. Stables, armouries and guardrooms opened on to a paved courtyard. Moreover, the plan of the imperial abode was similar to that of other Hittite dwellings, large or small, namely a collection of rooms arranged round a central square.

An officer greeted Uri-Teshup and led him into a hall with heavy columns where the emperor was accustomed to receive his guests. Stone lions and sphinxes guarded the door, as well as the entrance to the Hall of Archives where souvenirs of the Hittite army's victories were kept. In this room, which exhibited the invincibility of the empire, Uri-Teshup felt himself strengthened in his mission.

Two men entered the chamber. The first was Emperor Muwatallis, a fifty-year-old of average height, broad-chested with short legs. As he was susceptible to the cold, he was draped in a long cloak of red and black wool. His brown eyes were ceaselessly on the alert.

The second was Hattusilis, the emperor's younger brother. He was small and puny; his hair was bound with a head-band, he wore a silver necklace, a bracelet on his left elbow, and was dressed in a multicoloured length of material which left his shoulders bare. He was a priest of the sun goddess and had married the fair Putuhepa, the intelligent, influential daughter of the high priest. Uri-Teshup detested both of them, but the emperor listened willingly to their advice. In the eyes of the new commander-in-chief, Hattusilis was nothing but an intriguer who hid in the shadows in order to seize power at a suitable moment.

Uri-Teshup knelt before his father and kissed his hand.

'Did you find General Baduk?'

'Yes, father, he was hiding in the fortress at Masat.'

'What explanation did he give for his behaviour?'

'He attacked me and I killed him. The governor of the fortress was a witness.'

Muwatallis turned to his brother.

'A terrible tragedy,' Hattusilis commented. 'But no one will bring this vanquished general back to life. His death seems like a punishment from the gods.'

Uri-Teshup could not hide his surprise. For the first time, Hattusilis was on his side!

'Wise words,' pronounced the emperor. 'The Hittite people do not like defeats.'

'I am for the immediate invasion of Amurru and Canaan,' recommended Uri-Teshup, 'then for attacking Egypt.'

'The King's Wall forms a solid line of defence,' objected Hattusilis.

'That's just an illusion. The forts are too far apart. We shall isolate and capture them all in one assault-wave.'

'Such optimism seems excessive to me. Egypt has just proved how formidable her army is.'

'She has only defeated cowards! When the Egyptians come face to face with the Hittites, they will flee.'

'Aren't you forgetting Ramses?'

The emperor's question curbed his son's impatience.

'You will lead your army to victory, Uri-Teshup, but you must prepare for your triumph. To wage war far from our bases would be a mistake.'

'But then where shall we launch the offensive?'

'At a spot where the Egyptian forces will themselves be far from their bases.'

'You mean . . . ?'

'At Kadesh. That is where the great battle will take place, the battle that will see the defeat of Ramses.'

'I'd prefer to attack Pharaoh's protectorates.'

'I have studied our informers' reports and drawn conclusions from Baduk's failure. Ramses is a true war-leader, much more formidable than we thought. We shall need long preparation.'

'We're wasting time needlessly!'

'No, my son. We must strike with strength and precision.'

'Our army is greatly superior to a collection of Egyptian soldiers and mercenaries! We already have the strength; as for precision, I shall prove this by executing my own plans. Everything is prepared in my head; more talk is useless. I need only to give the command to sweep my troops along in an irresistible momentum!'

'I rule Hatti, Uri-Teshup. You will act on my orders, and only on my orders. For the moment, prepare yourself for the ceremony; I shall address the court in less than an hour.'

The emperor left the Hall of Columns.

Uri-Teshup turned defiantly to Hattusilis. 'You're the one who's trying to block my initiatives, aren't you?'

'The army's no concern of mine.'

'Are you trying to make a fool of me? Sometimes I wonder if you aren't the one who really rules the empire.'

'Don't insult the greatness of your father, Uri-Teshup; Muwatallis is the emperor, and I do my best to serve him.'

'While waiting for him to die!'

'Watch your words; you're letting your tongue run away with you.'

'This court is a web of intrigues, and you are the one behind it all. But don't hope to get away with anything.'

'You're attributing false intentions to me. Are you capable of admitting that a man may not have boundless ambitions?'

'That's not true of you, Hattusilis.'

'It's useless to try to convince you, I suppose.'

'Completely useless.'

'The emperor has appointed you commander-in-chief, and he was right. You're an excellent soldier and our troops trust you; but I hope you won't act as you please and without control.'

'You forget one essential fact, Hattusilis: among the Hittites, it's the army that lays down the law.'

'Do you know what most people in our country love? Their houses, their vines, their herds of cattle.'

'Are you advocating peace?'

'We aren't at war, as far as I know.'

'Anyone who speaks in favour of peace with Egypt will be considered a traitor.'

'I forbid you to put such an interpretation on my words.'

'Don't stand in my way, Hattusilis, or you'll regret it.'

'Threats are the weapon of the weak, Uri-Teshup.'

The emperor's son grasped the hilt of his sword.

Hattusilis faced him. 'Would you dare raise your sword against the brother of Muwatallis?'

Uri-Teshup uttered a cry of rage and stamped furiously out of the great hall.

31

Uri-Teshup, Hattusilis, Putuhepa, the high priest of the god of storms, the high priest of the sun goddess, the workers' leader, the inspector of markets and all the other dignitaries of the empire had gathered to listen to the emperor's address.

There was much disquiet over the failure of the plan to destabilize the Egyptian protectorates. No one doubted that the guilty person was General Baduk, who had met such a tragic death. But what policy would Muwatallis advocate? The military clan, urged on by the hot-headed Uri-Teshup, wished for a direct, speedy confrontation with Egypt. The merchants, whose financial power was considerable, preferred to prolong the state of 'neither war nor peace', favourable to the development of commercial exchanges. Hattusilis had received their representatives and advised the emperor not to neglect their point of view. Hatti was a land through which goods passed, where caravans circulated, which paid heavy taxes to the Hittite state and thus fed the military clan. Did not one donkey transport the weight of a man in mixed goods and of a heavy man in textiles? In cities and villages alike, merchants had established regular commercial centres and set up an efficient economic system, thanks to the lists of goods, transport directives, contracts, acknowledgment of debts and specific judicial procedures. If, for example, a merchant was convicted of murder, he could

189

avoid trial and imprisonment by purchasing his liberty at great cost.

The army and commerce: such were the two pillars of the emperor's power. He could not do without either. Since Uri-Teshup was becoming the idol of the military, Hattusilis took care to be the favoured representative of the merchants. As for the priests, they were under the thumb of Hattusilis's wife, Putuhepa, whose family was the wealthiest of the Hittite aristocracy.

Muwatallis was too clear-sighted not to be aware of the intensity of the furtive struggles of his son and his brother, pitted against each other. By granting each a sphere of influence, he satisfied their ambitions and remained in control of the situation, but for how long? Soon a decision would have to be reached.

Hattusilis was not against the conquest of Egypt, insofar as it did not cause Uri-Teshup to be recognized as a hero and future emperor. So it was imperative for him to win more friendships for himself in the army and erode Uri-Teshup's power. Wouldn't a heroic death in battle be the most enviable fate for the son of the emperor?

Hattusilis valued Muwatallis's method of ruling, and would have been pleased to serve him if Uri-Teshup had not become a threat to the equilibrium of the empire. Muwatallis could not expect either respect or gratitude from his son; with the Hittites, family ties were of comparatively minor importance. Under the law, incest was an acceptable practice, in as much as it harmed no one. As for rape, it did not carry heavy penalties, and did not even involve any sanction if consent could be assumed on the part of the girl or woman in question. For a son to murder his father in order to seize power did not strike a blow at public morality.

To entrust the high command of the army to Uri-Teshup was a stroke of genius; so long as the son of the emperor was busy establishing his prestige, he would not think, at least in the immediate future, of doing away with his father. But in the long run the danger would re-surface. It was up to Hattusilis to make the most of this period and reduce Uri-Teshup's capacity for doing harm.

An icy north wind blew through the upper town, announcing the early onset of winter. The dignitaries were invited to enter the audience chamber, which was heated by braziers.

The atmosphere was heavy and tense. Muwatallis liked neither speeches nor gatherings; he preferred to work in the shadows and manipulate his subordinates individually, avoiding burdening himself with the presence of a council.

In the front row, Uri-Teshup's brand-new armour contrasted with Hattusilis's modest attire. Putuhepa, the latter's wife, was magnificent in her scarlet gown, as dignified as a queen; she was covered in jewels, including gold bracelets from Egypt.

Muwatallis was seated on his throne, a seat of rough-hewn, unpolished stone. On his rare appearances, everyone was astonished that this insignificant, harmless-looking man was the emperor of such a bellicose nation; but an attentive observer would soon perceive, in his look and his attitudes, a suppressed aggressiveness ready to find extremely violent expression. Muwatallis combined brute strength with cunning, and knew how to strike like a scorpion.

'It is to me, and to me alone,' declared the emperor, 'that the god of storms and the sun goddess have entrusted this land, its capital and its cities. I, the emperor, shall protect them, since the power and the war chariot have been conceded to me and to none other.'

By using the ancient ritual words, Muwatallis reminded his son and brother that he alone would make decisions, and that they, whatever their influence, owed him absolute obedience. At the first false step, they would be ruthlessly eliminated and no one would contest his decision.

191

'To the north, to the south, to the east and to the west,' he continued, 'the Anatolian plateau is bounded by mountains which protect us. Our frontiers are inviolable. But the destiny of our people is not to remain shut away inside our land. My predecessors declared, "May the country of the Hittites be bounded by the sea on both sides." And I declare, "May the banks of the Nile belong to us."'

Muwatallis rose to his feet, his speech finished.

In those few words he had just announced war.

The reception organized by Uri-Teshup to celebrate his appointment was brilliant and greatly appreciated. Governors of fortresses, high-ranking officers and elite soldiers talked of past exploits and future victories. The prince announced he would be taking the chariot corps in hand and renewing its equipment. The intoxicating smell of violent, fierce conflict floated in the air.

Hattusilis and his wife left their places when a hundred young female slaves burst in. Uri-Teshup was offering them to his guests as dessert, and they had been ordered to submit to the guests' every whim, on pain of a flogging and being sent to the salt mines, one of the sources of Hatti's wealth.

'You are leaving already, my friends?' exclaimed the prince in astonishment.

'We have a busy day tomorrow,' replied Putuhepa.

'Hattusilis ought to have a little relaxation. There are some sixteen-year-old Asian girls among this lot, pretty little fillies. The man who sold them to me promised they would give exceptional performances. You go home, dear Putuhepa, and allow your husband this little distraction.'

'Not all men are pigs,' she retorted. 'In future, spare us such invitations.'

Hattusilis and Putuhepa returned to the wing of the palace where they lodged. The setting was austere, scarcely enlivened by the few multicoloured woollen rugs and the trophies, heads of bears and crossed spears on the walls.

Putuhepa was nervous; she dismissed her maid and removed her make-up herself.

'That Uri-Teshup is a dangerous fool,' she commented.

'But don't forget that he's the emperor's son.'

'But *you* are his brother!'

'In many people's eyes, he is Muwatallis's designated successor.'

'Designated . . . Could the emperor have made such a blunder?'

'It's still only a rumour.'

'Why not block it?'

'It doesn't worry me too much.'

'Your calmness seems rather forced.'

'No, my dear; it is the result of logical analysis of the situation.'

'Would you be good enough to enlighten me?'

'Uri-Teshup has obtained the post he dreamed of; he no longer needs to plot against the emperor.'

'Are you becoming gullible? It's the throne he's after.'

'That is obvious, Putuhepa, but is he capable of getting it?'

The priestess gazed attentively at her husband. Puny and unattractive though he was, Hattusilis had won her by his intelligence and perspicacity. He had the making of a great statesman.

'Uri-Teshup cannot think clearly,' declared Hattusilis, 'and he is unaware of the enormity of his task. To command a Hittite army demands skills he does not possess.'

'But he's an excellent warrior and completely fearless.'

'True. But a commander-in-chief must know how to judge between different tendencies – indeed, sometimes between conflicting ones. That sort of thing calls for experience and patience.'

'That's not exactly the picture of Uri-Teshup you're painting!'

'What could be more heartening? It won't be long before this hot-head makes serious mistakes by displeasing one general or another. The present factions will be strengthened and divided, clashes will occur, and ravenous beasts will set about devouring a tyrant who commands no respect.'

'But the emperor has announced war, and has put Uri-Teshup in overall command!'

'In appearance, only in appearance.'

'Are you sure of that?'

'I repeat, Uri-Teshup has illusions about his own ability. He will discover a complex, cruel world. His warrior's dreams will be shattered against footsoldiers' shields and crushed under chariot wheels. But that's not all . . . '

'Don't keep me on tenterhooks, my dear husband.'

'Muwatallis is a great emperor.'

'Does he intend to exploit his son's shortcomings?'

Hattusilis smiled. 'The empire is both strong and fragile. Strong, because its military might is considerable; fragile, because it is threatened by envious neighbours ready to take advantage of its slightest weakness. Attacking and occupying Egypt is a good plan, but improvisation would lead to disaster. Vultures would take advantage of that to feed on our spoils.'

'Can even Muwatallis control a warmonger like Uri-Teshup?'

'Uri-Teshup doesn't know his father's real plans, nor the way he intends to realize them. The emperor has told him enough to give him confidence, but hasn't revealed the essentials to him.'

'And you? Has he revealed them to you?'

'I have that honour, Putuhepa. And the emperor has also entrusted me with a mission: to implement his plan of action, without warning his son.'

From the terrace of his official residence in the upper town,

Uri-Teshup gazed at the new moon. She held the secret of the future, his future, So he spoke to her at length and confided his desire to lead the Hittite army to victory by crushing anyone who opposed his progress.

The emperor's son raised a dish filled with water to the night star. By means of this mirror he hoped to penetrate the secrets of the heavens. All Hittites practised the art of divination; but to address the moon directly involved a risk which few dared take. If her silence were violated, the moon became a curved sword which cut the throat of her assailant and his broken body would be found at the foot of the ramparts. To her lovers, on the other hand, she granted good fortune in battle.

Uri-Teshup worshipped the faithless, arrogant queen of the night.

For an hour she remained silent. Then ripples began to appear on the surface of the water, which now seethed and bubbled. The dish became boiling hot, but Uri-Teshup clung on to it.

The water became calm again. On the smooth surface, there appeared the head of a man wearing the double crown of Upper and Lower Egypt.

Ramses!

Such was the great destiny announced to Uri-Teshup: he would kill Ramses and make Egypt his docile slave.

32

Clad in a heavy tunic, his beard impeccably trimmed, Raia presented himself at the office of Ahmeni, Pharaoh's private secretary, who received him immediately.

'I'm told you've been looking for me all over the city,' Raia declared, his voice shaking slightly.

'That's correct. Serramanna was instructed to bring you here, by force if you didn't come willingly.'

'By force? But on what grounds?'

'There are serious suspicions hanging over you.'

The Syrian seemed stunned. 'Suspicions . . . about me?'

'Where were you hiding?'

'I *wasn't* hiding! I was at the port, in a warehouse, preparing a shipment of luxury preserves. As soon as I heard the incredible rumour, I hurried here! I'm an honest tradesman. I've been settled in Egypt for many years and I've not committed any sort of offence. Ask people who know me, ask my customers. You should know that I'm extending my business and I'm about to buy a new boat to transport my goods. My preserves are served at the best tables and my valuable vases are works of art which adorn the finest houses in Thebes, Memphis and Pi-Ramses – I'm even purveyor to the palace!' Raia's words poured out, but his voice was strained.

'I don't doubt your virtues as a trader,' said Ahmeni.

196

'But . . . What am I accused of?'

'Do you know a certain Nenophar, a woman of easy virtue, living in Pi-Ramses?'

'No.'

'You're not married?'

'My business doesn't leave me much leisure to look after a wife and family.'

'You must have some amorous affairs.'

'My private life . . . '

'In your own interests, answer.'

Raia hesitated. 'I have some lady friends, here and there. To tell the truth, I work so hard that my favourite distraction is sleep.'

'So you deny having met this Nenophar?'

'I do.'

'Do you ackowledge that you have the use of a storehouse in Pi-Ramses?'

'Naturally. I rent a big warehouse on the quay, but it will soon be too cramped. So I decided to rent another one, in the town itself. I shall start using it next month.'

'Who owns it?'

'An Egyptian colleague, Renuf. A good fellow and an honest trader, who had bought the place in the hope of extending his business. As he isn't using it, he offered it to me at a reasonable rent.'

'At the moment the premises are empty?'

'Yes.'

'Do you go there often?'

'I've only been once, with Renuf to sign the lease.'

'Nenophar's dead body was discovered there.'

The merchant seemed stunned by this revelation.

'The poor girl had been strangled,' Ahmeni went on, 'because she was about to reveal the name of the man who had forced her to offer forged evidence.'

Raia's hands trembled and his lips were white. 'Murder —

here, in the capital! What an abomination . . . Such violence
. . . I'm overwhelmed.'

'What is your country of origin?'

'Syria.'

'Our investigation has convinced us that the guilty person
was a Syrian.'

'There are thousands of Syrians in Egypt!'

'You are a Syrian and Nenophar was murdered on your
premises. Disturbing coincidences, aren't they?'

'Just coincidences, that's all!'

'This crime is linked to another extremely serious offence.
That is why the king has asked me to proceed promptly.'

'I'm just a merchant, a humble merchant! Is it because I'm
beginning to make my fortune that I'm the target of slanders
and jealousies? If I'm growing rich, it's thanks to constant
hard work! I've never robbed anyone.'

If this Raia really is the man we're looking for, thought
Ahmeni, he's a first-rate actor.

'Read this,' demanded the scribe, handing the Syrian the
report on the discovery of Nenophar's body; it gave the date
of the crime. 'Where were you on that day and that night?'

'Let me think. I'm so upset . . . And with all my travels,
I'm a bit lost . . . Ah, I've got it! I was stocktaking in my
Bubastis store.'

Bubastis, the pretty town dedicated to the cat goddess
Bastet, was situated downriver from Pi-Ramses. With a fast
boat and a strong current, it was only five to six hours away.

'Did anyone see you there?'

'Yes, my head storekeeper and my sales supervisor for the
region.'

'How long did you stay in Bubastis?'

'I got there the evening before the tragedy and I left the
next day for Memphis.'

'A perfect alibi, Raia.'

'Alibi . . . ? But it is simply the truth!'

198

'What are the names of these two men?'

Raia wrote them on a used piece of papyrus.

'I shall check,' Ahmeni promised.

'You'll find I'm innocent!'

'I must ask you not to leave Pi-Ramses.'

'Are you . . . Are you arresting me?'

'It may be necessary to question you again.'

'But my business! I have to leave for the provinces to sell my vases.'

'Your customers will have to wait a little.'

The merchant was on the verge of tears. 'I risk losing the trust of wealthy families. I always deliver on the agreed day.'

'I'm afraid that can't be helped. Where are you staying?'

'In a small house behind my warehouse on the quay. How long will this persecution last?'

'Be assured we shall soon have the matter settled.'

The Sardinian giant needed a good three beakers of strong beer to cool his anger on his return from his lightning journey to Bubastis.

'I've questioned Raia's employees,' he informed Ahmeni.

'And they confirm his alibi?'

'They do.'

'Will they take the oath before a tribunal?'

'They are Syrians, Ahmeni! What does the judgment of the dead matter to them? They will lie shamelessly in exchange for a big enough reward. For them the Rule doesn't count. If I were allowed to question them in my own way, like when I was a pirate—'

'You're not a pirate any more, and justice is Egypt's most precious possession. Ill-treating a human being is an offence.'

'Isn't it an offence to let a criminal go free when he's also a spy?'

The arrival of an orderly put an end to the argument.

Ahmeni and Serramanna were summoned to Ramses' vast office.

'How far have we got?' asked the king.

'Serramanna is convinced that the Syrian merchant is a spy and a murderer.'

'And you?'

'I think so too.'

The Sardinian looked gratefully at the scribe. Every trace of friction between them had been dispelled.

'Any proof?'

'None at all, Majesty,' admitted Serramanna.

'If Raia is arrested simply on suspicion, he'll ask to be heard by a tribunal and he'll be acquitted.'

'We're aware of that,' deplored Ahmeni.

'Leave it to me, Majesty,' begged Serramanna.

'Must I remind the commander of my personal bodyguard that any bodily harm inflicted on a suspect carries a heavy sentence – for the aggressor?'

Serramanna sighed.

'We're at a dead end,' admitted Ahmeni. 'Raia is probably a member of a network of pro-Hittite spies, possibly even their leader. The man is intelligent, cunning and an actor. He can control his reactions, become tearful or indignant at will, and give the impression of being an honest, hard-working merchant, whose whole life is devoted to work. The fact still remains that he travels throughout Egypt, goes from town to town, and meets a great number of people. Is there any better way of observing what is happening in our country in order to pass on detailed information to the enemy?'

'Raia was sleeping with Nenophar,' declared Sarramanna, 'and he paid her to lie. He thought she'd keep her mouth shut; that was his mistake. She tried to blackmail him and he killed her.'

'According to your report,' noted Ramses, 'the Syrian strangled this woman in commercial premises he rented. Why be so foolhardy?'

'The premises weren't in his name,' Ahmeni reminded him. 'Tracing them to the owner, who is above suspicion, and then to Raia wasn't easy.'

'Raia must certainly have thought of getting rid of the owner,' Serramanna added, 'for fear he'd reveal his name. But we intervened in time. Otherwise no one would have known about this Syrian. In my opinion, Raia didn't intend to murder Nenophar. By meeting her in this discreet spot, in a district where no one knew him, he ran no risk. A stern warning, he thought, should be enough to keep her quiet. But the situation became acrimonious; the girl had the idea of screwing a small fortune out of him in exchange for her silence. Otherwise she threatened to reveal everything to the police. Raia killed her and fled without being able to dispose of the body. But he forged himself an alibi, thanks to his Syrian accomplices.'

'If we are on the eve of war with the Hittites,' commented Ramses, 'the presence of a spy network in our lands is a serious problem. Your reconstruction of the facts is convincing, but the most important thing is to find out how Raia transmits messages to the Hittites.'

'A good interrogation . . . ' suggested Serramanna.

'A spy won't talk.'

'What does Your Majesty suggest?' asked the scribe.

'Question him again, then release him. Try to convince him that we have no charge against him.'

'He won't be taken in.'

'No,' the king admitted, 'but when he feels the net closing round him he'll be forced to communicate with Hatti. I want to know how he manages it.'

33

It was the end of November, the beginning of the season when the first shoots of the cereals appeared. The sown seeds were proclaiming their victory over darkness and offering the Egyptian people the life they bore within them.

Ramses helped Homer down from the litter and into an armchair, set at a table laden with provisions in the shade of palm trees beside a canal. Close by was a ford where the herds could cross. The mild sunshine of the first days of winter caressed the old poet's brow.

'Does this meal in the open country appeal to you?' asked the king.

'The gods have granted Egypt great favours.'

'The pharaohs have built them great dwellings where they are worshipped.'

'This land is a mystery, Majesty, and you yourself are a mystery. This serenity, this gentle way of life, the beauty of these palm trees, the limpid clarity of this air, the exquisite taste of this food . . . there is something magical in all this. You Egyptians have created a miracle and you live in magic. But how long will it endure?'

'As long as we value the Rule of Ma'at above all else.'

'You forget the outside world, Ramses. It cares naught for this Rule. Do you believe that Ma'at will halt the Hittite army?'

'She will be our best bulwark against adversity.'

'I have gazed on warfare with my own eyes, I have seen the cruelty of men, seen fury unleashed, murderous folly take hold of beings who seemed level-headed. War . . . It is the vice hidden in men's blood, the defect that destroys all forms of civilization. Egypt will be no exception to that rule.'

'She will, Homer. Our country is a miracle, you are right, but a miracle that we build every day. And I shall crush the invasion, wherever it comes from.'

The poet closed his eyes. 'I am no longer in exile, Majesty. I shall never forget Greece, its ruggedness and its charm, but it is here, on this black and fertile soil, that my spirit communes with the heavens, the heavens that war is about to rip apart.'

'Why this pessimism?'

'The Hittites dream only of conquest. Fighting is their sole reason for existence, as it was for many Greeks, who were determined to tear one another to pieces. Your recent victory won't deter them.'

'My army will be ready to fight.'

'You're like one of the great cats, Majesty. I thought of you when I composed these lines: "A panther which confronts a hunter does not tremble but maintains a steady heart, even when it hears the howls of a pack of hounds; even when wounded by a javelin, it continues to struggle and attacks in order to live or die."'

Nefertari reread the astonishing missive Shaanar had had delivered to her. Messengers on horseback had brought it from Hatti to southern Syria, then it was relayed by others into Egypt, where it had been delivered to the Foreign Affairs secretariat.

To my sister, the very dear Queen of Egypt, Nefertari.
I, Putuhepa, wife of Hattusilis, brother of the Emperor

*of the Hittites, send you my friendly greetings. We are far
from each other; our countries and our peoples are very
different, but do they not aspire to the same peace? If you
and I succeed in promoting good understanding between
our peoples, shall we not have accomplished a good deed?
For my part, I shall devote myself to this. May I beg my
illustrious sister to do likewise?*

*To receive a letter from her hand would be a pleasure
and an honour. May the gods protect her.*

'What can this strange message mean?' the queen asked
Ramses.

'The form of the two dried-mud seals and the handwriting
leave no doubt about the letter's authenticity.'

'Should I reply to Putuhepa?'

'She isn't a queen, but must be considered as the first lady
of the Hittite Empire since the death of Muwatallis's wife.'

'Will her husband, Hattusilis, be the next emperor?'

'Muwatallis's preference is for his son, Uri-Teshup, a
determined partisan of war against Egypt.'

'So this letter is almost meaningless.'

'It reveals the existence of another faction, encouraged by
the priests and the merchants – whose financial power is far
from negligible, according to Ahsha. They fear a war that
would cripple their businesses.'

'Are they influential enough to prevent the war?'

'Definitely not.'

'If Putuhepa is sincere, I ought to help her. There's still a
faint hope of avoiding thousands of deaths.'

Raia fingered his beard nervously.

'We have checked your alibi,' declared Ahmeni.

'All the better.'

'All the better for you, indeed. Your employees have
confirmed your statement.'

'I spoke the truth and have nothing to hide.'

Ahmeni toyed with a writing-brush. 'I have to admit . . . perhaps we made a mistake.'

'At last, the voice of reason!'

'You must acknowledge that the circumstantial evidence against you was overwhelming. Nevertheless, I offer you my apologies.'

'In Egypt justice is not an empty word.'

'We are all proud of it.'

'Am I free to go where I please?'

'You are at complete liberty to resume your work.'

'Am I cleared of all accusations?'

'You are, Raia.'

'I appreciate your frankness and I hope you find that poor girl's murderer as quickly as possible.'

Raia's mind was not on his work as he pretended to busy himself with delivery notes and paced up and down the quay between his warehouse and his boat.

That performance hadn't taken him in for a moment. Ahmeni was far too persistent to let go so quickly, claiming to believe the evidence of two Syrians. Instead of using violence, the scribe was setting a trap: he hoped that Raia, believing his innocence proved, would resume his secret activities and lead Serramanna to the members of his network.

When he thought about it, the situation seemed much more serious than he'd realized. Whatever he did, his network seemed doomed. Ahmeni would soon discover that nearly all Raia's employees worked for Hatti, forming a veritable shadow army, terribly effective. A wave of arrests would destroy it. To allay suspicion, he must continue trading as usual.

But this temporary solution would not take him far. He had to warn Shaanar immediately, without letting the slightest suspicion fall on him.

Raia delivered some valuable vases to several notables in Pi-Ramses. Shaanar, a regular customer, was on the list, so the Syrian went to his villa and met his steward.

'Lord Shaanar is not at home.'

'Ah. Will he be back soon?'

'I don't know.'

'Unfortunately I can't wait, as I have to leave for Memphis. A few incidents recently have greatly delayed me. Would you be so good as to deliver this object to Lord Shaanar?'

'Certainly.'

'Give him my greetings, please. Oh, I nearly forgot. The price is very high, but the quality of this little work of art justifies it. We can settle this minor problem on my return.'

Raia visited three other regular customers before embarking for Memphis.

He had made up his mind: given the urgency of the situation, he had first to shake off Serramanna's men who were following him, and then contact his master to ask his advice.

The scribe at the Foreign Affairs secretariat who was responsible for drawing up dispatches ran to Shaanar's office, forgetting both the dignity of his position and his wig. His colleagues watched him critically: the most important quality of a man of letters was supposed to be self-control.

Shaanar was not there.

A terrible dilemma . . . Should he wait for the minister's return or skip a rung in the hierarchy and take the missive directly to the king? Risking probable blame, the official opted for the second solution.

His astounded colleagues saw him, still wigless, leave the secretariat – during working hours! – and jump into the official chariot, which took him to the palace in a few minutes.

Ahmeni received the official and understood his agitation. The letter, sent on by the diplomatic services of southern Syria, bore the seals of Muwatallis, Emperor of the Hitttites.

'As my minister was absent, I thought it right . . . '

'You did well. Have no fears for your career: the king will appreciate this spirit of initiative.'

Ahmeni weighed up the missive, a wooden tablet wrapped in material which bore the stains of several dried-mud seals and was covered with Hittite script. He closed his eyes, hoping that this was a nightmare. When he opened them, the message was still there and was still burning his fingers.

His mouth dry, he went slowly down the passageway separating his office from Ramses'.

After spending the day in the company of his minister for agriculture and those in charge of irrigation, the king was alone, busy preparing a decree aimed at improving the maintenance of the dykes.

'You seem upset, Ahmeni.'

The scribe held out his hands and presented the official missive from the Emperor of Hatti to Pharaoh.

'The declaration of war,' murmured Ramses.

34

Ramses unhurriedly broke the seals, tore off the protective wrapping and glanced through the message.

Once again, Ahmeni closed his eyes, savouring the last moments of peace before all hell broke loose, before the pharaoh dictated the reply which would mark the outbreak of war between Egypt and Hatti.

'Are you still as abstemious as ever, Ahmeni?'

The question astonished the scribe. 'Me, abstemious? Yes, of course!'

'A pity. We could have shared an exceptionally good wine. Read this.'

Ahmeni deciphered the tablet.

From the Emperor of Hatti, Muwatallis, to his brother Ramses, the Son of the Light, the Pharaoh of Egypt.

Are you in good health? I hope that your mother, Tuya, your wife, Nefertari, and your children are in good health. Your fame and that of the Great Royal Wife grow endlessly, and your valour is known to all the inhabitants of Hatti.

Are your horses in good condition? Here, we take good care of ours. They are magnificent animals, the finest in creation.

May the gods protect Hatti and Egypt.

A broad smile lit up Ahmeni's face. 'This . . . this is wonderful!'

'I am not convinced.'

'These are the usual diplomatic forms of words, and a declaration of war is still a long way off.'

'Ahsha is the only one who can tell us that.'

'You don't trust Muwatallis.'

'He founded his power on a combination of violence and cunning; in his eyes, diplomacy is only an additional weapon, not the path to peace.'

'What if he's weary of war? Your reconquest of Canaan and Amurru showed him that the Egyptian army has to be taken seriously.'

'He doesn't despise our army; that's why he's preparing for battle and trying to allay our fears with demonstrations of friendship. Homer, who's very far-sighted, doesn't believe in a lasting peace.'

'What if he's mistaken? What if Muwatallis has changed, or the merchants are prevailing over the warriors? Putuhepa's letter is to that effect.'

'The economy of the Hittite Empire is based on warfare; the people secretly love violence. The merchants will support the soldiers and a great war will give them the opportunity to make greater profits.'

'So you think the confrontation is inevitable?'

'I hope I'm wrong. If Ahsha notes no significant manoeuvres, nor a massive stock of weapons, nor general mobilization, I shall take hope again.'

Ahmeni was worried: a preposterous idea had just crossed his mind. 'Ahsha's official mission is to reorganize the defences of our protectorates. To obtain the information you want, won't he have to enter Hittite territory?'

'Correct,' Ramses acknowledged.

'That is madness! If he's captured . . . '

'Ahsha was free to accept or to refuse.'

'He's our friend, Ramses, our childhood friend, he's as loyal to you as I am, he—'

'I know, Ahmeni, and I value his courage at its full worth.'

'He has no chance of returning alive! Even if he manages to send some messages, he'll be captured.'

For the first time in his life, the scribe felt a little resentful towards Ramses. The pharaoh was right to consider the interests of Egypt of paramount importance. But he was sacrificing a friend, one of the elite, a man who would have deserved to live for one hundred and ten years, like the sages.

'I must dictate a reply, Ahmeni; let us reassure our brother the Emperor of Hatti about the state of my family's health and that of my horses.'

Shaanar half-heartedly nibbled an apple while gazing at the vase that his steward had placed before him.

'It was the merchant Raia himself who brought it to you?'

'Yes, my lord.'

'Repeat what he said to you.'

'He mentioned the high price for this work of art and believes you will settle that problem when he returns to the capital.'

'Give me another apple and see that I'm not disturbed.'

'My lord, you were supposed to receive a young lady.'

'Send her away.'

Shaanar stared at the vase. A copy. An ugly, clumsy copy that wasn't worth the price of a pair of cheap sandals. Even a little provincial nobody would have hesitated to put it on show in her reception chamber.

Raia's message was clear. The spy had been unmasked and would make no further contact with Shaanar. A vital component of his strategy was collapsing. Deprived of his contact with the Hittites, how would Shaanar be able to operate?

Two things reassured him.

210

First, at such a critical time the Hittites would certainly continue to maintain a network of spics on Egyptian soil; Raia would be replaced and his successor would make contact with Shaanar. Second, there was Ahsha's privileged position. While disorganizing the defence system of the protectorates, he wouldn't fail to link up with the Hittites and warn Shaanar. And there was also the magus Ofir, whose magic might well prove effective.

All in all, Raia's misfortune wasn't too much of a disadvantage. The Syrian would manage to extricate himself from this awkward situation.

The temples of Pi-Ramses were bathed in a warm ochre light. Ramses and Nefertari had celebrated the rites of the setting sun and now met in front of the Temple of Amun, which was still under construction. Every day the capital grew more beautiful, seemingly dedicated to peace and happiness.

The royal couple walked in the garden that had been planted in front of the sanctuary: perseas, sycamores and jujube trees grew between clumps of oleanders. Gardeners were watering the young saplings and talking lovingly to them. Everyone knew that plants appreciated their words as much as the water which nourished them.

'What do you think of the letters we have received?'

'I don't find them reassuring,' answered Nefertari. 'The Hittites are trying to dazzle us with the mirage of a truce.'

'I was hoping for more comfort from your opinion.'

'To deceive you would be to betray our love. I must tell you what I see, even if it has the disturbing colours of a stormy sky.'

'How can we be thinking of a war in which so many young men will lose their lives, just when we are enjoying the beauty of this garden?'

'We have no right to take refuge in this paradise and forget the storm that threatens to destroy it.'

'Will my army be able to resist the Hittite attacks? Too many old campaigners whose only thoughts are of their retirement, too many inexperienced young soldiers, too many mercenaries concerned only with their pay . . . The enemy knows our weaknesses.'

'Do we know theirs?'

'Our intelligence services are badly organized; it will need years of effort to make them efficient. We thought Muwatallis would respect the frontier laid down by my father when he reached the gates of Kadesh; but, like his predecessors, the emperor dreams of expansion and there is no finer prey than Egypt.'

'Has Ahsha sent you a report?'

'No, there's been no news.'

'You fear for his life, don't you?'

'I have entrusted him with a dangerous mission which forces him to enter enemy territory to gather as much information as possible. Ahmeni cannot forgive me for that.'

'Whose idea was it?'

'I shall never lie to you, Nefertari. It was mine, not Ahsha's.'

'He could have refused.'

'Who can refuse what the pharaoh proposes?'

'Ahsha has a strong character, capable of choosing his own destiny.'

'If he fails, I shall be responsible for his arrest and death.'

'Ahsha lives for Egypt, just as you do. By leaving for Hatti he hopes to save our counry from disaster.'

'We spent a whole night talking of this ideal. If he sends me any significant information about the Hittite army and their strategy, we shall perhaps succeed in driving back the invaders.'

'And what if you attacked first?'

'I'm considering it. But I must leave Ahsha room to manoeuvre.'

212

'The letters we received prove that the Hittites are trying to gain time, no doubt because of internal dissension. We must not let the right moment pass.'

In her sweet, musical voice, Nefertaru expressed the rigour and inflexible will of a Queen of Egypt. Just as Tuya had done at Seti's side, she was shaping the royal soul and nourishing its strength.

'I often think of Moses. How would he react, today, at a time when the very existence of the Two Lands is threatened? In spite of the strange ideas that haunted him, I am convinced he would fight with us to save the land of the pharaohs.'

The sun had set. Nefertari shivered. 'I miss my old shawl; it kept me so warm.'

35

Lying to the east of the Gulf of Aqaba and south of Edom, the land of Midian enjoyed a peaceful, isolated existence, sometimes visited by nomads passing through the Sinai peninsula. The people of Midian, attached to their pastoral existence, distanced themselves from the battles fought between the Arab tribes of the land of Moab.

An elderly priest, the father of seven daughters, governed the little community of Midianites, who complained neither of their poverty nor of the rigours of the climate. The old man was treating the foot of a ewe when his ear was struck by an unaccustomed sound.

Horses. Horses and chariots driven at great speed.

An Egyptian army patrol . . . Yet they never came to Midian, whose inhabitants possessed no weapons and did not know how to fight. They were so poor that they paid no taxes and the desert police knew that they would not risk sheltering Bedouin plunderers, for fear of seeing their oasis ravaged and themselves sentenced to deportation.

When the Egyptian chariots drove into the camp, men, women and children ran to hide in their tents of coarse canvas. The old priest rose and faced the strangers.

The leader of the patrol was an arrogant young officer. 'Who are you?'

'The priest of Midian.'

'Are you the head of this bunch of vermin?'

'I have that honour.'

'What do you live on here?'

'We rear sheep, eat dates and drink water from our well. Our little gardens provide us with a few vegetables.'

'Have you any weapons?'

'That is not our custom.'

'I've been ordered to search your tents.'

'They are open to you: we have nothing to hide.'

'You are said to give asylum to Bedouin criminals.'

'We wouldn't be so foolish as to arouse the pharaoh's anger. Although this scrap of land is poor and neglected, it is ours and we are attached to it. To break the law would bring about our ruin.'

'You are a wise old man, but I shall nevertheless proceed with the search.'

'I repeat, our tents are open to you. But first, will you agree to partake of a modest feast? One of my daughters has just given birth to a son. We shall eat lamb and drink palm wine.'

The Egyptian officer was embarrassed. 'It's not really allowed . . . '

'While your soldiers go about their duty, come and sit beside the fire.'

The frightened Midianites gathered round the old priest, who reassured them and asked them to facilitate the Egyptians' task.

The leader of the patrol agreed to sit and share in the festive meal. The mother was still confined to bed, but the father, a bearded man with craggy features, crouched down, cradling his baby in his arms.

'A shepherd who feared he could never beget a child,' explained the priest. 'This infant will be the light of his old age.'

The soldiers discovered neither weapons nor Bedouin.

'Continue to respect the law,' the officer told the priest,

'and your people will not be troubled.'

Chariots and horses drove off into the desert.

When the dust-cloud had settled, the father of the newborn baby rose to his feet. The officer would have been astonished to see a stunted shepherd transformed into a broad-shouldered giant.

'We are saved, Moses,' the old priest said to his son-in-law. 'They won't be back.'

At Thebes, on the west bank of the Nile, architects, stonecutters and sculptors were working tirelessly to build the House of Ramses, the Son of the Light's Temple of a Million Years. In accordance with the Rule, the construction had begun with the innermost shrine, where dwelt the hidden god whose form humans would never know. A vast number of blocks of sandstone, grey granite and basalt were deposited ready for use on the building site, where strict order reigned. The walls of the pillared halls were already going up; already the future royal palace was under construction. As Ramses had demanded, his temple would be a fabulous monument which would endure for centuries. There, the memory of his father would be honoured; there, the praises of his mother and wife would be sung; there would be transmitted the invisible energy without which it was impossible to exercise power justly.

Nebu, the high priest of Karnak, smiled. True, the weary, rheumatic old man had been made responsible for administering the greatest and wealthiest of all the Egyptian sanctuaries, and everyone had thought that Ramses' choice was cynical and strategic. Close to senility, Nebu would only be a straw man, elderly and servile, soon replaced by another of the monarch's creatures.

No one had foreseen that Nebu would age like granite. Bald, slow-moving, laconic, he governed fairly. Loyal to his king, he never dreamed, as certain of his predecessors had done, of conducting a policy of favouritism. Serving Ramses was what kept him young

But today Nebu forgot about the vast temple, its large staff, its priests, its lands and villages, to crouch over the acacia sapling Ramses had planted on the site of his Temple of a Million Years, in the second year of his reign. The high priest of Karnak had promised the monarch to watch over the growth of this tree. Its strength was impressive. Benefiting from the magic of the place, it rose up towards the sky much more quickly than others of its kind.

'Are you pleased with my acacia, Nebu?'

The high priest turned slowly round. 'Majesty . . . No one warned me of your arrival!'

'Don't reprimand anyone: the palace did not announce my journey. This tree is magnificent.'

'I don't think I've ever seen such an astonishing specimen. Have you passed some of your own strength on to it? I have the privilege of protecting its youth; you will gaze on it when it is fully grown.'

'I wanted to visit Thebes again, to see once more my Temple of a Million Years, my tomb and my acacia, before this turmoil comes upon us.'

'Is war then inevitable, Majesty?'

'The Hittites are trying to convince us that it is not, but who can trust their soothing declarations?'

'Here, everything is in order. The wealth of Karnak is yours, and I have brought prosperity to the lands you entrusted to me.'

'And how are you yourself?'

'As long as the canals of my heart aren't blocked, I shall carry out my duties. Nevertheless, if Your Majesty intended to replace me, I should not be displeased. To live near to the sacred lake and meditate on the flight of the swallows is my greatest ambition.'

'At the risk of disappointing you, I see no need to make

217

any changes in the present priesthood.'

'My legs are giving way, my ears are blocked up, my bones ache—'

'But your thinking remains as rapid as the flight of a falcon and as precise as that of the ibis. Continue to work like this, Nebu, and look after this acacia. If I do not return, you will be its guardian.'

'You will return. You must.'

Ramses visited the building site, recalling the time when he lived among the stone-cutters and the quarrymen. For his part, he was building Egypt one day at a time, while they were erecting the temples and dwellings of eternity, without which the Two Lands would have given way to the anarchy and wickedness natural to mankind. By worshipping the power of light and respecting the Rule of Ma'at, man would be taught uprightness and to turn aside from selfishness and vanity.

The king's dream was being realized. The Temple of a Million Years was taking shape; this formidable source of magic energy was beginning to operate independently, simply through the presence of the hieroglyphs and scenes engraved on the walls of the sanctuary. As he walked through the halls whose layout was marked out, while sunk in meditation where its shrines would be built, Ramses drew on the force of *ka*,* born of the union of heaven and earth. He absorbed it, not for himself but to give him the strength to confront the darkness into which the Hittites wished to plunge the land beloved of the gods.

Ramses felt that he bore the weight of all the dynasties, of this long line of pharaohs who had fashioned Egypt in the image of the cosmos. For one instant, the twenty-seven-year-old sovereign faltered; but the past became a source of strength, not a burden. In this Temple of a Million Years, his

*An individual's life force or spirit, which lived on after that individual's death.

predecessors were showing him the way.

Raia delivered some vases to the notables of Memphis. If the men who were shadowing him questioned his employees, they would learn that he intended to continue satisfying his customers and to remain the appointed purveyor to the noble families. So Raia went about his sales in his usual manner, which consisted of direct contacts, endless bargaining and flattery.

Then he left for the great harem of Mer-Ur, where he had not been to offer his wares for two years, certain that this visit would puzzle Ahmeni's and Serramanna's henchmen. They would think he had accomplices in that noble and ancient institution, and would waste time and energy following the wrong track.

Raia offered them another false trail by staying in a small village, near the harem, where he had discussions with peasants he did not know. Evidently more accomplices, the Egyptian investigators would think.

Abandoning the men who were following him to their confusion, he returned to Memphis to attend to the transport of several consignments of luxury preserves, some destined for Pi-Ramses, others for Thebes.

Serramanna was ranting and raving. 'This spy is making fools of us! He knows we're following him and he amuses himself leading us a fine dance.'

'Calm down,' recommended Ahmeni. 'He's bound to slip up.'

'How?'

'The messages he receives from Hatti are hidden either in his preserves or in his vases. I'd wager it's the latter, since most of them come from southern Syria and Asia.'

'Well, let's examine them!'

'That would be a thankless task. The important thing is to

find out how he sends his messages and the network he uses. Given the situation, he'll have to warn the Hittites that he can't carry on his activities. Let's watch out for the moment when he sends a consignment of objects to Syria.'

'I have another idea,' Serramanna said.

'Legal, I hope.'

'If I avoid all scandal and make it possible for you to arrest Raia quite legally, will you give me permission to act?'

The scribe toyed with his brush. 'How much time do you want?'

'I shall be done by tomorrow.'

36

In Bubastis they were celebrating the festival of intemperance. For a whole week girls and youths would enjoy love's first raptures under the kindly gaze of the cat goddess, Bastet, the embodiment of the pleasures of life. In the countryside, wrestling tournaments gave boys the opportunity of demonstrating their strength and charming the fair spectators by their enthusiasm for the contest

Raia's employees had been given two days off. The head storeman, a thin stooping Syrian, had bolted the door of the warehouse, which contained about a dozen vases of average value. He was not exactly displeased to be able to mingle with the crowd and try his luck with a lively lass, even if she wasn't in the first bloom of youth.

The storeman's mouth watered as he imagined the pleasure he would enjoy, and he hummed to himself as he started down the alleyway leading to the little square where people were already gathering in anticipation of the festivities.

An enormous fist grabbed him by the hair and pulled him backwards; a hand clapped over his mouth stifled his cry of pain.

'Don't make a sound,' ordered Serramanna, 'or I'll strangle you.'

The terrified Syrian was dragged into a shed filled with basketware.

'How long have you been working for Raia?' asked the Sardinian.

'Four years.'

'Does he pay you well?'

'He's rather tight-fisted.'

'Are you afraid of him?'

'A bit.'

'Raia is going to be arrested,' Serramanna said, 'and he'll be sentenced to death for spying for the Hittites. His accomplices will suffer the same punishment.'

'I'm only his employee!'

'Lying is a serious error.'

'He employs me as a storekeeper, not as a spy!'

'You were wrong to claim he was here in Bubastis when he was committing a murder in Pi-Ramses.'

'A *murder*! No, that's impossible . . . I didn't know!'

'Now you do know. Are you sticking to your statement?'

'No – Yes, otherwise he'll get his revenge!'

'You leave me no choice, my friend: if you continue to hide the truth I shall smash your head against the wall.'

'You wouldn't dare!'

'I've killed a dozen cowards like you.'

'Raia . . . He'd take his revenge on me.'

'You'll never see him again.'

'You're sure?'

'Certain.'

'Then, all right. He paid me to say he was here.'

'Can you write?'

'Not very well.'

'We'll go together to the office of the public scribe, and he'll record your statement. Then you can chase after the girls.'

Iset the Fair, the mother of little Kha, looked as young as ever. She was still graceful, lively and gay; her eyes were still bright green, her lips delicately made up. On this cool winter evening she had thrown a woollen shawl over her shoulders.

In the Theban countryside a strong wind was blowing. Nevertheless, Iset was keeping the appointment made in a strange letter: '*The reed hut. Look for one similar to that in Memphis, on the west bank, facing the temple of Luxor, beside a field of corn.*'

It was his handwriting; there was no mistaking it. But why this curious invitation and the reminder of such an intimate past?

Iset walked alongside an irrigation canal, spotted the field of corn gilded by the setting sun and found the hut. She was about to enter when a gust of wind lifted the bottom of her gown, which caught on a bush. As she stooped down to prevent the material being torn, a hand freed it and raised her up.

'Ramses!'

'You're still as beautiful as ever, Iset. Thank you for coming.'

'Your message overwhelmed me.'

'I wanted to see you far from the palace.'

She was infatuated with the king. His athletic body, his noble bearing, his piercing gaze aroused in her the same desire as before. She had never stopped loving him, although she knew she could never rival Nefertari. The Great Royal Wife filled Ramses' heart, over which she held undivided sway. Iset was neither jealous nor envious; she accepted her fate and felt proud to have given the king a son whose exceptional qualities were already evident.

Yes, she had hated Ramses when he married Nefertari, but that violent emotion was only a painful form of her love. Iset had opposed a plot that threatened the king and with which the conspirators had wished to associate her. Never would she betray the man who had given her so much happiness, bringing light to her heart and a glow to her body.

223

'Why this discretion – and the reminder of our first meetings in a hut like this one?'

'Nefertari wishes it so.'

'Nefertari? I don't understand.'

'She insists that we have another son to ensure the perpetuity of the kingdom, should any misfortune befall Kha.'

Iset swayed, and sank into Ramses' arms. 'This is a dream,' she murmured, 'a wonderful dream. You're not the king, I'm not Iset, we aren't in Thebes, we aren't going to make love to give Kha a brother. It's just a dream, but I want to live it in the depths of myself and preserve it for all eternity.'

Ramses removed his tunic and laid it on the ground. Feverishly Iset let him remove her garments.

The mad exaltation of that one moment when her body was creating a child for Ramses, the blinding flash of an ecstasy that she had ceased to hope for.

On the boat that took him back to Pi-Ramses, the king, withdrawn in his solitude, gazed at the Nile. Nefertari's face haunted him. Yes, Iset's love was sincere and her charm intact; but he did not feel for her that emotion, as imperious as the sun and as vast as the desert, which had swept through his whole being from his first meeting with Nefertari, that love whose intensity grew with every passing day. Just as the House of Ramses and the capital grew, thanks to the ceaseless work of the builders, so the passion Ramses felt for his queen constantly grew and was strengthened.

The king had not revealed to Iset what Nefertari had really asked: the queen wanted Iset to fulfil the true role of second wife and give the monarch several children, for his powerful, overwhelming personality risked discouraging several potential successors. Egypt had known a serious precedent: Pepy II, who lived to be more than a hundred, had outlived his

children and when he died had left the country in a vacuum
that became an acute crisis. If Ramses lived to a great age,
what would become of the kingdom if Kha or Meritamon, for
whatever reason, could not succeed him?

It was impossible for a pharaoh to lead the life of an
ordinary man. Even his loves and his family had to serve to
perpetuate the institution he embodied. But there was
Nefertari, first among women, and the sublime love she gave
him. Ramses wished neither to betray his duty nor to share his
desire with any other woman, even Iset.

It was the Nile that gave him the answer, the Nile whose
energy, at the time of the inundation, fertilized both banks
with inexhaustible generosity.

The whole court was gathered in the vast audience chamber
of Pi-Ramses, and rumours were flying. Like his father, Seti,
Ramses was rather sparing of this type of ceremony; he
preferred working privately with his ministers to pointless
discussions with a gathering whose members' only idea was
to heap praise upon him.

When the pharaoh appeared, holding in his right hand a
staff round which a cord was wound, many people held their
breath for a moment. This symbol indicated that Ramses was
about to promulgate a decree which would have immediate
force of law. The staff symbolized the Word, the cord the link
with reality which the king would cause to take effect when
he set out the terms of a decision he had reached after long
deliberation.

The court was in the grip of anguish. No one had any
doubt: Ramses would declare that they were at war with the
Hittites. An ambassador would be sent to Hatti and would
deliver Pharaoh's message to the emperor, announcing the
date of the beginning of hostilities.

'The words that I pronounce form a royal decree,' declared
Ramses. 'It will be carved on stelae, heralds will proclaim it

225

in towns and villages, every inhabitant of the Two Lands will be informed of it. From today until I draw my last breath, I shall elevate to the dignity of "Royal Son" and "Royal Daughter" all children who are educated in the palace school and receive the same teaching as my son Kha and my daughter Meritamon. Their number is unlimited and I shall choose my successor from among them, without informing him until the opportune moment.'

The court was stunned and delighted. Every father and every mother nursed the secret hope that their child would be elevated to this dignity. Some already thought of praising the merits of their offspring to influence the choice of Ramses and Nefertari.

Nefertari was recovering from a chill, and Ramses draped a large shawl round her shoulders.

'It comes from the finest workshops in Saïs; the high priestess of the temple wove it with her own hands.'

The queen's smile lit up the gloomy sky of the Delta. 'I would so have loved to leave for the South, but I know it is impossible.'

'I am sorry about that, Nefertari, but I must supervise the training of my troops.'

'Iset will give you another son, will she not?'

'The gods will decide.'

'It is well. When will you see her again?'

'I don't know.'

'But you promised me . . . '

'I have just promulgated a decree.'

'What has that to do with Iset?'

'Your wish has been granted, Nefertari: we shall have more than a hundred sons and daughters and my succession will be assured.'

37

'I've proof that Raia was lying,' declared Serramanna
excitedly.

Ahmeni remained unmoved.

'Did you hear what I said?'

'Yes, yes,' replied the scribe.

The Sardinian understood the reason for Ahmeni's lack of
response: once again he had slept for only two or three hours
and was not yet quite awake.

'I've got here a sworn statement from Raia's storeman,
signed and witnessed. He clearly shows that his employer
was not at Bubastis the day of Nenophar's murder and that
Raia paid him to give false evidence.'

'Congratulations, Serramanna. Nice work. Is your storeman . . . undamaged?'

'When he left the scribe's office he expressed a burning
desire to take part in the town's festivities and to meet a few
young women who might not be averse to his advances.'

'Nice work. I really mean it.'

'You haven't understood. Raia's alibi is destroyed. We can
arrest him and question him!'

'No, we can't.'

'We can't? Who's going to stop us?'

'Raia shook off the men who were following him and
vanished into an alleyway in Memphis.'

*

With Shaanar warned and out of danger, Raia had to get away. Convinced that Ahmeni would examine any consignment to southern Syria, even if it were only a jar of preserves, he could no longer get information to the Hittites. He judged it too risky to entrust a message to one of the members of his network. It was so easy to betray a man who was on the run and wanted by Pharaoh's police! The only solution he could see, from the moment he was suspected, was to contact the head of his network, although this was strictly forbidden.

It had not been easy to shake off the policemen who were following him round the clock. Thanks to the god of storms, who had unleashed his fury over Memphis as evening fell, he had managed to give them the slip by diving into a workshop that had another way out.

At the height of the storm, as lightning flashed across the sky and a violent wind blew clouds of dust through the empty streets, he had climbed over roofs and made his way into the house of the head of his network.

The house was plunged in darkness and seemed deserted. As Raia's eyes grew accustomed to the lack of light, he ventured tentatively into the living room without making a sound. A groan reached his ears.

He approached nervously.

Another groan, expressing intense but suppressed pain. There, a beam of light, under a door.

Had the head spy been arrested and tortured? No, that was impossible. Raia was the only one who knew who he was.

The door opened and the flame of a torch blinded him. He recoiled, protecting his eyes with his crossed hands.

'Raia! What are you doing here?'

'Forgive me, but I had no choice.'

The Syrian had only met the head of the network once, at Muwatallis's court, but he had never forgotten him: tall and thin, with prominent cheekbones, dark-green eyes and the look of a bird of prey.

Suddenly Raia was afraid that Ofir would do away with him on the spot. But the Libyan remained suspiciously calm.

In the laboratory Lita was still groaning.

'I was preparing her for an experiment,' explained Ofir, shutting the door.

The darkness threw Raia into a panic; was it not the realm of those who practised the black arts?

'We can talk here undisturbed. You have disobeyed your orders.'

'I know, but I was going to be arrested by Serramanna's men.'

'They are still in the city, I suppose?'

'Yes, but I gave them the slip.'

'If they've followed you, they'll soon burst in here. In which case I shall be obliged to kill you and say that I was attacked by a burglar.'

Dolora, who was sleeping upstairs after taking a sleeping-draught, would answer for Ofir's version of events.

'I know my job. They didn't follow me.'

'Let's hope so, Raia. What has happened?'

'A succession of mishaps.'

'A succession of stupid mistakes, more like.'

The Syrian gave his explanation, not omitting the smallest detail. With Ofir, it was better not to bend the truth, for the magus had the power to read people's minds.

A long silence followed Raia's explanation. Ofir was thinking hard before giving his verdict.

'You were unlucky, it's true; but we have to accept that your network is finished.'

'My stores, my stocks, the fortune I've amassed . . . '

'You'll get them back when Hatti has conquered Egypt.'

'We must pray that the demons of war hear your words!'

'Do you doubt our eventual victory?'

'Not for a moment! The Egyptian army is not ready.

According to my most recent information, its weapons programme is behind schedule and the senior officers are afraid of meeting the Hittites in battle. Soldiers who are afraid are already vanquished.'

'Too much confidence can lead to defeat,' objected Ofir. 'We must leave no stone unturned to bring about Ramses' downfall.'

'Will you contine to manipulate Shaanar?'

'Does Pharaoh suspect him?'

'He mistrusts him but cannot for a moment think that Shaanar has become our ally. How could he possibly imagine that an Egyptian, a member of the royal family and the minister for foreign affairs could betray his country? In my opinion, Shaanar remains an instrument essential to our plans. Who will replace me?'

'You don't need to know.'

'You are obliged to send a report on me, Ofir . . . '

'It will be fulsome. You have served Hatti loyally; the emperor will bear it in mind and reward you.'

'What will be my new mission?'

'I shall submit a plan to Muwatallis; he'll decide.'

'This Atonian party, is it serious?'

'I've no more time for the followers of Aton than for believers in any other god; but they are gullible sheep that it's easy to lead to the slaughterhouse. Since they eat out of my hand, why deprive them of their belief?'

'What about that girl?'

'A crank and a halfwit, but an excellent medium. She enables me to obtain valuable information which would be beyond my reach without her help. And I have great hopes of weakening Ramses' defences.'

Ofir was thinking of Moses, a potential ally whose flight and disappearance he regretted. By questioning Lita during a trance, he had become certain that the Hebrew was still alive.

'May I stay and rest here for a few days?' asked the Syrian.

230

'My nerves have been sorely tried.'

'Too risky. Go back to the port immediately, to the southern end, and board the barge which is leaving for Pi-Ramses.'

Ofir gave the Syrian the passwords and the names of the necessary contacts to get out of Egypt, cross Canaan and southern Syria and reach the Hittite zone of influence.

As soon as Raia had gone, the magus made sure that Lita was sound asleep and left the villa.

The continuing bad weather favoured him; he wouldn't be noticed and would be able to give orders for Raia's replacement to make his apppearance, and then quickly make his way back to his lair.

Shaanar was devouring food. Although his reason told him there was nothing to fear, he had to allay his anxiety by eating. He was gulping down a roast quail when his steward announced Meba, the former minister for foreign affairs.

Meba was one of those worthy and formal senior civil servants, scribes from generation to generation, used to finding their way about in the corridors of power, avoiding the day-to-day annoying matters and only interested in their own promotion. On becoming minister, Meba had reached a height where he hoped to remain until retirement; but Shaanar's unexpected intervention – which he would never know about – had deprived him of his post. Reduced to inactivity, the diplomat had retired to his vast estate in Memphis and contented himself with occasional appearances at the court of Pi-Ramses.

Shaanar washed his hands and rinsed his mouth, scented himself and checked that his headdress was in order. He knew his visitor was fussy about appearances, and he would be a match for him.

'My dear Meba! What a pleasure to see you in the capital. Will you do me the honour of attending the reception I'm giving tomorrow evening?'

'I shall be delighted.'

'I know that the moment is not exactly right for celebrations, but we mustn't give way to gloom. The king himself insists on not modifying anything in the palace routine.'

With his broad, reassuring face, his elegant gestures and calm voice, Meba was still a charmer. 'Are you satisfied with your job, Shaanar?'

'It's not easy but I do my best, for the glory of the country.'

'Do you know Raia, a Syrian merchant?'

Shaanar stiffened. 'He sells me valuable vases of outstanding quality and at rather high prices.'

'Don't you touch on any other subjects when you meet?'

'What's come over you, Meba?'

'You have nothing to fear from me, Shaanar. In fact, quite the contrary.'

'To fear? What do you mean?'

'You were expecting Raia's successor, weren't you? Here I am.'

'*You*, Meba?'

'I don't take easily to a life of idleness. And when the Hittite network contacted me, I seized the opportunity of getting my own back on Ramses. That the enemy chose you to succeed him doesn't bother me, so long as you give me back the Foreign Affairs secretariat when you take power.'

The king's elder brother seemed stunned.

'You'll give me your word, Shaanar.'

'You have it, Meba, you have it.'

'I shall let you know our friends' instructions. If you have a message for them, you will send it through me. Since, as from today, you are engaging me as your deputy, in place of Ahsha, we shall have the opportunity of seeing each other frequently. No one will suspect me.'

38

Icy rain was falling on Hattusa, the capital of the Hittite Empire. The temperature had fallen below freezing-point, and people were burning peat and wood to get warm. It was the time when many children died; boys who survived would make excellent soldiers. As for girls, who did not have the right to inherit, their only hope was for a good marriage.

In spite of the harsh climate, Uri-Teshup, the emperor's son and the new commander-in-chief, had stepped up the training. Dissatisfied with the footsoldiers' performance, he made them undertake forced marches for hours on end, laden with weapons and food, as if they were setting off on the roads for a long campaign. Several men had succumbed to exhaustion. Uri-Teshup had abandoned them on the roadside, judging that weaklings did not deserve burial. The vultures would feed on their corpses.

The prince didn't spare the chariot crews either, ordering them to urge on their horses and vehicles to their utmost limits. Numerous fatal accidents had convinced him that certain charioteers had not mastered the new equipment and had grown fat during the long period of peace.

There was no protest from the ranks. They all sensed that Uri-Teshup was preparing the troops for war and that victory depended on his rigorous discipline. Pleased with his growing popularity, he nevertheless bore in mind that

Muwatallis was still the supreme leader of the army. There were therefore risks in being so far from the court, directing manoeuvres in isolated corners of Anatolia: so Uri-Teshup had paid courtiers to let him have as much information as possible about what his father and Hattusilis were up to.

When he heard that the latter had left for a tour of inspection in those neighbouring countries which were under Hittite influence, the prince was both astonished and reassured. Astonished because the emperor's brother rarely left the capital; reassured because his absence prevented him from getting up to any mischief by disseminating treacherous counsels which would benefit the merchant clans.

Uri-Teshup detested the merchants. After his victory over Ramses, he would drive out Muwatallis, take over the throne of Hatti, send Hattusilis to perish in the salt mines and shut up his wife, the arrogant, intriguing Putuhepa, in a provincial brothel. As for the merchants, they would be forcibly recruited into the army.

He had planned the future of Hatti: it would become a military dictatorship, with him, Uri-Teshup, as its absolute master.

It would be premature to attack the emperor, whose prestige was still intact after several years of a skilful cruel reign; in spite of his fiery temperament, Uri-Teshup would curb his impatience and wait for his father's first mistake. Then, either Muwatallis would agree to abdicate, or his son would do away with him.

Tightly muffled in a thick woollen cloak, the emperor huddled close to a fire whose heat scarcely warmed him. As he grew older, he endured the rigours of winter less and less easily, but he could not do without the grand spectacle of the snow-covered mountains. Sometimes he was tempted to give up his policy of conquest and be content to exploit the natural riches of ɪis country: but the illusion soon vanished, for expansion was essential for the survival of his people. The conquest of Egypt would mean the possession of a treasure-house, whose administration he would entrust, in the first instance, to Ramses' elder brother, the ambitious Shaanar, in order to placate the Egyptian people. Then he would get rid of that traitor and impose on the Two Lands a Hittite government which would quickly stifle any inclination to rebel.

The principal danger was his own son, Uri-Teshup. The emperor needed him to restore the troops' vigour and fighting spirit, but he must prevent him from turning the results of his triumph to his own advantage. Uri-Teshup was an intrepid warrior but no statesman and would make a deplorable administrator.

Hattusilis was another matter. Although undersized and weakly, the emperor's brother possessed the qualities of a ruler and knew how to remain in the background, letting his real influence be overlooked. What did he really want? Muwatallis was unable to answer this question, and so was doubly distrustful of him.

Hattusilis presented himself to the emperor.

'A successful voyage, brother?'

'The results are up to our expectations.'

Hattusilis sneezed several times.

'Have you caught a chill?'

'The staging posts are badly heated; my wife has prepared me some mulled wine, and boiling-hot footbaths will soon relieve this nasty cold.'

'Did our allies honour you with a good reception?'

'My visit surprised them; they feared supplementary taxes were going to be levied.'

'It is good to maintain a climate of fear among our vassals. A lack of subservience is the first step to disobedience.'

'That is why I touched on the past errors of a certain prince, and mentioned the emperor's mercy, before entering into the main subject.'

'Blackmail remains the favourite weapon of diplomacy, Hattusilis; you appear to handle it with great skill.'

'A difficult art, which is never completely mastered, but whose effects turn out to be positive. All our vassals, without exception, have accepted our . . . invitation.'

'I am most pleased, brother. When will their preparations be completed?'

'In three or four months.'

'Will it be necessary to draw up official documents?'

'Better avoid that,' judged Hattusilis. 'We have infiltrated spies into the enemy's territory; the Egyptians may have done the same in ours.'

'It's unlikely, but prudence is necessary.'

'For our allies, the collapse of Egypt is a priority. By giving their word to Hatti's official representative, they have given it to the emperor. They will keep silent until the outbreak of hostilities.'

Bright-eyed with fever, Hattusilis appreciated the warmth of the room whose windows had been closed by wooden panels covered with cloth.

'How are our army's preparations going?'

'Uri-Teshup is carrying out his task perfectly,' replied Muwatallis. 'Our troops will soon be up to maximum efficiency.'

'Do you think that your letter and my wife's will have allayed the royal couple's suspicions?'

'Ramses and Nefertari have replied cordially and we shall continue our correspondence. At the very least, it will worry them. What has become of our spy network?'

'That of the merchant Raia has been dismantled and its members dispersed. But our principal agent, the Libyan, Ofir, continues to send very valuable information.'

'What's to be done with this Raia?'

'I think it would be a good solution to let him meet a violent end, but Ofir has had a better idea.'

'Go and have a well-deserved rest in the company of your delightful wife.'

The spicy mulled wine brought down Hattusilis's temperature and cleared his sinuses; the boiling-hot footbath gave him a feeling of well-being which rewarded him for the many hours of travel on the roads of Asia. A servant massaged his shoulders and neck and a barber shaved him under Putuhepa's supervision.

'Was your mission successful?' she asked when they were alone.

'I think so, my dear.'

'For my part I have fulfilled my own.'

'Your mission . . . ? What are you talking about?'

'It is not in my nature to remain idle.'

'Do please explain!'

'You, whose mind is so astute, haven't you understood yet?'

'Don't tell me that—'

'Oh yes, dearest diplomat! While you were carrying out the emperor's orders, I was taking care of your rival, your only rival.'

'Uri-Teshup?'

'Who else prevents your rise and tries to block your influence? His appointment has turned his head. He already sees himself as emperor.'

'It's Muwatallis who manipulates him, not the other way round.'

'Both you and he underestimate the danger.'

'You are mistaken, Putuhepa; the emperor knows what he's doing. If he has entrusted his son with this position, it is to infuse renewed energy into the army and make it completely efficient when it comes to fighting. But Muwatallis does not think Uri-Teshup capable of governing Hatti.'

'Has he said as much to you?'

'That is what I think.'

'That isn't enough for me. The prince is violent and dangerous. He hates both of us and dreams of keeping us out of power. Because you are the emperor's brother, he dare not attack you directly, but he will stab you in the back.'

'Be patient. He will condemn himself.'

'It's too late.'

'What do you mean, too late?'

'I've done what I had to do.'

Hattusilis was afraid to understand.

'A representative of the merchants is on the way to Uri-Teshup's headquarters,' Putuhepa told him. 'He will ask to speak to him, and to gain his confidence will tell him in secret that several wealthy merchants would be glad to see the end of Muwatallis and his son succeed him. Our man will stab the prince and we shall finally be rid of that monster.'

'Hatti needs him. It's too soon, much too soon! It is essential for Uri-Teshup to prepare our troops for war.'

'Will you try to save him?' Putuhepa asked ironically.

Aching all over, feverish, stiff-legged, Hattusilis rose. 'I'm leaving immediately.'

39

The elegant, refined Ahsha was unrecognizable in the guise of a courier, clad in a shabby, coarse mantle, riding through southern Syria on a sturdy donkey, leading two similar animals, each carrying a heavy load of documents. He had just entered the Hittite zone of influence.

He had spent several weeks in Canaan and Amurru, closely examining the defensive systems of both protectorates, had had discussions with the Egyptian officers responsible for organizing resistance to any Hittite attack, and had added the names of a good dozen resourceful young women to the list of his mistresses.

Benteshina, the Prince of Amurru, had been very appreciative of Ahsha's behaviour. The Egyptian had shown himself a considerate guest, a lover of good food, and had made no untoward demands, simply asking the prince to warn Ramses if he suspected any aggressive manoeuvres on the part of the Hittites.

Then Ahsha had set out back to Egypt; at least, that is what he had let be believed. As ordered, his escort had headed south along the coast road, while the diplomat had got rid of his Egyptian garments and, armed with perfectly forged Hittite credentials, had slipped into a courier's costume and left for the north.

Given the contradictory reports couched in vague

language, how was he to form a realistic opinion of Hatti's true intentions except by exploring the country himself? Since Ramses' wish corresponded with his own, Ahsha had accepted the mission without balking; once in possession of first-hand information, he would be free to call the tune.

Did the Hittites' greatest strength lie in letting it be believed that they were invulnerable and prepared to conquer the world? That was the crucial question that had to be answered, based on hard facts.

The Hittite frontier post was guarded by some thirty sinister-looking armed soldiers. For several long minutes, four of them hovered round Ahsha and his three donkeys. The false courier stood with a vacant look.

A spear-point touched Ahsha's left cheek. 'Your credentials?'

Ahsha took out from his mantle a tablet written in Hittite script.

The soldier read it and passed it to a colleague, who read it in his turn.

'Where are you going?'

'I have to take letters and invoices to the merchants in Hattusa.'

'Show them.'

'They're confidential.'

'There's nothing confidential for the army.'

'I wouldn't like to get into trouble with the people they are addressed to.'

'If you don't do as you're told, you'll be in plenty of trouble.'

With fingers numbed with cold, Ahsha undid the cords that tied up the sacks of tablets.

'Commercial gibberish,' said the soldier. 'We shall search you.'

The courier carried no weapons. Greatly frustrated, the Hittites could find nothing against him.

'Before you enter any village, present yourself to the checkpoint.'

'That's something new.'

'You don't ask questions. If you don't present yourself at every checkpoint, you'll be considered an enemy and killed.'

'There aren't any enemies on Hittite soil!'

'Just do as you're told'

'All right, all right.'

'Clear off, we've had enough of you!'

Ahsha moved away unhurriedly, like an untroubled man who had done nothing illegal. He walked beside the leading donkey, keeping up with its easy pace, and set off on the road leading to Hattusa in the heart of Anatolia.

He looked round several times, searching for the Nile. He found it hard to get used to a tortured landscape, lacking the simplicity of the valley watered by the divine river. Ahsha missed the clear distinction between the cultivated land and the desert, the green of the fields and the gold of the sand, the sunsets with their myriad colours. But he had to forget these and concern himself solely with Hatti, this cold and hostile land whose secrets he would be fathoming.

The sky hung low; violent rainstorms broke out. The donkeys avoided the puddles and stopped whenever they pleased to enjoy munching the wet grass.

This landscape was not favourable to peace. There circulated in its veins a savagery which urged its inhabitants to think of existence as a war and the future as the destruction of other people. How many generations would it need to make fertile these desolate valleys watched over by harsh mountains, and transform soldiers into peasants? Here people were born to fight and would always fight.

The setting up of a checkpoint at the entrance to each village intrigued Ahsha. Did the Hittites fear the presence of spies in their land, although it was under the close control of their security forces? This unusual measure was by way of a clue. Was the army undertaking large-scale manoeuvres, not meant to be seen by curious eyes?

Twice mounted patrols checked Ahsha's documents and questioned him about his destination. When his answers were deemed satisfactory he was allowed to continue on his way. As he approached the first village he was again searched thoroughly at the checkpoint. The soldiers seemed tense and irritable, so he did not protest.

After spending a night sleeping in a cowshed, he ate some bread and cheese and continued on his journey, pleased to have confirmation that his disguise was completely credible. In mid-afternoon he took a path that cut across to a little wood, where he got rid of some tablets addressed to non-existent merchants. As he progressed towards the capital, he would gradually lighten his load.

The wood projected over a ravine in which lay enormous rocks, fallen from a peak eroded by rainfall and snow. The roots of gnarled oak trees clung to the slopes.

As he was opening one of the sacks carried by the leading donkey, Ahsha had the sensation of being watched. The animals were restless. Some robins were disturbed and flew off.

The Egyptian picked up a stone and a piece of dry wood, scarcely adequate weapons against a possible attacker. When he clearly caught the sound of horsemen, he hid face-down behind a log.

Four riders emerged from the undergrowth and surrounded the donkeys. They were not soldiers but bandits, armed with bows and daggers. Even in Hatti caravan-looters abounded; if they were captured they were executed on the spot. Ahsha flattened himself deeper into the mud. If the thieves spotted him they would cut his throat.

Their leader, a bearded man with a pockmarked face, sniffed the air like a hunting dog.

'Look,' said one of his companions, 'these are miserable

spoils. Nothing but tablets. Can you read?'

'Never had time to learn.'

'Are they worth anything?'

'Not to us.'

The brigand angrily smahed the tablets and threw the pieces down into the ravine.

'The owner of the donkeys – he can't be far away and he's sure to have some tin on him.'

'Let's spread out,' ordered the chief. 'We'll find him.'

Although chilled to the bone and paralysed by fear, Ahsha kept his head. A single bandit was coming towards him. The Egyptian crawled forward, clinging to a root. The bandit chief walked round him without seeing him.

Ahsha broke his neck with a large stone. The man fell forward, and landed with his face in the mud.

'Over there!' shouted one of his accomplices, who had seen what happened.

Ahsha seized his victim's dagger and hurled it with force and precision. The weapon buried itself in the thief's chest.

The two survivors bent their bows. Ahsha's only hope was to run for it. An arrow whistled past his ears as he hurtled down the slope towards the bottom of the ravine, gasping for breath, in an attempt to reach a tangle of shrubs and thorn bushes where he would be safe.

Another arrow grazed his right shin, but he managed to hurl himself into his temporary shelter. Covered with scratches, his hands bleeding, he struggled through an enormous bramble thicket, fell, picked himself up and began to run again.

When his breath finally gave out, he came to a standstill. If his pursuers caught up with him he wouldn't have the strength to fight. But in the ravine all was silent, except for the cawing of a flock of crows flying beneath the black clouds.

Still wary, Ahsha remained there until nightfall without

stirring. Then he climbed back up the slope and, finding his way along the edge of the ravine, returned to the spot where he had left the donkeys.

The animals had disappeared. Only the corpses of the two thieves still lay there.

Ahsha's wounds, though superficial, were painful. He washed in the water from a spring, picked three herbs at random and rubbed them on his bruises, climbed to the top of a sturdy oak tree and lay down to sleep on two thick, almost parallel branches.

Ahsha dreamed of a comfortable bed in one of his luxurious villas (Shaanar had given it to him in exchange for his collaboration), of a pond surrounded by palm trees, of a beaker of rare wine and a pretty lute-player who would charm his ears before offering him her body.

Icy rain woke him before dawn, and he resumed his journey to the north.

The loss of his donkeys and his tablets meant he'd have to adopt a new identity. A courier without dispatches and without transport animals would be considered suspicious and he would be arrested. So it was impossible for him to present himself at the next checkpoint and enter any village.

By travelling through the forests he would avoid patrols, but would he escape the bears, lynx and brigands who took refuge there? There was abundant water, but food would be difficult to find. With a bit of luck, he might manage to lay a trap for a travelling merchant and take his place.

His situation wasn't exactly wonderful, but nothing was going to stop him reaching Hattusa and discovering the true strength of the Hittite army.

40

Uri-Teshup was washing in cold water after a day spent on horseback directing the manoeuvres of the chariot corps. The increasingly intensive training was giving good results, but the prince was still not satisfied. The Hittite army must leave the Egyptian troops no chances and never hesitate during the various phases of the attack.

As he was drying himself in the wind, his subordinate let him know that a merchant from Hattusa wanted to speak to the commander-in-chief.

'Let him wait,' said Uri-Teshup. 'I'll see him tomorrow at dawn. Merchants are born to obey. What does this fellow look like?'

'Judging by his appearance, he's someone important.'

'He can wait, just the same. Let him sleep in the least comfortable tent.'

'And if he complains?'

'Let him.'

Hattusilis and his escort had galloped non-stop The emperor's brother ignored both his cold and his fever, in the grip of one obsession: to arrive at Uri-Teshup's headquarters before the irreparable deed was done.

When the military camp came in sight in the middle of the night, Hattusilis seemed calm. He introduced himself to the guards, who opened the wooden gate for him. He followed the officer responsible for security, and was admitted into Uri-Teshup's tent.

The latter woke up in a bad temper. The sight of his uncle gave him no pleasure. 'What is the reason for this unexpected visit?'

'Your life.'

'What does that mean?'

'There is a plot against your person. Some people want to kill you.'

'Are you serious?'

'I'm only just back from an exhausting journey, I have a temperature and my only wish is to rest. Do you think I'd have ridden so fast if it weren't serious?'

'Who wants to kill me?'

'You know my links with the merchant clan. During my absence one of its representatives confided to my wife that a madman had decided to do away with you to avoid war against Egypt and preserve their profits.'

'His name?'

'I don't know it, but I was anxious to put you on your guard without delay.'

'This war, you too would like to avoid it.'

'You are mistaken, Uri-Teshup, I think war is necessary. Thanks to your victory, our empire will continue to expand. The emperor has put you in charge of the army because of your skill as a warrior and your qualities as a leader.'

Hattusilis's words astonished Uri-Teshup, without dispelling his suspicions. The emperor's brother was a consummate master of flattery.

And yet, it was a merchant who had asked for an interview. If Uri-Teshup had received him immediately, perhaps he would no longer be in this world. There was a simple way of finding out the truth and judging Hattusilis's sincerity.

The merchant had spent a sleepless night, endlessly going

over in his mind what he would have to do. He would plant the dagger in Uri-Teshup's throat to prevent him crying out, leave the general's tent with the peaceful bearing of a man of property, mount his horse and leave the camp at a jog-trot. Then he would urge his mount on, before leaping on to the back of another horse, hidden in a little wood.

The risk was great, but the merchant hated Uri-Teshup. A year before, this brilliant warrior had caused the death of his two sons in the course of a ridiculous manoeuvre in which twenty young men had died from exhaustion. When Putuhepa had suggested this plan to him, he had expressed his enthusiasm. He did not care about the fortune she had promised him. Even if he were arrested and executed, he would have avenged his sons and done away with a monster.

At dawn, one of Uri-Teshup's officers came to fetch the merchant and take him to the commander-in-chief's tent. The would-be executioner had to control his excitement and speak warmly of his friends who hoped to oust the emperor and help his son to win power.

The officer searched him and found no weapon. The short double-bladed dagger was hidden under the harmless-looking woollen cap that a merchant usually wore in the cold season.

'Go in. The general is expecting you.'

Uri-Teshup was leaning over a map, with his back to the visitor.

'Thank you for receiving me, General.'

'Make it brief.'

'The merchant clan is divided. Some cling on to peace, others not. For my part, I am one of those who hope for the conquest of Egypt.'

'Go on.'

The opportunity was too good. Uri-Teshup did not turn round, busy tracing little circles on a map.

The merchant took off his cap, seized the handle of the little dagger and approached the soldier while still talking.

'My friends and I are convinced that the emperor is not capable of leading us to the triumph we hope for. You, on the other hand, you, the brilliant warrior, you—Die! Die for having killed my sons!'

The general turned round just as the merchant struck. In his left hand he too held a dagger. The merchant's blade entered the victim's neck, that of the general his attacker's heart. They fell dead together, their limbs entwined.

The real Uri-Teshup lifted the flap of his tent.

In order to know the truth, he had had to sacrifice the life of a private soldier of the same build as himself. The fool had reacted badly by killing the merchant, whom the general would have liked to question. But he had heard enough to know that Hattusilis had not lied.

So the emperor's brother, realistic and cautious, was coming over to his side, in the hope that Uri-Teshup, the victorious general and future master of Hatti, would not be ungrateful.

Hattusilis was mistaken.

Ahsha had stripped neither merchant nor traveller, for he had discovered a much better instrument for his purpose: a poor young widow, aged about twenty. Her husband, a footsoldier at Kadesh, had died accidentally when crossing the Orontes in flood. Alone, childless, she farmed with great difficulty a poor, barren piece of land.

When he collapsed, exhausted, in the doorway of her farmhouse, Ahsha had explained to her that brigands had robbed him of everything, and that he had fled, scratching himself on brambles and thorn bushes. Now destitute, he begged her to shelter him, at least for the night.

When he had washed in tepid water, which the peasant woman warmed in a basin placed on the hearth, her feelings suddenly changed. Her reserve was transformed into an imperious desire to caress the body of this man of distinction.

Deprived of love for many months, she hurriedly undressed. When the woman, who was in the full bloom of youth, put her arms round Ahsha's neck and pressed her breasts against his back, the Egyptian didn't shy away.

For two days the lovers didn't leave the farm. The woman was not very experienced, but was passionate and generous; she would be one of the rare mistresses of whom Ahsha retained a precise memory.

Outside, it was raining. Ahsha and the woman lay naked, close to the hearth. The diplomat ran his hands over the clefts and valleys of the young woman, who moaned with pleasure.

'Who are you really?'

'I told you, a merchant who has been robbed and ruined.'

'I don't believe you.'

'Why not?'

'Because you are too refined, too elegant. Your actions and language are not those of a merchant.'

Ahsha learned the lesson. The years spent at the Memphis Academy and in the Foreign Affairs secretariat seemed to have left their indelible marks.

'You aren't a Hittite. You haven't got their brutality. When you make love, you think about the other person; my husband only took his own pleasure. Who are you?'

'Will you promise to keep the secret?'

'I swear by the god of storms!' The young woman's eyes shone with excitement.

'It's difficult . . . '

'Trust me! Haven't I given you proof of my love?'

He kissed her nipples. 'I am the son of a Syrian noble,' he explained, 'and I dream of enlisting in the Hittite army. My father has forbidden this, because of the severity of the training. I have run away from home, wanting to discover Hatti, alone, without escort, and prove my valour in order to be recruited.'

'That is madness! The soldiers are bloodthirsty brutes.'

'I want to fight the Egyptians. If I don't act, they will seize my lands and rob me of all I possess.'

She rested her head on his chest. 'I hate war.'

'It's inevitable, isn't it?'

'Everyone is convinced it will happen.'

'Do you know where the soldiers are training?'

'It's a secret.'

'Have you noticed movements of troops hereabouts?'

'No, this is an isolated place.'

'Would you agree to accompany me to Hattusa?'

'Me, go to the capital? I've never been there!'

'This is a good opportunity. There I shall meet some officers and shall be able to enlist.'

'Please, give up this idea! Is death such a temptation?'

'If I don't act, my province will be destroyed. Evil must be fought, and Egypt is the evil.'

'The capital is a long way off.'

'There are a lot of clay pots in your shed. Did your husband make them?'

'He was a potter before he was forced to join the army.'

'We can sell them and live in Hattusa. They say that it is an unforgettable city.'

'My field . . . '

'It's winter, the soil is resting. We shall leave tomorrow.'

She lay down close to the hearth and stretched out her arms to embrace her lover.

41

In the Heliopolis House of Life, the oldest in the country, work was proceeding as usual. The ritualists were verifying the texts that would be used during the celebration of the mysteries of Osiris, the magicians strove to ward off spells and dangerous forces, the astrologists were polishing up their forecasts for the coming months, the healers preparing their potions. One unusual detail: the library containing thousands of papyri, including the original version of the *Texts of the Pyramids* and the Ritual for Pharaoh's Regeneration, was closed until the following day.

It sheltered a very special reader, Ramses in person.

The monarch had arrived during the night and shut himself up in the vast stone-walled library, with its store of all the important Egyptian lore relating to the visible as well as the invisible. Ramses had felt the need to consult the archives because of the state of Nefertari's health.

The Great Royal Wife was wasting away. Neither the court physician nor Setau had been able to discover the cause of her malady. The Queen Mother had suggested a disquieting diagnosis: an assault by the powers of darkness, against which medicine's usual remedies would be of no avail. That was why the king was searching through the archives, which so many monarchs had consulted before him.

After at least ten hours of research, he thought he could see a solution and immediately left for Pi-Ramses.

Nefertari had presided over the meeting of the weavers, who had come from all the temples in Egypt, and she had given the necessary instructions for making the ritual garments to last until the next inundation. The queen offered up to the gods red, white, green and blue lengths of material and left the temple supported by two priestesses. She managed to climb into a litter, which took her back to the palace.

Dr Pariamaku rushed to the Great Royal Wife's bedside and administered a stimulating potion, though without much hope of lifting the burden of fatigue which every day increasingly overwhelmed her. As soon as Ramses entered his wife's bedchamber the physician slipped away.

The king kissed Nefertari's forehead and hands.

'I'm exhausted.'

'Your burden of official duties must be reduced.'

'It isn't a passing weakness. I feel my life ebbing away like a trickle of water, growing ever less and less.'

'Tuya thinks that it's not a normal malady.'

'She's right.'

'Someone is attacking us from the realm of darkness.'

'My shawl – my favourite shawl! A magician is using it against me.'

'I have come to the same conclusion and I have asked Serramanna to do everything he can to identify the culprit.'

'He must hurry, Ramses, he must hurry . . .'

'We have other ways of fighting this, Nefertari; but we must leave Pi-Ramses tomorrow.'

'Where are you taking me?'

'To a place where you will be safe from our invisible enemy.'

Ramses spent long hours with Ahmeni, who reported nothing noteworthy regarding the affairs of state. The scribe was always anxious at the idea of a prolonged absence by the monarch and promised to take every precaution to avoid any mistake which might compromise the country's welfare. Ramses noticed that Ahmeni followed up every dossier with exemplary vigour and put together all essential information with an instinct for classification.

The king made numerous decisions and entrusted Ahmeni with seeing that they were carried out by his ministers. Serramanna, too, received confirmation of his various duties, not the least of which was to oversee the training of the elite troops quartered in the barracks at Pi-Ramses.

The monarch walked with his mother, Tuya, in the garden where she loved to meditate. She wore a pleated cape over her shoulders; earrings in the shape of lotus flowers and an amethyst necklace softened her severe countenance

'I am leaving for the south with Nefertari, mother. Here she is in too great danger.'

'You are right. As long as we cannot overcome the action of the fiend that is lurking in the shadows, it is better to take her away.'

'Watch over the kingdom; in any emergency Ahmeni will carry out your orders.'

'What is the situation regarding the threat of war?'

'Everything is quiet – too quiet. The Hittites are not reacting. Muwatallis simply writes empty formal letters.'

'Could they be an indication of internal dissent? Muwatallis did away with many opponents before seizing power, and there are some who still harbour a grudge against him'

'That is not exactly encouraging,' said Ramses. 'What better means than war to wipe out discord and rebuild unity?'

'In that case, the Hittites must be preparing a large-scale offensive.'

'I hope I'm wrong. Perhaps Muwatallis is weary of fighting and bloodshed.'

'You mustn't think like an Egyptian, my son; happiness,

peace and tranquility are not qualities prized by the Hittites. If the emperor does not advocate conquest and expansion, he will lose his throne.'

'If the attack begins in my absence, don't wait for my return to order the army to set out.'

Tuya's little square chin hardened. 'No Hittite will cross the border of the Delta.'

In the temple of Mut, the mother goddess, there were three hundred and sixty-five statues of the lioness-headed goddess Sekhmet, one for each day, to celebrate the rites for the appeasement of the morning, and a further three hundred and sixty-five for the evening rites. It was there that the great physicians of the realm came to search for the secrets of sickness and healing.

Nefertari chanted the ritual which transformed the lioness's deadly fury into creativity; her controlled violence was the source of the ability to master the constituent elements of life. The college of the seven priestesses of Sekhmet communed with the queen's spirit, which was offered up to cause light to shine forth in the darkness of the shrine where the fearsome goddess was enthroned.

The high priestess poured water over the lioness's head, which was carved out of hard shiny diorite. The liquid ran down over the goddess's body and was collected in a dish by an assistant.

Nefertari drank the healing water, absorbing the magic of Sekhmet, whose great energy would help her struggle against the weakness that had permeated her veins. Then the Great Royal Wife remained for a day and a night in silence and darkness, alone with the lion-headed goddess.

When she crossed the Nile, leaning affectionately against Ramses' shoulder, Nefertari felt less oppressed than during the recent weeks. The king's love was the source of a different magic, as potent as that of the goddess. A chariot bore them to the Sublime of Sublimes, a temple on terraces set against a cliff; it had been built by order of the female Pharaoh Hatshepsut. In front of it lay a garden, whose finest treasures were frankincense trees imported from the land of Punt. Here the goddess Hathor reigned, the lady of the stars, beauty and love. She was another form of the goddess Sekhmet.

One of the temple buildings was a convalescence centre, where patients took several baths a day and sometimes underwent a sleeping cure. Hieroglyphic texts on the base of the tubs of warm water warded off disease.

'A period of rest is essential, Nefertari.'

'My duties as queen . . . '

'Your first duty is to survive so that the royal couple remains the cornerstone of Egypt. Those who wish to destroy us try to separate us and so weaken Egypt.'

The garden of the temple of Deir el-Bahri seemed to belong to another world; the foliage of the incense trees shone in the soft winter sunlight. Pipes sunk just below the surface provided constant irrigation, regulated according to the temperature.

Nefertari felt that her love for Ramses was growing ever greater, that it spread like the boundless sky; and the look in the king's eyes proved that he shared this radiance. But this happiness was fragile, so fragile.

'Do not sacrifice Egypt for me, Ramses; if I should die you must take Iset the Fair for Great Royal Wife.'

'You are alive, Nefertari, and you are the one I love.'

'Swear to me, Ramses! Swear that Egypt alone will dictate your conduct. You have dedicated your life to Egypt, not to a human being, whoever that might be. The life of a people and, even more, of a civilization founded by our ancestors depends on your commitment. Without this, what would become of the world? It would be delivered into the hands of hordes of barbarians, to the reign of profit and injustice. I love you with all my might, and my final thought will be this love; but because you are Pharaoh I have no right to hold you in thrall.'

They sat down on a stone bench. Ramses clasped Nefertari tightly to him.

'You are the one who sees Seth and Horus in the same being,' he reminded her, using the ritual formula that had been applied to the queen since the First Dynasty. 'It is through your gaze that Pharaoh exists, that he is the receptacle of the light which he sheds on the Two Lands. The reigns of all my predecessors were nourished by the Rule of Ma'at, but none was like any other, for humans constantly invent new failings. Your gaze is unique, Nefertari; Egypt and Pharaoh have need of it.'

In the midst of her ordeal, she discovered fresh love.

'While consulting the archives in the Heliopolis House of Life, I discovered a way of fending off the invisible attacker. By the double action of Sekhmet and Hathor, and thanks to the rest you will have in this temple, your energy will not decline any more. But that is not enough.'

'Are you leaving again for Pi-Ramses?'

'No, Nefertari. There may be a complete cure for you.'

'What is it?'

'According to the archives, it is the Nubian stone placed under the protection of the goddess Hathor, in an isolated site neglected for centuries.'

'Do you know where it is?'

'I shall find it.'

'Your journey might be a long one . . . '

'Thanks to the strength of the current, I shall return rapidly. If I am fortunate enough to reach the site fairly quickly, my absence will be short.'

'The Hittites . . . '

'My mother is in charge. In case of attack she will warn you immediately and you will act.'

They embraced long, under the foliage of the incense trees.

She would have liked to keep him with her, to spend the remainder of her days near him, in the peace of the temple.

But she was the Great Royal Wife and he was Pharaoh of Egypt.

42

Lita looked imploringly at the magus, Ofir.

'It must be done, my child.'

'No, I am in too much pain . . . '

'That's the proof that the spell is working. We must continue.'

'My skin . . . '

'The king's sister will treat it. No trace of the burns will remain.'

Lita, the sole descendant of the heretic king Akhenaton, turned her back on the magus. 'No, I don't want to go on. I can't bear this suffering any more!'

'That's enough of your tantrums! Do as I tell you or I shall lock you in the cellar.' Ofir dragged her by the hair.

'Not that, I beg you, not that!' The young medium was claustrophobic and feared this punishment more than anything.

'Come into my laboratory, bare your chest and lie down on your back.'

Dolora, Ramses' sister, deplored the sorcerer's harshness, but sided with him. The latest news from the court was excellent: Nefertari was suffering from a mysterious incurable illness and had left for Thebes, where she would die at Deir el-Bahr, where the goddess Hathor held sway. Her slow death would break Ramses' heart and he, in turn, would die of sorrow.

For Shaanar, the road to power seemed open.

As soon as Ramses left, Serramanna visited each of the barracks in Pi-Ramses and ordered the senior officers to intensify the training. The mercenaries immediately demanded an increase in their pay, setting off a similar request from the Egyptian soldiers.

Faced with a problem which was beyond him, the Sardinian referred to Ahmeni, who appealed to Tuya, whose reply was immediate: either the soldiers and mercenaries obeyed, or she would replace them by young recruits. If Serramanna was satisfied with the progress shown during manoeuvres, she might consider a special allowance.

The soldiers gave way. Then the Sardinian devoted himself to another mission: to try to discover the magician for whom the steward Remet had stolen Nefertari's shawl. Ramses had told him of his suspicions, which confirmed the strange way Remet had died and the queen's no less strange illness.

If the cursed steward had survived, the former pirate would have had no difficulty in making him talk. True, torture was forbidden in Egypt, but an attempt on the lives of the royal couple, using supernatural powers, was surely enough to justify an exemption from the common law.

Remet was dead, taking his secret with him into a void inhabited by fiends, and the trail leading to the power behind him seemed to have gone dead. But what if this was only apparent? Remet had been outgoing, talkative. Perhaps he had used the services of an accomplice . . . possibly female?

Questioning Remet's intimates and staff might give results, on condition that he put questions to them with a certain persuasive force . . . Serramanna rushed off to see Ahmeni. He would talk the scribe into agreeing to his plan.

All the palace domestic staff were summoned to the northern

barracks. The queen's dressers and linen-maids, maids of the bedchamber, make-up assistants and hairdressers, the cooks, sweeps and all the other servants were rounded up in the armoury, guarded by Serramanna's stern-faced bowmen.

When the Sardinian appeared, in helmet and breastplate, hearts fell.

'There have been new thefts committed in the palace,' he revealed. 'We know that the person responsible is an accomplice of the steward Remet, that vile, despicable creature whom heaven has punished. I shall question you one by one. If I do not obtain the truth, you will all be deported to the oasis of Kharga and there the culprit will talk.'

It had taken a great effort on Serramanna's part to persuade Ahmeni to let him lie and make threats that had no legal basis. Any one of the domestic staff could contest his action and appeal to a tribunal which would condemn him. But the formidable appearance of the commander of the king's personal bodyguard, combined with the distressing nature of the place, deterred anyone from protesting.

Serramanna was in luck: the third woman who came into the room where he was proceeding with the questioning, talked freely.

'It was my job to replace the faded flowers with freshly cut bunches,' she revealed. 'I hated that Remet.'

'Why?'

'He made me go to bed with him. If I'd refused he'd have seen that I lost my job.'

'If you'd complained, he'd have been dismissed.'

'So you say, so you say . . . But then Remet had promised me a small fortune if I married him.'

'How had he got rich?'

'He wouldn't say very much, but in bed I managed to get him to talk a bit.'

'What did he tell you?'

'That he would sell some precious object for a high price.'

'Where did he expect to get it?'

'He'd obtain it thanks to a servant, a temporary linen-maid.'

'And what was this object?'

'I don't know. But I do know that that fat Remet never gave me anything, not even an amulet! Will I get a reward for telling you all this?'

A temporary linen-maid! Serramanna rushed back to Ahmeni and sent for the service rota for the week when the queen's shawl had been stolen.

In fact, a certain Nany had been taken on as temporary linen-maid, under the supervision of one of the queen's maids of the bedchamber. The latter described her and confirmed that she would have had access to Her Majesty's private apartments and been able to steal the shawl. The maid told them the address Nany had given her when she was engaged.

'Question her,' Ahmeni told Serramanna, 'but without any violence and with respect for the law.'

'That is my intention,' declared the Sardinian solemnly.

An old woman was dozing in the doorway of her house, in the eastern part of the capital.

Serramanna touched her gently on the shoulder. 'Wake up, grandma.'

She opened one eye and brushed away a fly with her callused hand. 'Who are you?'

'Serramanna, commander of Ramses' personal body-guard.'

'I've heard of you. Didn't you use to be a pirate?'

'No one really changes, grandma. I'm still as cruel as I used to be, especially if people lie to me.'

'Why should I lie to you?'

'Because I'm going to ask you some questions.'

'It's a sin to talk too much.'

'That depends on the circumstances. Today it's an

obligation to talk a lot.'

'Go on your way, pirate; at my age, I no longer have any obligations.'

'Are you Nany's grandmother?'

'Why should I be?'

'Because she lives here.'

'She's left.'

'When someone's been lucky enough to be taken on as a linen-maid at the palace, why should she run away?'

'I didn't say she'd run away, I said she'd left.'

'Where has she gone?'

'I've no idea.'

'I must remind you that I detest lies.'

'Would you hit an old woman, pirate?'

'To save Ramses, yes.'

She looked up at Serramanna anxiously. 'I don't understand. Is Pharaoh in danger?'

'Your granddaughter is a thief, perhaps a criminal. If you keep quiet, you will be her accomplice.'

'How could Nany be mixed up in a plot against Pharaoh?'

'She is. I have proof.'

The fly was bothering the old woman again; Serramanna squashed it.

'Death is welcome, pirate, when it relieves unbearable suffering. I had a good husband and a good son, but he made the mistake of marrying a horrible woman who gave him a horrible daughter. My husband is dead, my son got divorced, and I was the one left to bring up his cursed offspring – hours spent looking after her, feeding her, teaching her right from wrong, and you talk to me about a thief and a criminal!'

The grandmother paused for breath. Serramanna did not speak, hoping she would finish her story. If she said no more, he'd leave.

'Nany went to Memphis. She told me, scornfully and with pride, that she was going to live in a fine villa behind the school of medicine, whereas I would die in this little house!'

Serramanna told Ahmeni the results of his investigation.

'If you ill-treated that old woman, she'll make a complaint against you.'

'I didn't touch her; my men are witnesses to that.'

'What do you suggest?'

'She gave me a detailed description of Nany, which matches that given by the queen's maid of the bedchamber. As soon as I see her I shall recognize her.'

'How will you find her?'

'By searching all the villas in the district in Memphis where she is living.'

'And what if the old woman lied to you, to protect Nany?'

'That's a risk we must take.'

'Memphis isn't far, but you're needed here in Pi-Ramses.'

'You say yourself, Ahmeni, that Memphis is not far. But suppose I found this Nany and she led me to the sorcerer, don't you think Ramses would be pleased?'

'"Pleased" would be an understatement.'

'Then give me permission to act.'

43

Ahsha and his mistress had their breath quite taken away by their first sight of Hattusa. Hattusa, the capital of the Hittite empire, dedicated to the cult of war and power. As access to the three gates of the upper town – the King's Gate, the Gate of the Sphinx and the Gate of the Lions – was forbidden to merchants, the couple entered the city by one of the two gates to the lower town, guarded by soldiers armed with spears.

Ahsha showed his clay pots and even invited one of the fierce-looking guards to buy one at a reduced price. The soldier elbowed him away and told him to clear off. The couple made their way unhurriedly towards the artisans' and small traders' district.

The rocky peaks, the rows of stone terraces, the enormous blocks of stone used to build the temple of the god of storms, all made as deep an impression on the countrywoman as on her companion. But Ahsha deplored the lack of charm and elegance of the capital with its rugged architecture, surrounded by the harsh Anatolian mountains and dominated by a system of fortifications which made it impregnable. Peace and a comfortable life could not flourish in this place, where every stone exuded violence.

The Egyptian looked in vain for gardens, trees, lakes, while the biting north wind chilled him to the marrow. He could judge to what extent his own country was a paradise.

Several times he and his companion had to flatten themselves against the brick walls to let a patrol pass. Anyone who did not move aside in time, be it woman, old man or child, was jostled, even knocked over, by the groups of foot-soldiers passing at a run. The army was everywhere. At every street corner soldiers were on guard.

Ahsha offered a pot to a wholesaler dealing in household utensils. As was the custom in Hittite territory, his woman stood behind him and kept silent.

'It's good work,' said the wholesaler. 'How many do you make in a week?'

'I've a small stock that I made in the country. I'd like to settle here.'

'Have you got anywhere to stay?'

'Not yet.'

'I rent out premises in the lower town. I'll exchange your whole stock for a month's rent. That'll give you time to set up your workshop.'

'Agreed, if you add three pieces of tin.'

'You strike a hard bargain!'

'I have to buy food.'

'It's a deal.'

Ahsha and his mistress moved into a little house, damp and badly ventilated, with only hard-packed earth by way of a floor.

'I liked my farm better,' confessed the peasant. 'At least we were warm.'

'We shan't stay here long. Take a piece of tin and go and buy some blankets and something to eat.'

'And where are you going?'

'Don't worry. I'll be back tonight.'

Thanks to his perfect knowledge of the Hittite language, Ahsha could talk to the tradesmen, who pointed out a well-known tavern at the foot of a watch-tower. The smoke-filled establishment, lit by oil lamps, was frequented by merchants and artisans.

Ahsha got into conversation with two bearded men who proved quite talkative. They said they sold spare parts for war chariots and were carpenters who had given up making chairs to take up this much more lucrative activity.

'What a magnificent city,' Ahsha enthused. 'I never imagined it to be so grand.'

'Is this your first visit, my friend?'

'Yes, but I intend to open a workshop.'

'Then you must work for the army! Otherwise you'll have little to eat and nothing but water to drink.'

'Colleagues told me that preparations for war are being made.'

The carpenters burst out laughing. 'You're the last one to know! In Hattusa, it's no secret. Since Uri-Teshup, the emperor's son, was appointed commander-in-chief, manoeuvres have been carried on non-stop. And rumour has it that our assault troops will give no quarter. This time, Egypt's done for.'

'All the better!'

'That's debatable, at least among the merchants. Hattusilis, the emperor's brother, isn't in favour of war, but in the end he let himself be persuaded and he's just given his support to Uri-Teshup. For us, everything is profit, and we're even beginning to make our fortunes! At the present rate of production, Hatti will triple the number of its war chariots. There'll soon be more chariots than there are men to drive them!'

Ahsha drained his jar of harsh wine and pretended to be drunk. 'Long live the war! Hatti will polish off Egypt in no time. And we shall have some fun!'

'You'll have to be patient for a while, my friend, because the emperor doesn't seem in a hurry to start the offensive.'

'Ah . . . what is he waiting for?'

'We don't share the palace secrets! Go and ask Captain Kenzor.' The two carpenters laughed at their own joke.

'Who's Captain Kenzor?'

'The officer who carries messages between the commander-in-chief and the emperor – and a real lady-killer, believe me! When he stays in Hattusa, the pretty girls are all in a flutter. He's the most popular officer in the country.'

'Long live the war and long live the ladies!'

The conversation turned to feminine charms and the brothels in the capital. Finding Ahsha to their liking, the carpenters paid for the drinks.

Ahsha went to a different tavern every evening. He made a number of contacts, talked of frivolous subjects, and sometimes casually introduced Captain Kenzor's name into the conversation.

Eventually he picked up a valuable piece of information: the captain had just returned to Hattusa. If he could question this officer, he might save himself a great deal of time. He had to locate him, find a way to approach him and make him a proposal that he wouldn't refuse. An idea came into his mind . . .

Ahsha returned to his lodging, taking with him a gown, a mantle and a pair of sandals.

The peasant woman was filled with wonder. 'Are those for me?'

'Is there any other woman in my life?'

'They must have cost a lot.'

'I bargained.'

She wanted to touch the garments.

'No, not immediately!'

'When?'

'For a special outing when I shall have leisure to admire you. Give me time to arrange it.'

'As you will.' She threw her arms round his neck and

embraced him passionately.

'Do you know that you are just as pretty when you have no clothes on . . . ?'

As the royal ship sailed towards the south, Setau seemed rejuvenated. Clasping Lotus to him, he rediscovered with wonder the Nubian landscape, bathed in so pure a light that the Nile seemed a celestial river, of brilliant blue.

With his axe, Setau had cut a forked stick to capture a few cobras, whose poison he would pour into a copper flask. Pretty Lotus sat bare-breasted, wearing only a short loin-cloth that flew in the wind, and she eagerly breathed in the scented air of her native land.

Ramses himself acted as navigator. The experienced crew manoeuvred fast and with precision.

At midday the captain took over from the king. In the central cabin, Ramses, Setau and Lotus partook of dried beef, spiced salad and sweet papyrus roots, mixed with mild onions.

'You are a true friend, Majesty,' Setau acknowledged. 'You do us an enormous favour by taking us with you.'

'I need your talents and Lotus's.'

'Although we are isolated in the palace laboratory, unpleasant rumours reach our ears. Is war really imminent?'

'I'm afraid so.'

'Isn't it dangerous to leave Pi-Ramses in these troubled times?'

'Saving Nefertari is a matter of the highest importance.'

'I've been no more skilful than Doctor Pariamaku,' lamented Setau.

'There is a miraculous remedy hidden in Nubia, isn't there?' asked Lotus.

'According to the archives in the House of Life, yes: a stone created by the goddess Hathor, in an isolated place.'

'Any details, Majesty?'

'A vague indication: "In the heart of Nubia, in a creek of golden sand, where the mountains divide and are joined again".'

'A creek . . . So it must be close to the Nile.'

'We must hurry,' Ramses pointed out. 'Thanks to Sekhmet's power and the special treatment at the Deir el-Bahri temple, Nefertari won't lose all her physical strength. But the action of the forces of darkness has not been dispelled. Our hope resides in this stone.'

Lotus looked into the distance. 'This land loves you, as you love it, Majesty. Speak to it and it will speak to you.'

A pelican flew over the royal ship. Was not the magnificent bird one of the incarnations of Osiris, who triumphs over death?

44

Captain Kenzor had had too much to drink.

Three days' leave in the capital was a chance to forget the rigours of military life, drown his troubles in wine and deaden them with women. He was a tall fellow with a moustache and a hoarse voice. He despised girls and thought them only good for providing pleasure.

When his brain was fuddled with wine, Kenzor had an irresistible urge to make love. And that evening, after a full-bodied wine, the urge was both strong and insistent. On leaving the tavern, he stumbled off to find a brothel. The captain was impervious to the biting cold. He hoped that a virgin would be available and that she would be well and truly scared. It would be all the more amusing to deflower her.

A man approached him respectfully. 'May I have a word with you, Captain?'

'What do you want?'

'To offer you something really special,' Ahsha replied.

Kenzor smiled. 'What are you selling?'

'A young virgin.'

Captain Kenzor's eyes lit up. 'How much?'

'Ten best-quality pieces of tin.'

'That's expensive!'

'The goods are exceptional.'

'I want them immediately.'

'They are available.'

'I've only got five pieces of tin on me.'

'You can pay me the balance tomorrow morning.'

'You trust me?'

'After this one, I shall have other virgins to offer you.'

'You're a useful man. Let's go – I'm in a hurry.'

Kenzor was very excited, so the two men kept up a good pace. In the sleeping alleyways of the lower town, there was not a soul about.

Ahsha pushed open the door of his modest dwelling.

The peasant woman had done her hair nicely and put on the new clothes that Ahsha had bought her.

The captain, now aroused, sized her up. 'Say, merchant, isn't she a bit old to be a virgin?'

Ahsha lashed out violently at Kenzor and pinned him against a wall, knocking him almost senseless. The Egyptian took advantage of this to grab Kenzor's short sword and plant its point in the back of the officer's neck.

'Who . . . who are you?' stammered the Hittite.

'You are the link-officer between the army and the palace. Either you answer my questions or I kill you.'

Kenzor tried to free himself, but the sword-point dug into his flesh, drawing blood. The surfeit of wine had sapped the captain's strength so that he was at the mercy of his attacker. The horrified woman retreated to a corner of the room.

'When will the attack against Egypt take place?' demanded Ahsha. 'And why are the Hittites making so many chariots?'

Kenzor grimaced: this man already had valuable information. 'The attack . . . Military secret.'

'If you don't talk, you'll take the secret with you into your tomb.'

'You wouldn't dare!'

'You're wrong, Kenzor. I shan't hesitate to do away with you and I'll kill as many officers as necessary to obtain the truth.'

The sword-point dug deeper and brought a cry of pain from the officer. The woman looked away.

'The date of the attack . . . only the emperor knows it. I haven't been told.'

'But you know why the Hittite army needs so many chariots.'

With his neck so painful and his mind clouded with drink, the captain whispered a few words as if to himself.

Ahsha's hearing was sufficiently acute to catch the alarming admission and he did not need to make him repeat it.

He was furious. 'Have you gone mad?' he asked Kenzor.

'No, it's the truth.'

'Impossible!'

'It's the truth.'

Ahsha was stunned. He had just obtained an absolutely vital piece of information, information which could change the destiny of the world.

With one violent, well-aimed thrust, the Egyptian buried the sword in the back of Kenzor's neck and the captain dropped dead on the spot.

'Turn round,' Ahsha ordered the woman.

'No, leave me alone! Go away!'

He approached his mistress, holding the outstretched sword. 'Sorry, my girl, I can't let you live.'

'I didn't see or hear anything!'

'Are you quite sure?'

'He was muttering. I didn't hear anything, I swear!' She fell to her knees. 'Don't kill me, I beg you! I can be useful to you, to get out of the city!'

Ahsha hesitated. She was right. The city gates were closed during the night, and he would have to wait until dawn to leave, accompanied by his woman. He would use her to get through unnoticed, and then do away with her at a bend in some sunken lane.

Ahsha sat down near the body, unable to sleep. His one thought was to take the road back to Egypt as quickly as possible, and put his discovery to use.

The Nubian winter was delightful, once the coolness of the dawn was past. On the bank, Ramses had caught sight of a lion with its pride of lionesses. Monkeys climbed to the top of the dom-palms and greeted the passage of the royal ship with their shrieks.

At one place where they stopped, the villagers offered the monarch and his suite wild bananas and milk. Ramses took advantage of this impromptu feast to converse with the chief of the tribe, an old sorcerer whose hair had grown white in the course of his ninety years of peaceful existence, spent caring for his people.

When the old man tried to kneel before him, Ramses took him by the arm and prevented him.

'A light shines on my old age. The gods have allowed me to see Pharaoh! Is it not my duty to bow down before him and render homage?'

'It is my duty to respect your wisdom.'

'I'm only a village sorcerer.'

'Someone who has respected the Rule of Ma'at all his life is more worthy of respect than a false sage, lying and unjust.'

'Are you not the Lord of the Two Lands and of Nubia? I reign only over a few families.'

'Yet I need your memory.'

Pharaoh and the sorcerer sat down under a palm tree, where the old man was wont to shelter from the blazing sun.

'My memory . . . It is full of blue skies, children's games, women's smiles, gazelles leaping and beneficial inundations. You are now responsible for all that, Pharaoh. Without you, my memories would not exist, and future generations would produce none but heartless creatures.'

'Do you remember a holy place where the goddess of love

created a miraculous stone, an isolated place somewhere in the heart of Nubia?'

With his stick, the sorcerer drew a rough map in the sand. 'My father's father brought back a similar stone to my village. By touching it women regained their health. Unfortunately, nomads took it away.'

'Where did it come from?'

The stick pointed to a spot along the Nile. 'From this mysterious place, where the province of Kush begins.'

'What do you desire for your village?'

'Nothing but what is. But is that not a great deal to ask? Protect us, Pharaoh, and keep Nubia intact.'

'Nubia has spoken through your voice, and I have heard.'

The royal ship left the province of Uawat and entered Kush, where the mediation of Seti and then Ramses had brought peace; now, although the tribes were always prepared to attack each other, they maintained peace for fear of how Pharaoh's soldiers would react.

Here began a savage, magnificent land, which could not survive without the Nile. On either side of the river there was only a narrow strip of cultivated land, but there was shade under palm trees and dom-palms for the farmers who fought against the desert.

Suddenly, there were cliffs. Ramses had the sensation that the Nile was keeping all human presence at bay and that nature was retreating into an imposing emptiness.

A captivating scent of mimosa softened this impression of the end of the world.

Two almost parallel mountainous outcrops rose and fell towards the river, separated by a sandy valley. At the foot of the sandstone overhangs, there were acacias in flower. 'A creek of golden sand, where the mountains divide and are joined again' . . .

As if he were waking from a long sleep, as if he were

dragging himself free from a spell which had long clouded his vision, Ramses recognized the place. Why had he not thought of it before?

'Draw alongside,' he ordered. 'This is the place, it must be here.'

Lotus dived naked into the river and swam to the bank. Her body glistened with silvery drops as she ran, lithe as a gazelle, to a Nubian sleeping in the shade of the trees. She woke him, questioned him and ran again towards the mountain, picked up a piece of rock and returned to the boat.

Ramses was staring at the cliff. Abu Simbel . . . It was indeed Abu Simbel, where power and magic were combined, the place where he had decided to build temples, the realm of Hathor, which he had neglected and forgotten.

Setau helped Lotus back into the boat.

She held a piece of sandstone in her right hand. 'This is indeed the goddess's magic stone. But no one today knows how to use its curative power.'

45

A faint glimmer of light shone through the narrow window of the cold damp house. The peasant woman was woken by the sound of a patrol's footsteps. She started when she saw the captain's dead body. 'He's there! He's still there!'

'You're having a nightmare. Wake up,' Ahsha suggested. 'He won't testify against us.'

'*I* didn't do anything!'

'You're my woman. If I'm caught you'll be executed the same as me.'

The woman hurled herself at Ahsha and pounded his chest with her clenched fists.

'Last night,' he said, 'I was thinking.'

She stopped, panic-stricken. In her lover's icy gaze, she read her death. 'No, you've no right . . . '

'I've been thinking,' he repeated. 'Either I kill you immediately, or you help me.'

'Help you? How?'

'I'm an Egyptian.'

The Hittite stared at him as if he were a creature from the next world.

'I'm an Egyptian and I have to return to my own country as quickly as possible. If anything prevents me, I want you to cross the border and warn my employer.'

'Why should I run such a risk?'

'In exchange for comfort. Thanks to the tablet I shall give you, you'll be granted a home in the city, with a servant and an income for life. My master will be generous.'

Even in her wildest dreams, the woman had never imagined such a good life. 'Agreed.'

'We shall each leave by one of the gates of the city,' Ahsha insisted.

'Suppose you reach Egypt before I do?' she asked anxiously.

'Carry out your mission and don't worry about anything else.'

Ahsha composed a short message in hieratic, an abridged form of hieroglyphics, and handed the slim wooden tablet to his mistress.

When he embraced her she did not have the courage to resist.

'We shall meet again in Pi-Ramses,' he promised her.

When Ahsha reached the outskirts of the lower town, he was caught up in a throng of merchants who, like him, were trying to leave the capital.

Tense-looking soldiers were everywhere. It was impossible to turn back, on account of a squad of bowmen who were dividing the civilians into groups and subjecting them to a search. People were asking what was going on, complaining, pushing and shoving; donkeys and mules protested, but this agitation did not diminish the roughness of the sentinels who guarded the gate.

'What's happening?' Ahsha asked a tradesman.

'It's forbidden to enter the town and difficult to leave. They're looking for an officer who's said to have disappeared.'

'What's that got to do with us?'

'A Hittite officer doesn't disappear. Someone must have attacked him, possibly killed him. They're looking for the person responsible.'

'Any suspicions?'

'Another soldier, certainly. One more result of the quarrel between the emperor's son and brother. Eventually one of them will do away with the other.'

'But the guards are searching everyone.'

'They're making sure that the murderer, an armed soldier, doesn't try to leave the city disguised as a merchant.'

Ahsha relaxed.

The searching was slow and meticulous. A man of about thirty was hurled to the ground. His friends protested, saying that he sold cloth and had never been in the army. The merchant was released.

Then came Ahsha's turn.

A bony-faced soldier put a hand on his shoulder. 'Who are you?'

'A potter.'

'Why are you leaving the city?'

'I'm going to fetch more stocks from my farm.'

The soldier made sure he was not carrying any weapons.

'Can I go?'

The soldier made a scornful gesture.

The gate of the Hittite capital – freedom, the road to Egypt – was only a few yards away from Ahsha.

'One moment.' Someone had spoken, on Ahsha's left.

It was a man of average height, with inquisitive eyes, a weasel face and a little pointed beard. He wore a red woollen gown with black stripes.

'Arrest this man!' he ordered the guards.

An officer reacted indignantly. 'I'm the one who gives orders here.'

'My name is Raia,' said the man with the beard. 'I'm a member of the palace police.'

'What offence has this merchant committed?'

'He's neither a Hittite nor a potter. He's an Egyptian, his

name is Ahsha and he holds an important post at Ramses' court.'

Thanks to the powerful current and the slim lines of his ship, Ramses took only two days to travel the long distance from Abu Simbel to Elephantine, the tip of Egypt and its southern-most city. Two more days were needed to reach Thebes. The crew had proved extraordinarily efficient, as if each one was fully aware of the gravity of the situation.

During the voyage, Setau and Lotus worked endlessly on samples of the goddess's stone, a unique type of sandstone. As they drew near to the landing stage at Karnak, they could not hide their disappointment.

'I just don't understand the way this stone reacts,' admitted Setau. 'Its properties are abnormal; it is resistant to acids, takes on astonishing colours and seems charged with energy that I can't measure. How can we treat the queen if we don't know the ingredients and their proportions for this remedy and the exact dose to use?'

The monarch's arrival surprised the staff of the temple and went against protocol. Ramses hurried to Karnak's principal laboratory, accompanied by Setau and Lotus, who handed over the results of their own experiments to the doctors and alchemists.

The research began under the king's supervision. Thanks to the collection of scientific documents relating to the products of Nubia, the experts were able to draw up a list of substances to bring into contact with the goddess's stone, and so drive out the demons that drained a person's blood and caused death from exhaustion.

But they still had to choose the right ingredients and estab-lish the dosage of each component: several months would be needed to achieve this. The head of the laboratory expressed his regret and did not hide his perplexity.

'Set out all the substances on a stone table and leave me

alone,' Ramses commanded.

The king concentrated hard and took hold of the magic rod with which he and his father had discovered water in the desert. He passed the rod over each substance and when it gave a jerk, he isolated that substance. He confirmed the choice by passing the rod a second time, and then worked out the dosages by the same method.

The ingredients were acacia gum, anise, extract of sycamore fruits, a particular kind of cucumber, copper and particles of the goddess's stone.

Nefertari was carefully made up and looked smiling and happy. When Ramses approached her, she was reading the celebrated tale of Sinuhe, in a version written by an especially skillful scribe. She rolled up the papyrus, rose and nestled in the king's arms. Their embrace was long and passionate, while the hoopoes and nightingales sang soothing lullabies to them and the incense trees wafted their fragrance over them.

'I have found the goddess's stone,' said Ramses, 'and the Karnak laboratory has prepared a remedy.'

'Will it work?'

'I used my father's divining-rod to make up a forgotten formula.'

'Describe the place of the Nubian goddess to me.'

'A creek of golden sand, where the mountains divide and are joined again . . . Abu Simbel, the place I had forgotten. Abu Simbel where I have decided to erect a permanent monument to our love.'

The warmth of Ramses' powerful body restored the life which was gradually ebbing away.

'A construction manager and a team of stonecutters leave today for Abu Simbel,' the king continued. 'Those cliffs will become two temples, indivisible for all eternity, like you and me.'

'Shall I see this wonder?'

'Yes, you will see it.'

'May the will of Pharaoh be fulfilled.'

'If it were otherwise, would I still be worthy to reign?'

Ramses and Nefertari crossed the Nile to Karnak. In the sanctuary, they celebrated together the rites of the god Amon; then the queen went to meditate in the chapel of the goddess Sekhmet, whose smiling stone countenance seemed placated.

Pharaoh himself handed the Great Royal Wife the cup containing the one remedy for the supernatural malady from which she suffered.

The potion was warm and sweet. Nefertari was overcome with giddiness; she lay down and closed her eyes.

Ramses did not leave her bedside, struggling together with her throughout the interminable night during which the goddess's stone attempted to drive out the fiend that was draining the queen's blood.

46

Dishevelled, deathly pale, at a loss for words, Ahmeni tied his tongue in knots as he tried to explain.

'Calm down,' said Tuya.

'War, Majesty, it's war!'

'We have received no official document.'

'The generals are in a panic, the barracks are in a turmoil, contradictory orders can be heard everywhere.'

'What has caused this confusion?'

'I don't know, Majesty. I'm unable to control the situation. The soldiers don't listen to me any more!'

Tuya summoned the chief ritualist and two of the palace hairdressers. To emphasize the sacred character of her role, they placed on her head a wig in the form of a vulture, with wings sloping down from the middle of her forehead to her shoulders. The female vulture was the symbol above all else of the caring mother. Thus Tuya's appearance was as the protector of the Two Lands.

She wore gold bracelets on her wrists and ankles, and round her neck a collar of seven rows of semi-precious stones. In her long gown of pleated linen, held at the waist by a girdle with wide hanging ends, she personified supreme authority.

'Accompany me to the northern barracks,' she told Ahmeni.

'Do not go there, Majesty! Wait for the unrest to calm down.'

'Evil and chaos never destroy themselves. We must hurry.'

In Pi-Ramses all was noise and argument. Some declared that the Hittites were approaching the Delta, others were already describing the battles, while others again were getting ready to flee to the South.

The gate of the northern barracks was no longer guarded. The chariot bearing Ahmeni and the Queen Mother entered the great courtyard, where all discipline had vanished.

The horses halted in the centre of the vast space.

An officer of the chariot corps caught sight of Tuya and informed his colleagues, who warned other soldiers. In less than ten minutes hundreds of men had gathered to hear her words.

Small, frail Tuya was surrounded by armed giants, capable of trampling her underfoot in a few seconds. Ahmeni trembled, judging her intervention suicidal. She should have stayed in the palace, protected by the elite guard. Perhaps reassuring words would calm the tension a little, providing Tuya was diplomatic.

There was silence.

The Queen Mother looked around scornfully. 'I see none but cowards and weaklings,' she declared in a hard voice which resounded in Ahmeni's ears like thunder. 'Cowards and fools, unfit to defend their country, since they lend credence to the first rumour they hear.'

Ahmeni closed his eyes. Neither he nor Tuya would escape the soldiers' fury.

'Why do you insult us, Majesty?' asked one officer.

'Is it insulting to describe the facts? Your behaviour is ridiculous and despicable; the officers are more to blame than the troops. Who but Pharaoh will decide when we engage in war against the Hittites, and in his absence who but myself?'

The silence grew deeper. What the Queen Mother was

about to say would not be a rumour and would reveal the destiny of the whole nation.

'I have received no declaration of war from the Emperor of Hatti,' she announced.

Her words were greeted with cheers; Tuya had never lied. The soldiers exchanged congratulations.

As she remained standing motionless in her chariot, the gathering understood that she had not finished speaking. There was silence again.

'I cannot say that the peace will last, and I am even convinced that the Hittites' only aim is cold-blooded war. Its outcome will depend on your efforts. When Ramses is back in his capital – and his return is imminent – I want him to be proud of his army and confident in its ability to defeat the enemy.'

There was more applause. Ahmeni opened his eyes again; he too was swayed by Tuya's power of persuasion.

The soldiers made way for the chariot as it moved off, accompanied by chanting of Tuya's name.

'Are we returning to the palace, Majesty?'

'No, Ahmeni. I presume that the foundry employees have stopped work?'

Ahmeni lowered his eyes.

Through the impetus given by Tuya, the manufacture of weapons in Pi-Ramses resumed and was soon running at full speed, turning out spears, bows, arrowheads, swords, breast-plates, harness and chariot parts. No one doubted that war was now imminent, but a new and urgent requirement had arisen: to provide the army with equipment superior to that of the Hittites.

Tuya visited the barracks and had discussions with both officers and private soldiers. And she also went to the workshop where the chariots were assembled as they came out of the factory, and congratulated the artisans.

The capital had forgotten its fears and discovered a taste

for war.

How soft this lovely hand, with its long, delicate fingers, seemingly almost insubstantial, which Ramses kissed one by one, then clasped in his own hand, never to let them go. There was not one part of Nefertari's body which did not inspire love; the gods, who had placed on Ramses' shoulders the heaviest of burdens, had also given him the most sublime of wives.

'How do you feel this morning?'

'Better, much better. The blood is circulating again in my veins.'

'Would you like an excursion in the country?'

'I was dreaming of it.'

Ramses selected two very docile old horses, which he himself harnessed to his chariot. They made their way slowly along the paths on the west bank, beside the irrigation canals.

Nefertari's eyes drank in the vigour of the palm trees and the burgeoning green of the fields. She communed with the forces of the earth and succeeded, by her own willpower, in driving out the malady which had sapped her strength. When the Great Royal Wife alighted from the chariot and walked along beside the Nile, her hair blowing in the wind, Ramses knew that the goddess's stone had saved her and that she would live to see the two temples at Abu Simbel erected as monuments to their eternal love.

Lita smiled faintly at Dolora, who was removing the compress of honey, dried acacia resin and ground cucumber. The traces of burns had almost disappeared.

'I'm in pain,' she complained.

'Your wounds are healing.'

'Don't lie, Dolora. They'll never fade.'

'You're wrong. Our medicine is effective.'

'Ask Ofir to stop this experiment. I've had enough!'

'Your sacrifice will enable us to defeat Nefertari and Ramses; a little more courage and your ordeal will be at an end.'

Lita gave up trying to convince Ramses' sister, who was as fanatical as the Libyan magus. In spite of her apparent kindness, Dolora lived only for revenge. Her hatred predominated over all other emotions.

'I'll see it through,' the young medium promised.

'I was sure of it. Rest now before Ofir takes you to the laboratory. Nany will bring you something to eat.'

Nany, the only servant allowed to enter Lita's chamber, was her last resort. When she brought her a bowl containing a purée of figs and pieces of roast beef, the medium seized the girdle of her gown.

'Help me, Nany!'

'What do you want?'

'To get out of here, to escape!'

The servant pouted. 'It's dangerous.'

'Just unlock the street door.'

'I could lose my job.'

'Help me, I beg you!'

'How much will you pay me?'

Lita lied, 'My supporters have gold. I'll be generous.'

'Ofir is vindictive.'

'The followers of Aton will protect us.'

'I want a villa and a herd of milch cows.'

'You shall have them.'

Nany was greedy. She had extorted a good reward when she procured Nefertari's shawl for the magus, but what Lita was promising exceeded all her hopes.

'When do you want to leave?'

'At nightfall.'

'I'll try.'

'You must succeed! That's all you have to do to make your fortune, Nany.'

286

'It's really a huge risk. I want twenty lengths of best-quality cloth as well.'

'You have my word.'

Since morning Lita had been obsessed by a vision: a woman of sublime beauty, smiling, radiant, walking along beside the Nile, holding out her hand to a tall, athletic man. The medium knew that Ofir's evil spells had failed and that he was torturing her in vain.

Serramanna and his men explored the district behind the school of medicine and questioned the inhabitants without a break. The Sardinian showed them a drawing of Nany and threatened them with terrible penalties if they lied. The precaution was unnecessary, for just the sight of the giant provoked a stream of confessions; unfortunately, none was of any interest.

But the former pirate persisted and his gut instinct told him that his quarry was not far off. When a pedlar selling little round loaves was brought to him, Serramanna felt a twitch in the pit of his stomach, announcing a decisive moment.

He brandished the drawing. 'Do you know this girl?'

'I've seen her around. She's a servant. She hasn't been here long.'

'Which villa does she work in?'

'One of the big ones, near the old well.'

A hundred policemen surrounded the suspected houses. No one could escape from the net. The sorcerer guilty of attempting to murder the queen of Egypt would not elude Serramanna.

47

The sun was sinking on the horizon. Lita did not have much time to get away before the magus Ofir locked her in his laboratory. Why was Nany taking so much time?

The face of a beautiful woman, happy and radiant, continued to haunt the medium: the face of the Queen of Egypt. Lita owed her a debt, a debt she had to pay before she could regain her freedom.

The young woman moved noiselessly about in the silent house. Ofir was as usual consulting a book of magic spells. Dolora was tired and had gone to sleep.

Lita raised the lid of a wooden chest in which lay the last scrap of Nefertari's shawl. Another two or three sessions and it would be reduced to ashes. Lita tried to tear it, but it was too closely woven and she lacked the strength.

There was a noise in the kitchen. Lita hid the scrap of material in the sleeve of her gown; it immediately burned her arm.

'Is that you, Nany?'

'Are you ready?'

'I'll follow you . . . just a moment.'

'Hurry up.'

Lita held the remains of the shawl above the flame of an oil lamp. A splutter, followed by a curl of black smoke, marked the end of the evil spell intended to destroy the royal couple's supernatural defences.

'Oh, that's beautiful! What a beautiful sight!' Lita raised her arms to heaven, appealing to Aton, who would give her a new life.

'We must go,' insisted Nany, who had stolen all the blocks of copper she had been able to find in the house.

The two women ran to the back door, which opened on to an alleyway.

Nany collided with Ofir, who stood motionless, his arms crossed.

'Where are you going?'

Nany shrank back. Behind her stood Lita, terrified.

'Lita too? What's she doing with you?'

'She . . . she's ill,' replied Nany.

'Were you trying to escape?'

'She . . . Lita forced me.'

'What has she told you, Nany?'

'Nothing. Nothing at all!'

'You're lying, my girl.'

Ofir's fingers closed round the servant's neck. They squeezed so hard that she couldn't breathe and her protests were stifled in her throat. Nany tried in vain to free herself, to loosen the vice-like grip. She fell dead, strangled, her face distorted, at Ofir's feet. He kicked the corpse away,

'Lita, what has happened to you, my child?'

Near the oil lamp Ofir caught sight of the charred remains of a piece of cloth.

'Lita! What folly have you committed?' The magus seized a knife used for cutting up meat. 'You have dared to destroy Nefertari's shawl. You have dared ruin our work!'

The young woman tried to run. She bumped into the oil lamp and lost her balance. The magus pounced with the speed of a bird of prey, and grabbed her by the hair.

'You have betrayed me, Lita! I can no longer trust you. Tomorrow you will betray me again.'

'You are a monster!'

'A pity. You were an excellent medium.'

Lita fell to her knees and prayed, 'Aton creates life and wards off death, he—'

'I don't care a damn about your Aton, you little fool. Because of you, my plan has failed.'

With one swift stroke, he slit her throat.

Dolora burst into the room; her hair was dishevelled, her face crumpled. 'There are policemen in the alleyway! Oh, Lita! Lita!'

'She went out of her mind and attacked me with a knife,' explained Ofir. 'I was forced to defend myself and reluctantly had to kill her. Policemen, you say?'

'I heard them from the window of my room.'

'We must leave this house.'

Ofir dragged Dolora to a trapdoor hidden under a rug. It gave access to a passage which led to a warehouse. From now on, neither Lita nor Nany would give the game away.

'There's only one more villa,' a policeman told Serramanna. 'We knocked but there was no reply.'

'We must break down the door.'

'That's against the law.'

'It's a case of needs must.'

'We'd have to tell the owner and ask for his authorization.'

'I'm the authorization!'

'I need an indemnity; I don't want any trouble.'

Serramanna wasted a good hour legalizing the situation according to the requirements of the Memphis police. Finally, four sturdy men smashed the bolts and forced their way into the villa.

The Sardinian was the first to enter. He discovered the dead body of a young blonde woman, then that of the servant, Nany.

'It's a massacre,' murmured a policeman, visibly shaken.

'Two crimes committed in cold blood,' noted the Sardinian. 'Make a thorough search.'

Examination of the laboratory proved that this was indeed the sorcerer's hideout. Although he had arrived too late, one small find reassured Serramanna: the charred remains of some cloth, doubtless belonging to the queen's shawl.

Ramses and Nefertari entered a busy capital, which was less cheerful than usual. The feeling of military discipline was everywhere and the production of weapons and chariots was becoming the aim of the majority of the population. The city once devoted to the pleasures of life had become a throbbing, anxious war machine.

The royal couple immediately went to see Tuya, who was studying a report from the foundry.

'Have the Hittites officially begun hostilities?'

'No, my son, but I am certain that this silence hides something bad. Nefertari, are you cured?'

'My illness is now just a bad memory.'

'This episode has exhausted me. I no longer have the strength to govern this great country. Speak to the court and the army: they need your inspiration.'

Ramses had a long discussion with Ahmeni, then received Serramanna, who had returned from Memphis. What the Sardinian told him seemed to prove conclusively that there was no longer any supernatural threat to the royal couple's safety. However, the monarch asked Serramanna to pursue his inquiries and identify the real owner of the sinister villa. And who was the young blonde woman whose throat had been so savagely cut?

Pharaoh had other worries. On his desk was an accumulation of worried dispatches from Canaan and Amurru. The commanders of the Egyptian fortresses did not mention any serious incident, but they reported persistent rumours about the Hittite army's huge manoeuvres.

Alas, Ahsha had sent no report, not even a brief one, which might have helped clarify the situation. The outcome of the war would depend on where the battle with the Hittites took place. Without precise information, the king hesitated between reinforcing his lines of defence and adopting an offensive attitude which would lead to giving battle further to the north. In the latter case, he would have to take the initiative. But should he obey his instinct and take such a risk blindly?

The royal couple's presence inspired the army, from the generals to the lowliest soldiers, with confidence and energy. If he had defeated an invisible enemy, how could Ramses fail to triumph over Hittite barbarians? Seeing new weapons accumulate, the soldiers became aware of their potential and were less afraid of a head-on clash with the enemy. Ramses had himself tried out several war chariots in the presence of the elite of the chariot corps, and found them light, easy to handle and swift. Thanks to the skill of the carpenters, many technical details had been improved. Defences such as shields and breastplates also occupied the sovereign's attention, since they would save many lives.

The queen had reassured the court by resuming her many activities. Those who had already buried Nefertari were the first to congratulate her on her courage and assure her that her resistance to such a harsh ordeal was a guarantee of longevity.

This gossip left the Great Royal Wife indifferent. She concerned herself with the intensive production of new clothes for the soldiers, and settled a thousand and one details relating to the economic welfare of the country, based on Ahmeni's meticulous reports.

Shaanar greeted the king.

'You've put on weight,' observed Ramses.

'It's not for want of activity,' protested his brother.

292

'Anxiety doesn't suit me. These rumours of war, this army rabble everywhere . . . Is that what Egypt really is?'

'It won't be long before the Hittites attack us, Shaanar.'

'You are probably right, but my secretariat has no hard facts to support this fear. Do you still get friendly letters from Muwatallis?'

'Only to deceive us.'

'If we maintain the peace, thousands of lives will be saved.'

'Don't you think that is my dearest wish?'

'Surely moderation and prudence are the best counsellors.'

'Would you advocate sitting back and doing nothing, Shaanar?'

'Certainly not, but I fear a dangerous initiative on the part of some general greedy for fame.'

'Be reassured, brother, I have my army under control. There'll be no incident like that.'

'I am glad to hear you say so.'

'Are you satisfied with the services of Meba, your new deputy?'

'He is so pleased to be working in the secretariat again that he behaves like a docile, enthusiastic beginner. I'm not sorry to have brought him out of retirement. Sometimes you have to give an opportunity to a good professional. After all, generosity's the finest virtue, isn't it?'

48

Shaanar shut himself up in his office with Meba. His distinguished deputy had taken the trouble to bring some papyri with him, to give the impression that this was a normal working session.

'I've seen the king,' said Shaanar. 'He's undecided about what to do, because of the lack of reliable information.'

'Excellent,' noted Meba.

Shaanar could not admit to his accomplice that Ahsha's silence surprised him. Why was the young diplomat not reporting on what he'd found (this was essential for hastening Ramses' defeat). Something must have happened to him. Because of this worrying silence Shaanar, too, lacked any point of reference.

'Where do we stand, Meba?'

'Our spy network has been ordered to take no more action and to lie low. In other words, the hour approaches. Whatever Pharaoh decides to do, he no longer has any hope of winning.'

'What makes you so certain?'

'I am convinced that the might of the Hittites will be at its greatest. Every hour that passes brings you nearer to the supreme power. Shouldn't you take advantage of this period to develop your network of friends in the different secretariats?'

'That damned Ahmeni keeps an eye on everything.

Caution is essential.'

'Might you consider a . . . radical solution?'

'It's too soon, Meba. My brother's anger would be terrible.'

'Don't forget my advice: the weeks will pass quickly and you must be ready to reign, with the agreement of our Hittite friends.'

'I have waited so long for this moment . . . Don't worry, I shall be ready.'

Dolora had followed Ofir, in a state of total confusion. Lita's horrible death, the police, this precipitous flight . . . She was no longer capable of reasoning, no longer knew where to go. When Ofir had asked her to pretend to be his wife and to continue the struggle to restore the religion of Aton, the one and only god, she had accepted enthusiastically.

The couple had avoided the port of Memphis, which was under tight police control, and had purchased a donkey. Dressed as peasants, Ofir, who had shaved off his beard, and Dolora, without make-up, had started off towards the south. He knew they would be looked for to the north of Memphis and on the way to the border. Their only hope of eluding the river police and the police cordons set up on the roads was by doing the unexpected.

It might be advisable to seek asylum among the ardent followers of the heretic king Akhenaton, the majority of whom had gathered in Middle Egypt near his capital, the City of the Sun,* which had been abandoned. Ofir was not sorry to have acted a part which now was proving very useful. By making Dolora believe that his whole life was devoted to his love for the one and only god, Ofir retained an unquestioning ally and would enjoy a safe refuge among a circle of visionaries until the Hittites invaded Egypt.

*Akhetaton, meaning 'The Horizon of the Solar Disc'.

Fortunately, before slipping away, Ofir had received an important message whose contents he had passed on to Meba: the execution of Muwatallis's plan was going ahead. It only remained to await the final confrontation.

As soon as Ramses' death was announced, Shaanar would oust Nefertari and Tuya, and then mount the throne in order to receive the Hittites worthily. Shaanar did not know that Muwatallis was not in the habit of sharing power. Ramses' brother would be only a short-lived pharaoh, and the Two Lands would become the Hittites' granary.

Ofir was relaxed and enjoyed the serene beauty of the Egyptian countryside.

In view of his rank and position, Ahsha had not been thrown into one of the damp, dark dungeons of the lower town, where the average life expectancy was only a year, but shut in a stone prison in the upper town, reserved for special prisoners. The food was inferior and the bedding indifferent, but the diplomat made the best of it and kept up his physical condition by a series of daily exercises.

Since his arrest he had not been questioned at all. His imprisonment might well end in a brutal execution.

At last, his cell door opened.

'How do you feel?' asked Raia.

'Fine.'

'The gods were unkind to you, Ahsha. If it hadn't been for me you'd have got away.'

'I wasn't trying to escape.'

'You can't argue with facts.'

'Appearances can be deceptive.'

'You are indeed Ahsha, the childhood friend of Ramses! I've seen you in Memphis and Pi-Ramses, and I've sold rare vases to your family. The king entrusted you with a particularly audacious spying mission, and you've shown both courage and cunning.'

'You are wrong on one essential point. Ramses did indeed entrust me with this mission, but I serve another master. It is to him, not to the pharaoh, that I would have reported the results of my investigation.'

'Who do you mean?'

'Ramses' elder brother, Shaanar, Egypt's future pharaoh.'

Raia fingered his pointed beard, at the risk of disturbing the barber's perfect cut. So, Ahsha claimed to be the Hittites' ally . . . No! One crucial detail gave the lie to his claim.

'In that case, why were you disguised as a potter?'

The young diplomat smiled. 'As if you didn't know.'

'Enlighten me, just the same.'

'Muwatallis rules, it is true, but which faction does he rely on, and what is the true extent of his power? Are his son and his brother at each other's throat, or is the war of succession already settled?'

'Be quiet!'

'These are the vital questions to which I had to find answers. You see why I wanted to remain anonymous. By the way, what *are* the answers?'

Worried, Raia slammed out of the cell.

Ahsha had perhaps been wrong to provoke the Syrian; but by revealing his secret he hoped to save his skin.

Muwatallis left the palace; he was arrayed in his ceremonial robes and guarded by an escort which hid him from the sight of passers-by and protected him from any archer waiting in ambush on a rooftop. Thanks to the heralds' announcements, everyone knew that the ruler of Hatti was to go to the great temple in the lower town to implore the favour of the god of storms.

There was no more solemn way of declaring Hatti to be on a war footing and of mobilizing its strength for the final triumph.

In his cell, Ahsha heard the clamour that greeted the

emperor's passage. He, too, understood that an important decision had been taken.

All the Hittite divinities came under the authority of the god of storms. The priests washed the statues to avoid the wrath of heaven. No Hittite was to express any further doubts or criticisms: the time for action had come.

The priestess Putuhepa uttered the words which transformed the goddesses of fertility into formidable warrior women. Then she hammered into a pig ten iron nails, seven bronze ones and seven of copper, so that the future should obey the emperor's wishes.

During the chanting of the rites, Muwatallis's glance fell on his son, Uri-Teshup, who, in helmet and breastplate, was wild with joy at the thought of waging war and massacring the enemy. Hattusilis remained calm and inscrutable.

These two had gradually eliminated their rivals and formed, with Putuhepa, the small circle nearest to the emperor. But Uri-Teshup detested Hattusilis and Putuhepa; they fully returned his feelings.

The war against Egypt would allow Muwatallis to resolve internal dissension, expand his territory and strengthen his rule over the Orient and Asia, before attacking other lands. Did he not enjoy celestial favour?

When the ceremony was over, the emperor invited generals and senior officers to a banquet. It began with an offering of four portions of food: the palace cup-bearer placed the first on the royal throne, the second near the hearth, the third on the main table and the fourth in the doorway of the dining hall. Then the guests guzzled and drank themselves stupid, as if this were their last meal.

When Muwatallis rose, laughter and conversation ceased. Even the most drunken recovered a semblance of dignity.

One event and one alone could still delay the war.

The emperor and his retinue left the capital by one of the gates of the upper town, the Gate of the Sphinx, and made their way to a rocky mound.

Muwatallis, Uri-Teshup and Putuhepa climbed to the top. They stood motionless there, staring at the clouds.

'There they are!' exclaimed Uri-Teshup.

He bent his bow and aimed at one of the vultures that were circling the capital. The arrow found its mark in the bird's throat. An officer brought the carcass back to the commander-in-chief, who cut open its belly and with both hands drew out its steaming entrails.

'Read the augury,' Muwatallis said to Putuhepa, 'and tell us if fate is favourable to us.'

In spite of the affront to her nostrils, the priestess carried out her task by examining the vulture's entrails.

'Favourable.'

Uri-Teshup's war cry made the mountains of Anatolia tremble.

49

The meeting of Pharaoh's grand council, which included many important members of the court, threatened to be stormy. The ministers scowled, the senior officials deplored the absence of clear directives, the augurs predicted a military disaster. The rampart formed by Ahmeni and his scribes was not enough to protect Ramses, from whom everyone expected explanations.

When the pharaoh took his seat on his throne, the audience chamber was full. It was the duty of the most senior dignitary present to put the questions he had collected, so that there would be no confusion and the age-old dignity of the pharaonic institution would be preserved. Barbarians argued, shouted and interrupted each other; at the Egyptian court, on the other hand, people spoke in turn and listened to each other.

'Majesty,' declared the dignitary, 'the country is worried and wishes to know if war with the Hittites is imminent.'

'It is,' replied Ramses.

A long silence followed this brief, terrifying revelation.

'Is it inevitable?'

'Inevitable.'

'Is our army ready to fight?'

'The artisans have worked assiduously and are continuing their efforts. A few more months would have been welcome, but we do not have that much time.'

'Why, Majesty?'

'Because our army must set out for the north as soon as possible. The fighting will take place far from Egypt. Since our Canaanite and Amurru protectorates have been pacified, we shall pass through them safely.'

'Who are you appointing commander-in-chief?'

'I shall assume the command myself. During my absence the Great Royal Wife will rule over the Two Lands, assisted by the Queen Mother.'

The dignitary abandoned the other questions; they were no longer relevant.

Homer was smoking sage leaves stuffed into the snail shell which served him as a pipe. Seated under his lemon tree, he was basking in the spring sunshine, whose warmth relieved his rheumatism. His long white beard, scented by the barber, added dignity to his craggy, wrinkled face. Hector, the black and white cat, sat purring on his knees.

'I hoped to see you before you left, Majesty. It is the great war, isn't it?'

'The survival of Egypt is at stake, Homer.'

'This is what I have written: "Thanks to man's ministrations, a magnificent olive tree can be found, even in an isolated place, growing full of sap, watered by abundant waters and swaying in the wind, a tree covered in white blossom. But suddenly there blows a tornado, which uproots it and fells it to the ground."'

'And what if the tree stands firm in the tempest?'

Homer offered the king a cup of red wine flavoured with aniseed and coriander, and himself quaffed a long draught. 'I shall compose your epic, Ramses.'

'Will your writing leave you any leisure?'

'I am dedicated to singing of war and voyaging, and I love heroes. As a conquerer you will become immortal.'

'And if I am defeated?'

'Can you imagine the Hittites invading my garden, cutting down my lemon tree, smashing my writing desk, frightening Hector? The gods would not tolerate such a disaster. Where will you wage the decisive battle?'

'It's a military secret, but I can share it with you. It will be at Kadesh.'

'The battle of Kadesh . . . It's a good title. Many minor works will disappear, believe me, but that one will live in the memory of mankind. I shall put all my art into it. One detail, Majesty: I should like a happy ending.'

'I'll try not to disappoint you.'

Ahmeni was distraught. He had a thousand questions to put to Ramses, a hundred dossiers to show him, ten cases of conscience to submit to him, and Pharaoh alone could make the decisions. He was pale, short of breath, his hands trembled and he seemed at the end of his tether.

'You should rest,' recommended the king.

'But you are going to leave – and for how long? I risk making mistakes and weakening the kingdom.'

'I trust you, Ahmeni, and the queen will help you to make the right decisions.'

'Tell me the truth, Majesty: do you stand any chance, even the slightest chance, of defeating the Hittites?'

'Would I be leading my men into battle if I were beaten before we set out?'

'These barbarians are said to be invincible.'

'When you know who your enemy is, it is possible to overcome him. Take care of our country, Ahmeni.'

Shaanar was dining off grilled lamb chops, seasoned with parsley and celery; judging the flavour of the meat a little insipid, he sprinkled some spices on it. The red wine, although excellent, seemed mediocre to him. He summoned his cup-bearer but it was an unexpected guest who entered his dining hall.

'Ramses! Do you wish to share my meal?'

'Frankly, no.'

His curtness took Shaanar's appetite away and he thought it preferable to leave the table.

'We can adjourn to the arbour, if you like.'

'As you wish.'

Shaanar sat down on a garden chair, suffering from a slight attack of indigestion. Ramses remained standing, looking at the Nile.

'Your Majesty seems angry . . . The impending war?'

'I have other reasons for my displeasure.'

'Do they concern me?'

'Indeed, Shaanar.'

'Have you any reason to complain of my work at the secretariat?'

'You've always hated me, haven't you?'

'Ramses! There have been reasons for discord between us, but that time is over.'

'Do you think so?'

'You can be certain of it!'

'Your one aim, Shaanar, is to seize power, even at the cost of the basest treachery.'

Shaanar felt as if he had been punched in the stomach. 'Who has slandered me?'

'I don't listen to gossip. My opinion is based on facts.'

'Impossible!'

'In a house in Memphis Serramanna discovered the bodies of two women and the laboratory of a sorcerer who had tried to cast a spell on the queen.'

'Why should I be implicated in these terrible tragedies?'

'Because that house belongs to you, although you took the precaution of putting it in our sister's name. The officials at the registry are absolutely sure.'

'I own so many houses, especially in Memphis, that I don't even know how many exactly! How should I know what goes on in them?'

'Isn't one of your friends a Syrian merchant called Raia?'

'Not a friend, a supplier of exotic vases.'

'In reality he's a spy in the pay of the Hittites.'

'That . . . that's terrible! But how could I have known that? He sees hundreds of important people.'

'Your defence is clever, but I know that your overweening ambition has led you to betray your country and collaborate with our enemies. The Hittites needed accomplices in Egypt, and their main ally was you, my own brother.'

'What mad ideas have got into your head, Ramses? Only the vilest creature in the world could do such a thing.'

'That vilest of creatures is you, Shaanar.'

'You delight in insulting me without reason.'

'You made one fatal mistake: to think that anyone and everyone can be corrupted. You did not hesitate to go for those close to me and my childhood friends, but you didn't know that friendship can be as strong as granite. That is why you fell into the trap I set for you.'

Shaanar's face fell.

'Ahsha did not betray me, Shaanar, and he has never worked for you.'

Shaanar gripped the arms of his chair.

'My friend Ahsha has kept me informed of your plans and intrigues,' Ramses went on. 'You are evil through and through, Shaanar, and you will never change.'

'I . . . I demand a trial!'

'You shall have one, and you will be sentenced to death for high treason. As we are now at war, you will be incarcerated in the great Memphis prison, then in the penal colony at Kharga, while awaiting trial. According to the law, Pharaoh must suppress internal enemies before leaving for the front.'

Shaanar snarled, 'You don't dare kill me because I'm your

304

brother . . . The Hittites will defeat you! When you are dead, I shall be the one they put in power!'

'It is salutary for a king to have encountered evil and recognized its face! Thanks to you, Shaanar, I shall be a better warrior.'

50

The Hittite woman had told Ramses everything that had happened while she was with Ahsha and about how she had travelled to Egypt where, thanks to the diplomat's message, she had been well received and quickly taken to the pharaoh.

Ramses had fulfilled Ahsha's promise, giving the woman a house in Pi-Ramses and an income for life which would allow her to buy food and clothing and pay for a serving-maid. She was overcome with gratitude and would have liked to let the monarch know of Ahsha's fate, but she didn't know what had become of him.

Ramses had to face the facts: his friend had been arrested and probably executed. True, Ahsha could have used his final stratagem, letting it be believed that he was working for Shaanar, and so for the Hittites. But had he been given time to say anything and be convincing?

Whatever his fate, Ahsha had carried out his mission to the best of his ability. His brief message consisted of only three words, but they decided Ramses to go to war:

Kadesh. Quickly. Danger.

That was all Ahsha had written, for fear of his message being intercepted, and he had not confided in the woman, for fear of being betrayed. But those three words said enough.

When Meba was summoned to the great council, he rushed into his washroom and vomited. He had recourse to the

306

strongest perfumes, made from attar of roses, to mask his bad breath. Since Shaanar's arrest, which had left the court at a loss, the deputy minister for foreign affairs expected to be thrown into prison at any minute. Flight would be an admission of his complicity with Shaanar, and Meba was no longer able to warn Ofir, who had fled.

Meba tried to think clearly as he made his way to the palace. What if Ramses did not suspect him? He was not regarded as a friend of Shaanar, who had taken his place as minister, had long kept him out of things and had recalled him with the sole and obvious intention of humiliating him. That was the court's opinion and it might also be Ramses'. Would he see Meba as a victim to whom fate was doing justice by punishing his persecutor, Shaanar?

Meba had to behave discreetly and not ask for the post that had become vacant. The correct attitude was to maintain his dignity as a senior official, let himself be forgotten and wait for the moment when fate would pronounce in favour of Ramses or the Hittites. In the latter case he would be able to profit from the situation.

All the generals and some senior officers attended the grand council. Pharaoh and the Great Royal Wife took their places on their thrones, side by side.

'On the grounds of information that has reached us,' announced Ramses, 'Egypt declares war on Hatti. Our troops will set out for the north tomorrow morning, under my command. We have just sent a dispatch to Emperor Muwatallis, announcing the official start of hostilities. We pray that we may vanquish the forces of darkness and maintain the Rule of Ma'at in our land.'

The shortest session of the grand council since Ramses' reign had begun was not followed by any discussion. Courtiers and soldiers left in silence.

Serramanna passed Meba without seeing him. Back in his

office, the latter drank a full jar of white oasis wine.

Ramses embraced his children, Kha and Meritamon, who
rushed off on a silly game, accompanied by Wideawake, the
king's dog. Under the guidance of Nedjem, the former
gardener promoted to minister for agriculture, they were
perfecting their knowledge of hieroglyphs and they often
played the game of Snakes, which consisted of trying to avoid
the dark squares to reach the land of the light. For the little
boy and girl this day would be like any other; they cheerfully
followed gentle Nedjem, who would be obliged to read them
a story.

Ramses and Nefertari sat on the grass, enjoying a moment
of intimacy, gazing at the acacias, tamarisks, willows,
pomegranates and jujube trees which overhung beds of cornflowers, irises and larkspur. The spring sunshine revived the
forces hidden in the earth. The king was clad only in a kilt, the
queen in a short gown whose shoulder straps hung just below
her bare breasts.

'How can you bear your brother's treachery?'

'It's loyalty from him which would have surprised me. I
hope that, thanks to Ahsha's courage and cleverness, I have
severed the head of the monster, but there still remain some
dark areas. We have not found the sorcerer, and Shaanar
probably had other allies, Egyptians or foreigners. Be very
careful, Nefertari.'

'I shall think of the kingdom, not of myself, while you are
risking your own life to protect it.'

'I have ordered Serramanna to stay in Pi-Ramses and to
ensure your protection. His only thought was of massacring
Hittites, and he is still fuming.'

Nefertari rested her head on Ramses' shoulder, her
loosened hair lightly brushing the king's arms. 'Hardly have
I emerged from the abyss when you are exposed to danger.
Shall we ever know a few years of peace and happiness, as

your father and mother did?'

'Perhaps, providing we defeat the Hittites. If we didn't wage this war, Egypt would be condemned to destruction. If I don't return, Nefertari, you must become Pharaoh, you must rule and resist adversity. Muwatallis has enslaved all the peoples he has conquered. May the inhabitants of the Two Lands never be reduced to that!'

'Whatever our fate, we shall have known happiness, the happiness that is created at every moment, ephemeral as perfume or the murmur of the wind in the leaves of a tree. I am to you, Ramses, like a wave of the sea, like a flower opening out in a sunny field.'

The left strap of Nefertari's gown slipped down from her shoulder. The king's lips kissed the warm, scented skin, while he slowly undressed the queen and she abandoned herself to him.

A skein of wild geese flew over the palace in Pi-Ramses, while Ramses and Nefertari came together in their passionate desire.

A little before dawn Ramses dressed in the place of purity in the Temple of Amon and made sacred the liquid and solid food which would be used during the celebration of the rituals. Then the pharaoh left the place of purity and watched the birth of the sun, his protector, whom the goddess of heaven had swallowed at nightfall for him to be reborn in the morning, after a hard combat with the forces of darkness. It was this same combat that the son of Seti was preparing to wage against the Hittite hordes. The reborn day-star appeared between the two hills on the horizon, on which, according to ancient legend, grew two huge turquoise trees, which drew aside to let the light pass.

Ramses repeated the prayer that each of his predecessors had repeated before him: 'Greetings to thee, light which is born from the primeval waters, light which appears on the back of the earth, which illuminates the Two Lands and its beauty. Thou art the living soul which comes to life by itself, and no one knows thy origin. Thou flyest across the heavens in the shape of a falcon with many-coloured plumage and thou drivest away evil. The ship of night is on thy right, the ship of day on thy left; the crew of the ship of light rejoices.'

Perhaps Ramses would never again hand on this message if death awaited him at Kadesh; but another voice would succeed him and the words of light would not be lost.

In the four barracks of the capital, the final checks were being carried out before the departure. Thanks to the monarch's continuous presence during the preceding weeks, morale was good, despite the men's foreknowledge that the battle would be savage. The quality and quantity of weapons reassured the most anxious.

While the troops were leaving the barracks to march to the main gate of the capital, Ramses rode in his chariot from the Temple of Amon to that of Set, built in the oldest part of the city where, many centuries before, the Hyskos invaders had settled. In order to exorcise misfortune, the pharaohs had kept a sanctuary there, dedicated to the most powerful force in the universe. Seti, the man of the god Set, had succeeded in mastering this force and had handed on the secret to his son.

Today Ramses was coming not to challenge the god but to perform a magic act, which consisted of identifying Set with the Syrian and Hittite god of storms, in order to appropriate the power of the thunder and to strike his enemies with it.

The confrontation was rapid and intense.

Ramses stared into the red eyes of the statue, which represented a man standing, with a dog-like head with long snout and huge ears.

'Set, thou who art my strength, link me with thy *ka* and give me thy power.'

The light shining in the red eyes grew dim. Set had agreed to the pharaoh's request.

310

*

The priest of Midian and his daughter were worried. Moses, who led the tribe's largest flock of sheep out to pasture, should have been back two days ago. The old man's son-in-law was solitary and unsociable, wont to meditate in the mountains. He sometimes mentioned strange visions but refused to answer his wife's questions and scarcely gave a thought to playing with his son, whom he had named 'Exiled'.

The priest knew that Moses thought endlessly about Egypt, that wondrous land where he had been born, and where he had held important posts.

'Will he go back there?' his daughter asked him anxiously.

'I don't think so.'

'Why did he take refuge in Midian?'

'I don't know and I prefer to remain in ignorance. Moses is an honest, hardworking man. What more could we want?'

'My husband seems so distant, so secretive . . . '

'Accept him as he is, daughter, and you will be happy.'

'If he comes back, father.'

'Have confidence and look after the child.'

Moses returned, but his expression had changed. His face was marked with deep lines and his hair had turned white.

His wife threw her arms round his neck. 'What has happened, Moses?'

'I saw a flame leap out of a bush. The bush burned with fire but was not consumed. God called to me from the midst of the bush. He revealed His name to me and entrusted me with a mission. God is He who Is, and I must obey Him.'

'Obey him . . . Does that mean you're going to leave me and my child?'

'I shall carry out my mission, for no one must disobey God. His commandments are beyond our understanding. Who are we, if not the instruments to serve His will?'

'What is your mission, Moses?'

'You will know when the time comes.'

The Hebrew retreated alone to his tent, and there relived his encounter with the angel of Yahveh, the God of Abraham, Isaac and Jacob.

Shouts disturbed his meditation. A man on horseback burst into the camp and, his words tumbling over each other, said that an immense army, commanded by Pharaoh in person, was leaving for the north, in order to confront the Hittites.

Moses thought of Ramses, his childhood friend, of the tremendous energy which drove him. At that moment he wished for his victory.

51

The Hittite army deployed before the ramparts of the capital. The priestess Putuhepa looked on from the top of a watchtower as the chariots lined up, with the bowmen behind them, then the footsoldiers. Their perfect discipline embodied the invincible might of the empire, thanks to which the Egypt of Ramses would soon be a subject province.

As expected, Muwatallis had replied to Ramses' declaration of war with an identical letter, drawn up in formal terms.

Putuhepa would have preferred to keep her husband at her side, but the emperor had insisted on Hattusilis, his principal adviser, being present on the battlefield.

The commander-in-chief, Uri-Teshup, marched towards his soldiers, holding a torch. He lit a huge fire and had a chariot brought near, a brand-new chariot which had never been used. He smashed it to pieces with a sledgehammer and burned the fragments.

'So shall be destroyed any soldier who retreats before the enemy; so shall the god of storms consume him with fire!'

By this magic ceremony, Uri-Teshup gave his troops a cohesion which no fighting, however fierce, could weaken.

The prince held out his sword to Muwatallis as a sign of his submission.

The imperial chariot set off towards Kadesh, which would

be the burial ground of the Egyptian army.

The royal chariot, drawn by Ramses' two superb horses Victory-in-Thebes and The-Goddess-Mut-is-Content, headed an army consisting of four divisions, each of five thousand men, placed under the protection of the gods Amon, Ra, Ptah and Set respectively. The general commanding each division had under him company leaders, captains and standard-bearers. Then there were the five hundred chariots, divided into five regiments. The soldiers' accoutrements consisted of tunics, shirts, breastplates, leather greaves, helmets and small double-bladed axes, not to mention the countless weapons that the scribes of the supply caravan would distribute when the time came.

Ramses' armour-bearer, Menna, was an experienced soldier who knew Syria well. He was not particularly happy about the presence of Invincible, the enormous Nubian lion, who marched alongside the chariot, his mane blowing in the wind.

In spite of Ramses' remonstrances, Setau and Lotus had insisted on remaining in charge of the medical unit, even in the heat of battle. As they did not know the area around Kadesh, they hoped to discover a few rare snakes.

The Egyptian army left the capital at the end of the month of April in the fifth year of Ramses' reign. The weather was clement, and no incident delayed their progress. After crossing the border at Sileh, Ramses followed the coast road, which was lined with water-holes guarded by small forts; then the army marched through Canaan and Amurru.

At the place called the Abode of the Valley of Cedars, near Byblos, the king ordered the three thousand men who had been stationed there, in order to cordon off access to the protectorates, to proceed north as far as the heights of Kadesh, and to approach the site of the battle from the north-east. The generals had been opposed to this strategy, arguing that this auxiliary army would meet strong resistance and would be blocked at the coast. But Ramses had dismissed their arguments.

The route the king had chosen to reach Kadesh crossed the plain of Bekaa, a depression between the mountain ranges of Canaan and Eastern Syria, a disquieting, savage landscape which depressed the Egyptian soldiers. Some of them knew that the muddy water-courses teemed with crocodiles and that the dense forests covering the mountains were the haunt of bears, hyenas, wild cats and wolves.

The foliage of the cypresses, firs and cedars was so dense that when the soldiers were crossing a wooded area they could no longer see the sun and became terrified. A general intervened to put a stop to the incipient panic and convince the men that they were not going to die of suffocation.

The Amon regiment marched in the van, followed by those of Ra and Ptah. The Set division was in the rear. A month after setting out, the Egyptian troops approached the colossal Kadesh fortress, built on the left bank of the River Orontes, at the exit from the Bekaa valley. This stronghold marked the border of the Hittite Empire and served as a base for the raiding parties in charge of destabilizing the provinces of Canaan and Amurru.

Towards the end of May rain set in and the soldiers complained of the wet. But, as food proved abundant and of good quality, their full stomachs caused them to forget this inconvenience.

A few miles from Kadesh, just before the dense, dark Labni forest, Ramses halted his army. This seemed a likely place for an ambush: the chariots would be immobilized and the infantry would be unable to deploy. Keeping Ahsha's message 'Kadesh. Quickly. Danger' continually in mind, the king avoided acting precipitously.

Allowing only a basic camp to be set up, protected by a first line of chariots and archers, he summoned his war council. Among those present was Setau, who was very popular with the soldiers, whom he cured of their thouand and one minor ailments, with Lotus's assistance.

Ramses called his equerry, Menna. 'Unroll the big map.'

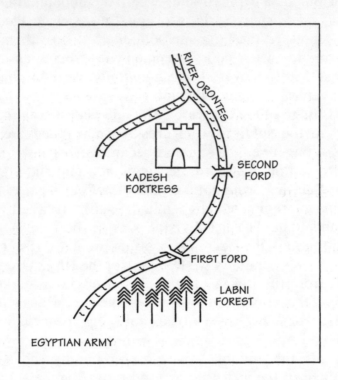

'We are here,' said Ramses, pointing, 'on the edge of the Labni forest, on the east bank of the Orontes. At the exit from the wood there is a first ford which will allow us to cross the river, out of reach of the Hittite archers posted on the towers of the fortress. The second ford, more to the north, is much too close. We shall pass wide of the stronghold and set up our camp to the north-east, so as to take it from the rear. Are you satisfied with this plan?'

The generals nodded in agreement.

The king's eyes flashed. 'Are you all stupid?'

'This forest is certainly something of an embarrassment,' suggested the general commanding the Amon division.

'Well observed! And do you think the Hittites will let us calmly cross that ford and pitch camp? This plan is the one you, my generals, submitted to me, and it leaves out one small detail: the presence of the Hittite army.'

'They'll all be in the fortress, sheltered behind its walls,' objected the commander of the Ptah division.

'If Muwatallis were a second-rate warrior, that is indeed what he would do. But he is the Emperor of Hatti! He will attack us simultaneously in the forest, at the ford and in front of the fort; he will isolate our divisions and prevent us from retaliating. The Hittites will not make the mistake of remaining on the defensive. Do you really think they'll keep their attack troops immobilized in a fortress? You have to admit that such a decision would be absurd!'

'The choice of the terrain is critical,' argued the commander of the Set division. 'Fighting in a forest is not our speciality – far from it. A flat, open place would suit us better. So let us cross the Orontes before we get to the Labni forest.'

'Impossible, there is no ford.'

'Well then, let's burn this cursed forest!'

'For one thing, the winds might turn against us and, for another, the charred and fallen tree trunks could hinder our advance.'

'It would have been better to follow the coast road,' observed the general of the Ra division, not hesitating to contradict himself, 'and attack Kadesh from the north.'

'Rubbish,' declared his colleague from the Ptah division. 'Saving the respect owing to Your Majesty, the auxiliary army has no chance of joining up with us. The Hittites are suspicious: they'll have posted many soldiers at the exit from the coast road so as to repel any possible attack. The best strategy is the one we have adopted.'

'That's true,' commented the commander of the Set

division ironically, 'but we can't advance! I suggest we send a thousand footsoldiers into the forest and see how the Hittites react.'

'What would we learn from a thousand dead?' asked Ramses.

The commander of the Ra division was crushed. 'Must we retreat before we have fought? We'd be the laughing-stock of the Hittites and Your Majesty's authority would be seriously damaged.'

'What would become of my reputation if I let my army be wiped out? It is Egypt, not my own fame, that must be saved.'

'What do you decide, Majesty?'

Setau broke his silence. 'In my capacity as a snake-charmer, I like to act alone or with my one companion. If I walked about accompanied by a hundred soldiers, I wouldn't see a single cobra.'

'Get to the point,' insisted the commander of the Set division.

'Let us send a small group into this forest,' suggested Setau. 'If they succeed in getting through it, let them observe the strength of the enemy. We shall then know how to attack.'

Setau himself headed a party of a dozen young, well-trained soldiers, armed with slings, bows and daggers. They all were adept at moving silently.

As soon as they entered the forest of Labni, where semi-darkness still reigned at midday, they scattered, frequently looking up to the tops of the trees to try to spot archers who might be lying flat on their stomachs on the high branches.

With all his senses on the alert, Setau could perceive no hostile presence. He was the first to emerge from the forest and squatted down in the tall grass, soon to be joined by his companions, who were astonished at having walked through peacefully.

They could see the first ford. There wasn't a single Hittite soldier in the area. In the distance was the fortress of Kadesh, standing on its rise. In front of the stronghold, an empty plain. The Egyptians gazed at it, stunned.

Unable to believe their eyes, they remained for more than an hour without moving. Eventually they had to accept the fact: the Hittite army was not at Kadesh.

'Over there,' Setau said, pointing to three oak trees near the ford. 'Something moved.'

The members of the party rapidly surrounded the spot. One of them remained behind; if his comrades fell into a trap, he would go back and warn Ramses. But the operation proceeded without a hitch and the Egyptians took two prisoners who, judging by their attire, were chiefs of Bedouin tribes.

52

The two prisoners were terrified. One was tall and thin, the other of average height, bald and bearded. Neither of them dared lift their eyes to look on the pharaoh of Egypt.

'What are your names?'

'I am Amos,' replied the bald man. 'My friend's name is Baduch.'

'Who are you?'

'Chiefs of Bedouin tribes.'

'Why are you here in this country?'

'We were supposed to meet a Hittite dignitary at Kadesh.'

'For what reason?'

Amos bit his lip. Baduch lowered his head still more.

'Answer!' demanded Ramses.

'The Hittites were suggesting we form an alliance against Egypt, to attack caravans in Sinai.'

'And you agreed.'

'No! We wanted to discuss it further.'

'What was the result of your discussions?'

'There weren't any discussions, Majesty, because there's not a single Hittite dignitary at Kadesh. There are now only Syrians in the fortress.'

'Where is the Hittite army?'

'They left Kadesh more than two weeks ago. According to the commander of the fortress, the army is deployed before the city of Aleppo, more than three days' march from here, so as to be able to manoeuvre with their hundreds of new chariots. My comrade and I were unwilling to undertake such a journey.'

'Weren't the Hittites expecting us here, at Kadesh?'

'Yes, Majesty. But some nomads, like us, let them know of the enormous number of your troops. They weren't expecting you to have such a formidable force and prefer to meet you on more favourable ground.'

'So you and other Bedouin warned them of our arrival!'

'We implore your pardon, Majesty! Like many others, I believed in the Hittites' superiority. And you know these barbarians leave us no choice: either we obey them or they massacre us.'

'How many men are there in the fortress?'

'At least a thousand Syrians, all convinced that Kadesh is impregnable.'

The council of war met again. In the generals' eyes Setau had become a respectable person, worthy of a decoration.

'The Hittite army has retreated,' the commander of the Ra division declared proudly. 'Is that not a victory, Majesty?'

'A very flimsy one. The question is: shall we lay siege to Kadesh?'

Opinions were divided, but the majority were for a rapid advance on Aleppo.

'If the Hittites have abandoned the idea of meeting us here, it is the better to draw us on to their terrain,' suggested Setau. 'Would it not be wise to seize this stronghold and use it as our rear base, instead of launching all our divisions into battle and so playing the enemy's game?'

'We risk wasting precious time,' objected the commander of the Ra division.

'I disagree. Since the Hittite army is not defending Kadesh, we shall be able to seize it rapidly. Perhaps we shall even manage to persuade the Syrians to surrender in exchange for their lives.'

'We shall besiege Kadesh and take it,' decided Ramses. 'From now on, this land will be under Pharaoh's authority.'

The king led the Amon division through the forest and across the first ford, then on to the plain, where they halted to the north-west of the imposing fortress. From its crenellated walls and five towers, the Syrians watched the Ra division take up its position facing the stronghold. The Ptah division camped near the ford, while the Set division remained on the edge of the forest. The next day, after resting for a night and a morning, the Egyptian troops would join forces, ready to surround Kadesh and launch their first assault.

The engineers promptly set up Pharaoh's camp. They first formed a rectangle with their tall shields and then pitched the sovereign's huge tent, which comprised a sleeping area, an office and an audience chamber. A number of other more modest tents were reserved for the officers. The private soldiers would sleep in the open air or, in the event of rain, under canvas shelters. At the entrance to the camp a wooden gate, flanked by two statues of lions, gave access to a central path leading to a shrine where the king would worship the god Amon.

As soon as the commanding generals gave their divisions permission to lay down their weapons, the men all busied themselves with the various tasks assigned to them according to the units to which they belonged. Horses, donkeys and oxen were tended, clothes washed, wheels damaged on rough tracks were repaired, daggers and spears sharpened, rations distributed and a meal prepared. The aroma of the dishes made them forget Kadesh, the Hittites and the war, and they began to joke, tell stories and gamble, wagering their pay. The hot-heads organized a bare-hands wrestling contest.

Ramses himself fed his horses and his lion, whose appetite

was as sound as ever. The camp fell asleep, the stars took possession of the sky, the king stared at the enormous fastness which his father had thought it better not to take. For him to seize it would be a serious blow to the Hittite Empire; by installing an elite garrison there, Ramses would protect his country from invasion.

Ramses lay down on his bed, which had feet shaped like a lion's paws, and rested his head on a cushion embroidered with papyrus and lotus flowers. The refinement of this decoration made him smile: how distant were the sweet and pleasant Two Lands!

When the king closed his eyes, Nefertari's sublime countenance appeared before him.

'On your feet, Shaanar!'

'Do you know who you are talking to, jailer?'

'To a traitor who deserves to die.'

'To the elder brother of the king!'

'You are nothing any more; your name will vanish for ever. Get up, or you'll feel the sting of my whip.'

'You have no right to ill-treat a prisoner.'

'A prisoner, no. But you . . . !'

Shaanar took the threat seriously and got to his feet.

In the big Memphis prison he had suffered no ill treatment. Unlike the other prisoners, who were condemned to hard labour in the fields or repairing dykes, the king's brother had been kept locked up in a cell and fed twice a day.

The jailer pushed him into a corridor. Shaanar thought that he would be riding in a wagon to the oases, but surly guards propelled him into an office where he found the man he hated most after Ramses and Ahsha: Ahmeni, the faithful scribe, the utterly incorruptible.

'You have chosen the wrong path, Ahmeni, that of the defeated; your triumph will be short-lived.'

'Will your heart ever be free of spite?'

'Not until I've plunged a dagger into yours! The Hittites will defeat Ramses and free me.'

'Your imprisonment has made you lose your reason, but perhaps not your memory.'

Shaanar scowled. 'What do you want from me, Ahmeni?'

'You must have had accomplices.'

'Accomplices? Yes, I have, and many of them! The entire court is my accomplice! When I mount the throne, everyone will prostrate themselves at my feet and I shall punish my enemies.'

'Give me the names of your accomplices, Shaanar.'

'You are curious, little scribe, too curious. Don't you think I was strong enough to act alone?'

'You were used, Shaanar, and your friends have abandoned you.'

'You're wrong, Ahmeni. Ramses is living his last days.'

'If you talk, Shaanar, the conditions of your imprisonment will be eased.'

'I shan't remain a prisoner for long. In your place, little scribe, I should be making a run for it! My vengeance will spare no one, especially not you.'

'One last time, Shaanar, will you reveal the names of your accomplices?'

'May all the fiends of hell claw your face and tear out your entrails!'

'Hard labour will loosen your tongue.'

'You will crawl at my feet, Ahmeni.'

'Take him away.'

The guards pushed Shaanar into a wagon, drawn by two oxen. A policeman took the reins. Four colleagues on horseback would accompany him to the penal colony.

Shaanar was seated on a rough-hewn wooden floor and felt every jolt. But he was indifferent to the pain and discomfort. The thought of having been so close to supreme power and of having fallen so low kept alive in him an insatiable desire for revenge.

Shaanar dozed until the middle of their journey, dreaming of triumphant morrows.

Grains of sand whipped his face. He knelt and looked out in astonishment. A huge ochre cloud hid the sky and filled the desert. A sandstorm was developing with incredible speed.

Two of the horses were maddened and threw their riders; while their comrades tried to help them, Shaanar knocked out the driver of the wagon, threw him out on to the path, took his place and drove headlong straight for the whirlwind.

53

The morning was misty and it was some time before the Kadesh fortress loomed out of the fog. Its formidable mass continued to defy the Egyptian army; it seemed impregnable, protected as it was both by the River Orontes and by wooded hills. From the height where he and the Amon division had taken up their position, Ramses could see the Ra division in the plain which extended in front of the stronghold, and the Ptah division between the forest of Labni and the first ford. Soon they would cross it, followed by the Set division. Then the four divisions would launch a victorious assault on the fortress.

The soldiers checked their weapons: daggers, spears, swords, short sabres, clubs, battle-axes and bows which they were burning to use. As the combat drew nearer, the horses were becoming restive. On orders from the scribes of the supply caravan, the camp was cleaned up and the cooking utensils thoroughly washed. The officers passed the troops in review, and sent to the barber those who were unshaven. Slovenly attire was not tolerated and the culprits were given several days' punishment duties.

A little before noon, under a hot sun which had finally emerged, Ramses had the order given by visual signal for the Ptah division to move. They set out and began to cross the ford. A messenger warned the Set division, which soon began to make its way through the Labni forest.

Suddenly, there was a rumble of thunder. Ramses looked up at the sky, but there wasn't a cloud in sight.

Roars rose up from the plain. The incredulous pharaoh then discovered the true cause of the terrifying din which filled the area round Kadesh.

A tide of Hittite chariots had just crossed the second ford, near the fortress, and were bearing down on the flank of the Ra division. Another swift, gigantic wave was attacking the Ptah division. Behind the chariots ran thousands of foot-soldiers, covering the hills and the valley, like a cloud of locusts.

This huge army had been hiding in the forest, to the east and west of Kadesh, and were bearing down on the Egyptian troops just when they were most vulnerable.

Ramses was stunned by the number of the enemy. When Muwatallis himself appeared, he understood.

The Emperor of Hatti stood in his chariot, surrounded by the princes of Syria, Mitanni, Aleppo, Ugarit, Karkemish, Arzawa and the chiefs of several small principalities which Hattusilis, on the emperor's orders, had persuaded to join with the Hittites to crush the Egyptian army. By distributing vast quantities of gold and silver, Muwatallis had united, in the greatest coalition that had ever existed, all the barbarian lands as far as the shores of the sea.

Forty thousand men and three thousand five hundred chariots advanced on the Egyptian forces, which were badly positioned and stupefied. Hundreds of footsoldiers from the Ptah division fell under the enemy arrows; their chariots were overturned and blocked the ford. The survivors ran to take refuge in the forest, preventing the Set division from intervening. That section of the Egyptian army could take no further part in the battle, and was at risk of becoming easy prey for the combined enemy archers.

Almost all the chariots of the Ptah division were destroyed;

those of the Set division were immobilized. In the plain the situation was becoming catastrophic. The Ra division was cut in two, and so had become powerless, and its men were scattering. The united enemy forces were massacring the Egyptians. Bones were broken and flesh pierced by iron weapons, spears plunged into sides, daggers ripped bellies open.

The allied princes applauded Muwatallis.

The emperor's strategy had proved to be brilliantly effective. Who would have thought that Ramses' arrogant army could be wiped out like that, without even having fought? The survivors were fleeing like frightened rabbits, and owed their survival only to the speed of their flight.

All that remained was to strike the final blow.

The Amon division and the pharaoh's camp were still intact but would not hold out for long against the shrieking hordes which were racing towards them. Then Muwatallis's victory would be complete; with the death of Ramses, the Egypt of the pharaohs would finally bow its head and become the slave of Hatti. Unlike his father, Ramses had fallen into the trap of Kadesh, and he would pay for this mistake with his life.

A dishevelled warrior pushed past two princes and faced the emperor.

'Father, what is happening?' asked Uri-Teshup. 'Why was I not advised of the time of the offensive? Am I not the commander-in-chief of our army?'

'I entrusted you with a specific role: to defend Kadesh with our reserve battalions.'

'But the fortress is not in danger!'

'Those are my orders, Uri-Teshup, and you are forgetting one essential fact: I did not put you in command of the allied forces of the coalition.'

'Who then—'

'Who but my brother, Hattusilis, could perform this

difficult task? He is the one who negotiated long and patiently to persuade our allies to agree to an exceptional war effort, so to him falls the honour of commanding the coalition.'

Uri-Teshup looked at Hattusilis with hate in his eyes, and grasped the hilt of his sword.

'Return to your post, my son,' Muwatallis ordered curtly.

The Hittite horsemen overturned the rampart of shields which protected Pharaoh's camp. The few Egyptian soldiers who tried to resist fell, their bodies transfixed by lances. An officer of the chariot corps shouted to the fleeing soldiers to resist; a Hittite arrow pierced his mouth and he died biting vainly on the dart that killed him.

More than two thousand chariots were preparing to charge at the royal tent.

'My lord,' exclaimed the armour-bearer, Menna, 'you who protect Egypt on the day of battle, you who are the lord of valour, look! We shall soon be isolated in the midst of thousands of enemies! We must not stay here. We must flee!'

Ramses glanced scornfully at him. 'Since cowardice has seized your heart, get out of my sight.'

'Majesty, I beg you! This is folly, not bravery. Save your life: the country has need of you.'

'Egypt does not need a defeated man. I shall fight, Menna.'

Ramses donned the Blue Crown and his short breastplate, which combined a kilt and corslet covered with little metal plates. On his wrists he wore golden bracelets whose clasps represented lapis-lazuli ducks with golden tails.

Calmly, as if it promised to be an uneventful day, the monarch caparisoned with red, blue and green trappings his two horses, the stallion, Victory in Thebes, and the mare, The Goddess Mut is Content. Their heads were decked with magnificent red plumes tipped with blue.

Ramses climbed into his chariot; it was six cubits long, made of wood plated with gold, and its caisson rested on an axle-tree and a shaft. The pieces had been curved in fire, covered with gold leaf and held together with tenons. The parts exposed to friction were covered with leather. The framework of the open-backed caisson was made of planks plated with gold; the floor was of intertwined thongs.

On the sides of the chariot were figures of Asians and Nubians kneeling in submission: the dream of a kingdom about to be shattered, the ultimate affirmation of the power of Egypt, of its domination over both North and South.

The chariot was equipped with two quivers, one for arrows, the other for bows and swords. With these derisory weapons, Pharaoh was preparing to fight an entire army.

Ramses tied the reins round his waist, in order to leave his hands free. The two horses were intelligent and brave; they would race straight into the fray. A low growl comforted the king; his lion, Invincible, would remain loyal to him and would fight at his side to the death.

A lion and a couple of horses: such were the last three allies of the king of Egypt. The chariots and footsoldiers of the Amon division were scattering before the enemy.

'If you make one mistake,' Seti had said, 'blame no one but yourself and rectify your error. Fight like a bull, a lion and a falcon, be as a flash of lightning in a storm. Otherwise you will be defeated.'

With a deafening din, raising a cloud of dust, the chariots of the allied armies rode up to attack the hill where the Pharaoh of Egypt stood in majesty in his chariot.

Ramses was overcome by a deep sense of injustice. Why had fate turned against him? The surviving forces of the Ptah and Set divisions were blocked on the east bank of the Orontes. As for the Amon division, which counted in its ranks the elite of the chariot corps, the men had behaved with sickening cowardice. At the first charge of the combined armies, the division had collapsed. There remained not one senior officer, not one shield-bearer, not one archer, ready to

330

fight. Whatever their rank, the soldiers had thought only of saving their own lives, forgetting Egypt. Menna was on his knees, his head in his hands so as not to see the enemy swoop down on him.

Five years of his reign, five years during which Ramses had tried to remain faithful to the spirit of Seti and to continue to build a rich and happy country, five years which were ending in disaster, the prelude to the invasion of the Two Lands and enslavement of their inhabitants. Nefertari and Tuya would put up only a brief resistance to the host of predators who would sweep down on the Delta, and then devastate the valley of the Nile.

As if they could perceive their master's thoughts, the horses wept.

Then Ramses rebelled. Casting his eyes up to the the sun, he addressed Amon, the god hidden in the light, whose real form no man would ever know.

'I call on thee, father Amon! Can a father forget his son, alone in the midst of a host of enemies? How has it come about that thou behavest thus? Have I disobeyed thee even once? All foreign lands are in league against me; my soldiers, although great in number, have fled and I am here alone, without aid. But who are these barbarians, if not cruel beings who do not practise the Rule of Ma'at? For thee, my father, I have built temples; I have had offerings brought to thee daily with the most delicate blossoms for thy delight; I have erected huge pylons to thee; I have raised up masts with banners to announce thy presence in the sanctuaries; I have caused obelisks to be dug out from the quarries of Elephantine to be raised up to thy glory. I call on thee, father Amon, for I am alone, absolutely alone. I have acted for thee with a loving heart; in this moment of my distress, act for the one who acts. Amon will be worth more to me than thousands of soldiers and hundreds of chariots. The valour of a multitude is worthless. Amon is of more help than an army.'

The fence that guarded access to the centre of the camp gave way, leaving the way open for the chariots to charge. In less than a minute Ramses would have ceased to live.

'My father,' cried Pharaoh, 'why hast thou abandoned me?'

54

Muwatallis, Hattusilis and the allied princes all expressed admiration for the pharaoh's attitude.

'He will die a warrior,' said the emperor. 'A sovereign of this quality almost deserves to be a Hittite. Our victory will be yours, Hattusilis.'

'The two Bedouin acted their parts perfectly. It was their lies that convinced Ramses our troops were far from Kadesh.'

'Uri-Teshup was wrong to oppose your plan and to recommend a battle in front of the stronghold. I shall remember his mistake.'

'Isn't the most important thing to see the coalition triumph? The conquest of Egypt will ensure our prosperity for many generations.'

'Let us witness the death of Ramses, betrayed by his own troops.'

The sun was suddenly twice as fierce, blinding the Hittites and their allies. In the clear blue sky thunder rumbled. They all thought themselves victims of a hallucination . . .

A voice as enormous as the whole universe rang out from the heavens. A voice whose message Ramses alone could understand: 'I am Amon, thy father; my hand is in thy hand; I, the master of victory, am thy father.'

The pharaoh was bathed in light, making his body glow like gold lit up by the sun. Ramses, the son of Ra, took on the strength of the day-star and sped towards his dumbfounded assailants.

He was no longer a defeated, solitary leader, waging his final battle, but a king of matchless power and indefatigable strength, a devastating flame, a glittering star, a fierce wind, a savage, sharp-horned bull, a falcon whose talons would tear any opponent to pieces. Ramses shot arrow after arrow, killing the drivers of the Hittite chariots. Their horses reared, out of control, falling foul of each other; the chariots overturned in a confused mass.

Invincible was responsible for wholesale slaughter. He launched his massive body into the battle, his claws mauled his opponents and his long fangs sank into necks and skulls. With his suberb mane blazing, his paws struck viciously and precisely.

Between them, Ramses and Invincible halted the enemy momentum and breached their lines. The leader of the footsoldiers brandished his spear but had no time to complete his action: Pharaoh's arrow embedded itself in his left eye. At the same moment, the lion's jaw closed over the terrified face of the leader of the imperial chariot corps. In spite of their numbers, the Hittites' allies retreated and raced down the slope towards the plain.

Muwatallis turned deathly pale. 'This is not a man,' he exclaimed, 'but the god Set in person, a unique being who has the power to defeat thousands of warriors! Look, when any man tries to attack him, his hand grows powerless, his body is paralysed and he cannot handle spear or bow!'

Hattusilis, normally so cool-headed and imperturbable, was struck dumb. One would have sworn that flames shot out from Ramses' body and engulfed anyone who tried to approach him.

A gigantic Hittite managed to grasp the edge of the chariot and brandish a dagger; but his coat of mail seemed to catch fire and he died screaming, his flesh charred. Neither Ramses nor the lion slackened his pace. Pharaoh sensed that the hand of Amon guided him, that the god of victory was just behind him and lent him more strength than a whole army. Like a hurricane, the King of Egypt felled his opponents as if they were wisps of straw.

'He must be stopped!' shouted Hattusilis.

'Our men are panic-stricken,' replied the Prince of Aleppo.

'You must rally them,' ordered Muwatallis.

'Ramses is a god—'

'He is only a man, even if his courage seems superhuman. Act, Prince, restore our soldiers' confidence and this battle will be over.'

The Prince of Aleppo reluctantly spurred his horse and rode down from the promontory on which the allied commanders were stationed. He was resolved to put an end to the mad venture of Ramses and his lion.

Hattusilis stared at the hills in the west. What he saw petrified him. 'Majesty, look over there! Egyptian chariots approaching at full speed!'

'Where are they coming from?'

'They must have taken the coast road.'

'How could they have forced their way through?'

'Uri-Teshup refused to block the approach, on the grounds that no Egyptian would dare come that way.'

The relief army sped over the open space and, meeting no opposition, deployed across the whole width of the plain to hurl themselves into the breach made by Ramses.

'Do not run!' shouted the Prince of Aleppo. 'Kill Ramses!'

A few soldiers obeyed; no sooner had they turned round than their faces and chests were mauled by the lion.

When the Prince of Aleppo saw Ramses' golden chariot bearing down on him, he stared in terror and fled from the battle in his turn. His horse trampled his Hittite allies underfoot as he tried to escape from the pharaoh. In his panic the prince let go of the reins; his horse bolted and plunged into the Orontes, where many chariots were already engulfed, piled up on top of each other, before sinking beneath the water or being carried away by the current. Soldiers were suffocating in the mud; some were drowning, others trying to swim; all preferred to leap into the river rather than face the terrifying deity who resembled fire from heaven.

The relief army completed Ramses' work by slaughtering a great number of the allies and forcing the fugitives into the Orontes. An officer of the chariot corps hauled the Prince of Aleppo out by the feet, who spat out the water he had swallowed.

Ramses' chariot drove up close to the mound occupied by the enemy commanders.

'We must retreat,' Hattusilis advised the emperor.

'We still have the units on the west bank.'

'They won't be enough. Ramses is capable of clearing the ford and freeing the Ptah and Set divisions.'

The emperor wiped his brow with the back of his hand. 'What is happening, Hattusilis? Can one man destroy a whole army?'

'If that man is Pharaoh, if he is Ramses . . . '

'The one who overpowers the multitude? That is only a myth, and we are on a battlefield!'

'We are defeated, Majesty, we must fall back.'

'A Hittite does not retreat.'

'We must think of saving your life and continuing the fight differently.'

'What do you suggest?'

'That we take refuge inside the fortress.'

'We shall be trapped there!'

'We have no choice,' replied Hattusilis. 'If we flee to the north, Ramses and his troops will pursue us.'

'Let us hope that Kadesh really is impregnable.'

'It is not a fortress like others, Majesty. Seti himself abandoned the attempt to capture it.'

'That will not be the case with his son!'

'We must hurry, Majesty!'

Muwatallis reluctantly raised his right hand and held it high for interminable seconds, thus giving the order to retreat.

Biting his lips till they bled, Uri-Teshup looked on powerlessly at the rout. The Hittite troops who blocked the access to the first ford, on the east bank of the Orontes, retreated to the second one. The survivors of the Ptah division dared not follow them for fear of falling into a new trap; the general preferred to protect his rear by sending a messenger to the Set division to let them know that the way was clear and they could cross the Labni forest.

The Prince of Aleppo pulled himself together, freed himself from the soldier who had rescued him, swam back across the river and rejoined his allies, who were marching towards Kadesh. The archers of the relief army shot down the fugitives by the hundred.

The Egyptians marched over the corpses and cut off a hand of each in order to make a macabre calculation of the number of dead, which would be entered in the official archives.

No one dared approach the pharaoh; Invincible lay like a sphinx in front of the horses. Ramses, bloodstained, alighted from the gilded chariot, stood for a long time patting his lion and his two horses, and spared not the briefest glance for the soldiers who stood still, awaiting the monarch's reaction.

Menna was the first to approach the king. The trembling armour-bearer had difficulty putting one foot in front of the other.

Beyond the second ford, the Hittite army and the survivors among the allies were fast making their way towards the great gate of Kadesh. The Egyptians had no time to intervene to prevent Muwatallis and his troops from reaching shelter.

'Majesty,' said Menna softly, 'Majesty, we have won.'

Ramses stood like a granite statue, staring at the fastness.

'The great Hittite leader has yielded to Your Majesty,'

Menna continued. 'He has fled. Alone you have killed thousands of men! Who will be able to sing your praises?'

Ramses turned towards him. Terrified, Menna prostrated himself, afraid he'd be struck dead by the power emanating from the sovereign.

'Is that you, Menna?'

'Yes, Majesty, it is indeed me, your loyal armour-bearer. Forgive me, forgive your army. Should not victory let mistakes be forgotten?'

'A pharaoh does not forgive, loyal servant. He rules and he acts.'

55

The Amon and Ra divisions had been decimated, that of Ptah weakened; the Set division was still intact. Thousands of Egyptians had died, greater numbers of Hittites had lost their lives, but only one fact was important: Ramses had won the battle of Kadesh.

True, Muwatallis, Hattusilis, Uri-Teshup and some of their allies, such as the Prince of Aleppo, were alive, confined in the fortress. But the myth of Hittite invincibility was dead. A number of the princes, committed to fighting beside the Emperor of Hatti, had perished, either drowned or shot through by arrows. Henceforth, the principalities, large or small, would know that Muwatallis's shield was not strong enough to protect them from Ramses' wrath.

The pharaoh summoned to his tent all the surviving officers, including the generals commanding the Ptah and Set divisions.

In spite of their delight in victory, there were no smiles. As he sat on his wooden throne, Ramses' expression was that of an angry falcon ready to pounce on its prey.

'All of you here,' he declared, 'were responsible for a command. You have all enjoyed the privileges of your rank. You all behaved like cowards! Well fed, well housed, exempt from taxes, respected and envied, you, the army's officers and commanders, fled when the time came to fight; you were all united in cowardice.'

The general of the Set division stepped forward. 'Majesty—'

'Do you wish to contradict me?'

The general returned to his place.

'I can no longer trust you. Tomorrow you will again take to flight, you will scatter like sparrows at the approach of danger. That is why I am stripping you of your rank. Be glad that you can remain in the army as private soldiers, able to serve your country, draw your pay and receive a pension.'

No one protested. The majority had feared a more severe punishment. That same day the king appointed new officers, chosen from the relief army.

The day after his victory, Ramses launched the first assault on the Kadesh fortress. Hittite pennants flew from the tops of the towers.

The Egyptian bowmen's shots were ineffective. Their arrows shattered against the battlements behind which the besieged men were sheltering. Unlike those of other Syrian fortresses, the tops of Kadesh's towers were out of range.

Wishing to prove their valour, the footsoldiers climbed the rocky spur on which the stronghold was built and placed wooden ladders against the walls. But the Hittite archers decimated them and the survivors were forced to give up. Three more attempts: as many failures.

The next day and the day after, a few daring men succeeded in climbing halfway up the wall, but a hail of stones wiped them out.

Kadesh seemed impregnable.

In sombre mood Ramses called a new council of war, whose members vied with each other in zeal in order to shine in the king's eyes. Weary of their chatter, he dismissed them, keeping only Setau with him.

'Lotus and I will be able to save dozens of lives, providing we don't die of exhaustion ourselves. At the rate we're working, we shall soon run out of remedies.'

'Come to the point.'

'We must return to Egypt, Ramses.'

'Forgetting Kadesh?'

'We were victorious.'

'As long as Kadesh is not in Egyptian hands, the Hittite menace will remain.'

'Such a conquest would demand too much effort and too many dead. Let us return to Egypt to treat the wounded and rebuild our army.'

'This fortress must fall, like the others.'

'What if you're wrong to persist?'

'The land around us is extremely rich. You and Lotus will find the necessary ingredients for your remedies.'

'And what if Ahsha is imprisoned in this stronghold?'

'All the more reason to take possession of it and free him.'

Menna ran up and prostrated himself. 'Majesty, Majesty! A lance has been thrown down from the top of the ramparts with a message tied to its tip!'

'Give it to me.'

Ramses deciphered the text.

To Ramses, the Pharaoh of Egypt, from his brother Muwatallis, the Emperor of Hatti.

Before continuing to fight each other, would it not be good to meet and parley? Let a tent be set up in the plain, halfway between your army and the fortress.

I shall go there alone, and my brother will go there alone, tomorrow when the sun is at its zenith.

In the tent, two thrones face to face. Between them a low table on which stood two drinking-cups and a small pitcher of fresh water.

The two sovereigns sat down simultaneously, eyeing each other. In spite of the heat, Muwatallis wore a long black and red woollen cloak.

'I am happy to meet my brother, the Pharaoh of Egypt, whose fame never ceases to grow.'

'The reputation of the Emperor of Hatti spreads dread in many lands.'

'As far as that is concerned, my brother Ramses need not envy me. I had formed an invincible coalition; you defeated it. What divine protection did you enjoy?'

'That of my father, Amon, whose arm was substituted for my own.'

'I could not believe such power could dwell in a man, even Pharaoh.'

'You did not hesitate to use lies and trickery.'

'They are weapons of war like any other. They would have defeated you had you not been possessed by a supernatural force. It was the soul of your father, Seti, which sustained your insane courage, which made you forget fear and defeat.'

'Are you ready to surrender, Muwatallis?'

'Is it my brother Ramses' custom to speak so plainly?'

'Thousands of men are dead because of Hatti's policy of expansion. So it is no longer the time for empty talk. Are you ready to surrender?'

'Does my brother know who I am?'

'The Emperor of Hatti, trapped in the Kadesh fortress.'

'With me are my brother, Hattusilis, my son, Uri-Teshup, my vassals and my allies. To surrender would be to cut off the head of the empire.'

'A man who is vanquished must bear the consequences of his defeat.'

'You have won the battle of Kadesh, it is true, but the fortress remains intact.'

'Sooner or later it will fall.'

'Your first attacks have proved ineffectual; by continuing

in this way you will lose many men, without making even a
scratch on the walls of Kadesh.'

'That is why I have decided to adopt another strategy.'

'Since we are speaking as brothers, will you reveal it to
me?'

'Have you not guessed it? It depends on patience. There
are many of you inside the fastness. We shall wait until food
runs out. Would not an immediate surrender be preferable to
long suffering?'

'My brother Ramses little knows this fortress. Its vast
storehouses contain a huge quantity of food, which will allow
us to hold out under siege for many months. So we shall enjoy
more favourable conditions than the Egyptian army.'

'Mere bragging.'

'Certainly not, my brother, certainly not! You Egyptians
are a long way from your bases and will experience more and
more difficult times. Everyone knows that you detest living
far from your country and that Egypt is reluctant to be long
deprived of its pharaoh. Autumn will come, then winter,
bringing cold and disease. There will be disillusion and
weariness too. Be certain of this, my brother Ramses: we
shall be privileged by comparison with you. And do not count
on the lack of water: the tanks in Kadesh are brimming full
and we have the benefit of a well dug in the middle of the
stronghold.'

Ramses took a drink of water, not because he was thirsty
but in order to interrupt the discussion and have time to think.
Muwatallis's arguments were not without merit.

'Would my brother like to quench his thirst?'

'No, I can stand the heat well.'

'Are you perhaps afraid of poison, so frequently used at the
Hatti court?'

'That custom has fallen into disuse; but I still prefer my
cup-bearer to taste dishes intended for me. My brother
Ramses must know that one of his childhood friends, the

young and brilliant diplomat Ahsha, was arrested, dressed as a merchant, while carrying out a spying mission. If I had applied our laws he would be dead. But I presumed you would be pleased to save the life of one who is dear to you.'

'You are mistaken, Muwatallis. In me, the king takes precedence over the man.'

'Ahsha is not only your friend but also the real head of the Egyptian diplomatic service and the person who knows Asia best. Even if the man remains insensible, the king will not sacrifice one of the principal pieces in his game.'

'What are you proposing?'

'Is not peace, even temporary peace, better than a disastrous war?'

'Peace? Impossible!'

'Think, brother Ramses. I did not engage the whole of my army in this battle. It will not be long before relief forces come to my help and you will have other battles to wage, while continuing the siege. Such efforts will exhaust your reserves of men and weapons and your victory will be transformed into a disaster.'

'You lost the battle of Kadesh, Muwatallis, and you dare ask for peace!'

'I am prepared to ackowledge my defeat by drawing up an official document. When it is in your possession you will raise the siege and the border of my empire will be fixed for ever at Kadesh. My army will never take possession of Egypt.'

56

The door of Ahsha's cell opened. In spite of his imperturbability, the young diplomat started; the two guards' inscrutable expression was an ominous sign.

Since his imprisonment Ahsha had expected every day to be executed. The Hittites showed no mercy to spies. The axe, the dagger or a forced jump from the top of a cliff? He hoped his death would be sudden and swift, rather than the occasion for a cruel spectacle.

Ahsha was shown into a cold, austere hall, decorated with shields and lances. As always in Hatti, one was reminded of the presence of war.

'How do you feel?' asked the priestess Putuhepa.

'I lack exercise and I'm not keen on the food, but I'm still alive. Is that not a miracle?'

'In some ways, yes.'

'I have the feeling that my reserves of luck are running out ... However, your presence reassures me. Would a woman be so ruthless?'

'Do not count on the weakness of a Hittite woman.'

'So my charm would not work?'

The priestess looked furious. 'Do you fully appreciate your situation?'

'An Egyptian diplomat knows how to die with a smile, even if he is trembling in every limb.'

Ahsha thought of the anger of Ramses, who would reproach him, even in the next world, for not having succeeded in escaping from Hatti to give him a description of the enormous coalition assembled by the emperor. Had the peasant woman transmitted his three-word message? He did not really believe so, but if she had, the pharaoh would have been sufficiently perceptive to detect its meaning.

Deprived of information, the Egyptian army had been destroyed at Kadesh and Shaanar had mounted the throne of Egypt. All things considered, it was better to die than to suffer the tyranny of such a despot.

'You did not betray Ramses,' said Putuhepa, 'and you never took orders from Shaanar.'

'That's for you to decide.'

'The battle of Kadesh has taken place,' she disclosed. 'Ramses defeated the allied troops.'

Ahsha felt intoxicated. 'You're mocking me!'

'I am not in the mood for joking.'

'He defeated the allied troops . . . ' repeated Ahsha, dumbfounded.

'Our emperor is alive and free,' Putuhepa added, 'and the fortress of Kadesh is still intact.'

The diplomat's mood darkened. 'What fate have you in store for me?'

'I would gladly have had you burned as a spy, but you have become one of the stakes in the negotiations.'

The Egyptian army camped in front of the fortress, whose walls were still grey in spite of the warm early-June sunshine. Since the meeting between Ramses and Muwatallis, Pharaoh's soldiers had launched no new assault against Kadesh. From the top of the ramparts, Uri-Teshup and the Hittite archers watched their opponents spending their time in peaceful pursuits. They tended horses, donkeys and oxen, they improved their skill in board games, organized bare-hand wrestling matches and atc a good variety of dishes prepared by the regimental cooks to the accompaniment of mutual invective.

Ramses had given only one order to the senior officers: to see that discipline was respected. To none of them had he given the slightest hint of the pact arranged with Muwatallis.

The new general of the Set division took the risk of questioning him. 'Majesty, we feel helpless.'

'Are you not delighted at having won a great victory?'

'We realize that you alone are the victor of Kadesh, Majesty. But why are we not attacking the fortress?'

'Because we have no hope of seizing it. Wc would have to sacrifice at least half our troops without being sure of success.'

'How long must we sit here staring at this accursed fortress?'

'I have concluded an agreement with Muwatallis.'

'Do you mean . . . peace?'

'Conditions have been laid down; if they are not fulfilled we shall resume hostilities.'

'What time limit have you prescribed, Majesty?'

'The end of this week. I shall then know if the Hittite emperor's word is worth anything.'

In the distance, on the road from the north, a cloud of dust. Several Hittite chariots were approaching Kadesh, chariots which perhaps formed the vanguard of a relief army, hurrying to free Muwatallis and his allies.

Ramses calmed the agitation which seized the Egyptian camp. Climbing into his chariot, drawn by Victory in Thebes and The Goddess Mut is Content, the king, accompanied by his lion, drove out to meet the Hittite soldiers.

The Hittite archers kept hold of their reins. The reputation of Ramses and Invincible had already spread through the wholc of Hatti.

A man alighted from a chariot and advanced briskly towards the pharaoh.

Ahsha, still elegant, a thin, neat moustache adorning his aristocratic countenance, forgot protocol and ran towards Ramses. The king and his friend embraced.

'Was my message useful, Majesty?'

'Yes and no. I wasn't able to make use of your warning, but the magic of fate played in Egypt's favour. And thanks to you I was able to intervene rapidly. It was Amon who won the victory.'

'I thought I'd never see Egypt again; Hittite prisons are grim. I did try to convince the enemy that I was Shaanar's accomplice, and that must have saved my life. Then things happened fast. It would have been an inexcusable error of taste to have died there.'

'We must decide between a truce and continuing hostilities. I shall find your advice useful.'

Back in his tent, Ramses showed Ahsha the document the Hittite emperor had sent him.

I, Muwatallis, am your servant, Ramses, and I recognize you as the Son of the Light, descended from him, truly descended from him. My country is your servant, we are at your feet. But do not abuse your power!

Your authority is implacable, you have proved this by winning a great victory. But why should you continue to exterminate your servant's people? Why should you be driven by malice?

Since you are victorious, admit that peace is better than war, and give the Hittites the breath of life.

'Nice diplomatic style,' Ahsha declared appreciatively.

'Does the message seem to you sufficiently explicit to cover all the countries in the region?'

'A veritable masterpiece! For a Hittite sovereign to be

defeated in battle is something new. For him to acknowledge his defeat is a fresh miracle to his credit.'

'I didn't manage to seize Kadesh.'

'Why is this stronghold so important? You have won a decisive battle. The invincible Muwatallis now considers himself your vassal, at least in words. This access of forced humility will be extremely useful to your reputation.'

Muwatallis had kept his word by drawing up an acceptable document and freeing Ahsha. So Ramses gave the order to his army to strike camp and set off on the road back to Egypt.

Before leaving the site where so many of his compatriots had lost their lives, Ramses turned towards the fortress from which Muwatallis, his brother and his son would depart unharmed. The pharaoh had not suceeded in destroying this symbol of Hittite power, but what would remain of that power after the coalition's bitter defeat? Muwatallis, declaring himself the servant of Ramses . . . Who would have imagined such a success? Never would the king forget that it was only the help of his heavenly father, whom he had called to his aid, that had allowed him to transform a disaster into a triumph.

'Not a single Egyptian remains on the Kadesh plain,' declared the chief lookout.

'Send scouts to the south, east and west,' Muwatallis ordered his son. 'Ramses may have learned his lesson and hidden his troops in the forest to attack us as soon as we leave the fortress.'

'How long shall we continue to flee?'

'We must return to Hattusa,' opined Hattusilis, 'to rebuild our army and reconsider our strategy.'

'I'm addressing the Emperor of the Hittites,' exclaimed Uri-Teshup furiously, 'not a defeated general.'

'Calm down, my son,' interrupted Muwatallis. 'I consider that the commander-in-chief of the allied forces did not show himself unworthy. We all underestimated the personal might of Ramses.'

'If you had let me act, we would have won!'

'You are mistaken. The Egyptian weaponry is of excellent quality, Pharaoh's chariots are as good as ours. The battle on the plain that you recommended would have turned against us, and our troops would have suffered heavy losses.'

'And you are content with this humiliating defeat!'

'We retain this fortress, Hatti has not been invaded, the war with Egypt will continue.'

'How can it continue after the infamous document you signed?'

'It is not a question of a peace treaty,' Hattusilis explained, 'but a simple letter from one monarch to another. The fact that Ramses is satisfied with it proves his lack of experience.'

'Muwatallis declares unequivocally that he considers himself Pharaoh's vassal!'

Hattusilis smiled. 'When a vassal has the necessary troops at his disposal, nothing prevents him rebelling.'

Uri-Teshup looked straight at Muwatallis. 'Ignore this weakling, father, and give me full military powers! The niceties and tricks of diplomacy will lead nowhere. I and I alone am capable of crushing Ramses.'

'Let us return to Hattusa,' decided the emperor. 'The air of our mountains will favour reflection.'

57

Ramses took a mighty leap into the pool where Nefertari was bathing. He swam under water and grabbed his wife by the waist. Feigning surprise, she let herself be pulled under and, entwined, they rose slowly to the surface. Wideawake, the king's yellow dog, ran barking round the pool, while Invincible slept in the shade of a sycamore tree, wearing round his neck a fine gold collar, the reward for his bravery.

Ramses could not look at Nefertari without coming under the spell of her beauty. Besides the attraction of the senses and their physical affinity, they were united by a mysterious bond, stronger than time and death. The soft autumn sun bathed their faces with its kindly light as they glided through the blue-green waters of the pool. When they emerged, Wideawake stopped barking and licked their legs. He detested water and could not understand why his master delighted in getting wet like this. When he had had enough of being petted by the royal couple, Wideawake nestled down between the paws of the huge lion and took a well-earned rest.

Nefertari was so desirable that Ramses' hands became impassioned: with the eagerness of an explorer entering an unknown country, they played feverishly over the young woman's body, in all its perfection. Passive at first, content to be dominated, she responded to her lover's invitation.

*

Throughout the country, Ramses was now known as 'Ramses the Great'. On his return to Pi-Ramses, a huge crowd had acclaimed the victor of the battle of Kadesh, the pharaoh who had succeeded in routing the Hittites and driving them back to their own territory. Several weeks of festivities in villages and towns had allowed this tremendous victory to be fittingly celebrated. With the spectre of invasion dispelled, Egypt gave itself up to its instinctive joy in life and, to crown it all, there was an excellent rise in the water level, with the promise of abundant crops.

The fifth year of the reign of the son of Seti ended in triumph. The new military commanders were totally devoted to the monarch and a subdued court deferred to him. Ramses' youth was at an end; the man of twenty-eight who ruled over the Two Lands had the calibre of the greatest sovereigns and was already putting his indelible seal on his era.

Homer came to meet Ramses, leaning on a staff. 'I have finished, Majesty.'

'Would you like to lean on my arm and walk a little, or sit beneath your lemon tree?'

'Let us walk a little. My head and my hand have worked hard recently; it's the turn of my legs now.'

'This new work means you've had to interrupt the composition of the *Iliad*.'

'True, but you have given me a magnificent subject.'

'How have you treated it?'

'By respecting the truth, Majesty. I have hidden neither the cowardice of your army nor your solitary, desperate fight, nor your appeal to your divine father. The circumstances of this extraordinary victory have fired my imagination as if I were a young poet writing his first work! The lines sang on my lips, the scenes organized themselves. Your friend Ahmeni helped me a great deal, particularly over avoiding grammatical mistakes. Egyptian is not an easy language, but its flexibility and precision are a joy to a poet.'

'The account of the battle of Kadesh will be carved on the outer wall of the great Hall of Pillars of the temple of Karnak,' Ramses told him, 'on the outer walls and the façade of the pylon-gateway of the temple of Luxor, on the outer walls of the temple of Abydos, and in the outer courtyard – which is yet to be built – of my Temple of a Million Years.'

'Thus the stone of eternity will preserve the memory of the battle of Kadesh for ever.'

'It is the hidden god whom I wish to honour, Homer, the victory of order over disorder, the Rule's ability to ward off chaos.'

'You astonish me, Majesty, and your country astonishes me a litle more every day. I did not think your famous Rule would help you defeat an encmy determined to destroy you.'

'If my thoughts and my will ceased to be inspired by love of the Rule, my reign would soon end and Egypt would be wedded to another.'

In spite of the enormous quantities of food he consumed, Ahmeni did not put on weight. Still as slight, pale and sickly as ever, he never left his office and, with a small team, dealt with an impressive number of dossiers. In direct communication with the vizier and all the ministers, Ahmeni knew everything that happened in the country, and saw to it that every senior official carried out correctly the tasks entrusted to him. For Ramses' childhood friend, a healthy administration could be summed up in one simple precept: the higher the post and the greater the responsibilities, the more severe should be the punishment in case of mistakes or inadequacy. From ministers to heads of departments, everyone was responsible for the mistakes of his subordinates, and paid the price for them. Ministers dismissed and officials demotcd had experienced Ahmeni's severity to their cost.

353

When the sovereign was in residence in Pi-Ramses, Ahmeni, his most trusted adviser, saw him every day. When the monarch left for Thebes or Memphis, Ahmeni prepared detailed reports, which the king read attentively. He was the one who settled matters and took decisions.

The scribe was explaining to the king his plan for reinforcing the dykes for the coming year, when Serramanna was admitted to the office, whose shelves were laden with meticulously classified papyri. The Sardinian giant bowed to the sovereign.

'Are you still angry with me?' asked Ramses.

'I wouldn't have abandoned you in the battle.'

'Looking after my wife and my mother was a mission of the greatest importance.'

'I can't deny that, but I'd have preferred to be with you and to kill a few Hittites. The arrogance of those people exasperates me. When you claim to represent the elite among the warriors, you don't go and take refuge in a fortress!'

'Our time is valuable,' interrupted Ahmeni. 'What are the results of your investigations?'

'Nothing,' replied Serramanna.

'No trace?'

'I found the wagon and the bodies of the Egyptian policemen, but not Shaanar's. According to the evidence of some merchants who sheltered in a stone hut, it was an unusually long and violent sandstorm. I went as far as the Khanga oasis and I can assure you that I and my men searched the desert thoroughly.'

'Shaanar would have had to stumble blindly along,' suggested Ahmeni, 'so he could have fallen into the bed of a dried-up wadi and be buried under a ton of sand.'

'That's the general opinion,' Serramanna admitted.

'It's not mine,' declared Ramses.

'He had no chance of getting out of that hell, Majesty. If he left the main track he'd have got lost and couldn't have held out for long against the raging wind, the sand and thirst.'

'His hatred is so intense that it will have served him as food and drink. Shaanar is not dead.'

The king placed a bunch of lilies and papyrus on the altar as an offering, then stood deep in thought before the statue of Thoth, the god of knowledge, at the entrance to the Foreign Affairs secretariat. The statue depicted a seated baboon, whose head was surmounted by the crescent moon, looking up to the heavens, beyond human affairs.

The officials of the secretariat rose and bowed as Ramses passed them. Ahsha, the new minister, himself opened the door of his office. The king and his friend, now a hero in the eyes of the court, embraced. The arrival of the sovereign was a clear mark of the esteem which confirmed Ahsha in his role as head of the Egyptian diplomatic service.

His office was very different from Ahmeni's. Bunches of roses imported from Syria, arrangements of narcissi and marigolds, slender alabaster vases placed on round pedestal tables, tall lamps, acacia-wood chests, coloured hangings, formed a sophisticated colourful setting, which gave the impression of the private rooms of a luxurious villa rather than a workplace.

His eyes sparkling with intelligence, elegant, wearing a light, scented wig, Ahsha looked like a guest at a banquet, frivolous, worldly and somewhat supercilious. Who would have supposed that this member of high society had been able to transform himself into a spy, disguise himself as a merchant, and travel along the hostile roads of Hittite territory? No accumulation of dossiers disturbed the new minister's luxurious environment, for he preferred to store all essential information in his prodigious memory.

'I think I shall be obliged to hand in my resignation, Majesty.'

'What offence are you guilty of?'

'Inefficiency. My department has spared no effort, yet Moses' whereabouts remain unknown. It's curious. Usually tongues wag. To my mind, there's only one answer: he's taken refuge in some isolated spot and hasn't moved. If he's changed his name and joined a family of Bedouin, it will be very difficult, if not impossible, to identify him.'

'Continue your investigations. And what about the Hittite spy network that had infiltrated our territory?'

'The body of the young blonde woman was buried without being identified. As for the sorcerer, he has disappeared – he probably managed to get out of Egypt. There, too, no gossip, as if the members of the network vanished in just a few days. We escaped a terrible danger, Ramses.'

'Has it really been dispelled?'

'It would be over-confident on our part to say so,' Ahsha acknowledged.

'Don't relax your vigilance.'

'I'm wondering about the Hittites' ability to react,' Ahsha confessed. 'Their defeat has humiliated them and their internal divisions are profound. They won't remain satisfied with peace, but they'll need several months, if not years, to prepare for renewed action.'

'How is Meba behaving?'

'My august predecessor is a zealous deputy, who knows his place.'

'Be wary of him. As a former minister, he is bound to be jealous of you. What have you heard from the commanders of our garrisons in southern Syria?'

'Everything is dead calm, but I have only limited confidence in their judgment. That's why I'm leaving tomorrow for the province of Amurru. We must immediately organize a force there, ready to intervene and check any invasion.'

58

To calm her fury, the priestess Putuhepa shut herself up in the
most sacred place in the Hittite capital, the subterranean
chamber dug out of the rock in the upper town, near the
acropolis on which the emperor's residence stood. After the
defeat at Kadesh, Muwatallis had decided to keep his brother
and his son at an equal distance, and he strengthened his
personal power by declaring that he alone was capable of
maintaining the balance between the rival factions.

The ceiling of the subterranean chamber was vaulted and
the walls decorated with reliefs depicting the emperor as a
warrior and as a priest surmounted by a winged sun. Putuhepa
approached the altar of the Underworld, on which lay a
bloodstained sword.

She had come here to seek the necessary inspiration to save
her husband from Muwatallis's wrath and to allow him to win
back his favour. For his part, Uri-Teshup, who still had the
ear of the most bellicose military clans, would not remain
inactive, and would try to do away with Hattusilis, or even
kill the emperor.

Putuhepa remained deep in reflection until midnight,
thinking only of her husband.

The god of the Underworld gave her the answer.

The limited council, attended only by Muwatallis, Uri-

Teshup and Hattusilis, was the occasion of a fierce clash.

'Hattusilis alone was responsible for our defeat,' declared Uri-Teshup. 'If I had commanded the allied troops, we would have crushed the Egyptian army.'

'We did crush it,' Hattusilis reminded him, 'but who could have predicted Ramses' intervention?'

'I would have defeated him!'

'Don't boast,' interrupted the emperor. 'No one could have controlled the force that galvanized him on the day of the battle. When the gods speak, one must listen to their voices.'

His assertion prevented his son from continuing along his chosen path. So the prince launched an offensive on different ground.

'What do you predict for the future, father?'

'I am reflecting.'

'The time for reflection is over! We were made a laughing-stock at Kadesh. It's vital that we react as quickly as possible. Entrust me with the command of the remnants of the allied troops and I will invade Egypt.'

'Absurd,' declared Hattusilis. 'Our first concern must be to retain our alliances. The armies of the coalition have lost many men, the thrones of many princes may totter if we don't support them financially.'

'Empty words from a defeated man!' retorted Uri-Teshup. 'Hattusilis is trying to gain time to mask his cowardice and his mediocrity.'

'Moderate your language,' demanded Muwatallis. 'Insults won't help.'

'Enough shilly-shallying, father. I demand full powers.'

'I am the emperor, Uri-Teshup. It's not your place to dictate my conduct.'

'Remain with your bad adviser if you prefer. I'm going back to my apartments until you order me to lead our troops to victory.' He strode out of the audience chamber.

'He's not altogether wrong,' admitted Hattusilis.

'What do you mean?'

'Putuhepa has consulted the gods of the Underworld.'

'And their answer?'

'We must wipe out the failure of Kadesh.'

'Have you a plan?'

'It presents risks which I shall assume.'

'You are my brother, Hattusilis, and your life is precious to me.'

'I don't believe I made a mistake at Kadesh, and the greatness of the empire is my most passionate concern. I shall do what the gods of the Underworld demand.'

Nedjem was not only Ramses' minister for agriculture but also the tutor to his son, Kha. Fascinated by the child's talent for reading and writing, he had allowed him to satisfy his taste for study and research. The minister and the king's son got on extremely well, and Ramses was most pleased with this type of education.

Now, for the first time, peaceable Nedjem felt obliged to oppose an order from Ramses, knowing that this lack of respect could entail his fall.

'Majesty . . . '

'Speak out, my good Nedjem.'

'It's about your son.'

'Is he ready?'

'Yes, but . . . '

'Is he ill?'

'No, Majesty, but—'

'Then let him come immediately.'

'With respect, Majesty, I am not sure that such a young child can confront the danger you wish to expose him to.'

'Let me be the judge of that, Nedjem.'

'The danger . . . The danger is considerable!

'Kha must meet his fate, whatever it may be. He is not a child like others.'

The minister understood that any effort on his part would be in vain. 'I regret that sometimes, Majesty.'

The cold north wind was blowing through the Delta, but did not succeed in driving away the huge black rain clouds. Seated behind his father on a magnificent grey horse, little Kha shivered.

'I'm cold, father. Can't we go more slowly?'

'We're in a hurry.'

'Where are you taking me?'

'To look on death.'

'The beautiful goddess of the West, with the gentle smile?'

'No, that death is for the righteous. And you are not yet one of them.'

'I want to become one!'

'Well, you must take the first step.'

Kha gritted his teeth. He would never disappoint his father.

Ramses halted at a place where a canal branched off from an arm of the Nile; the junction was marked by a small granite sanctuary. All seemed peaceful.

'Is death here?' asked Kha.

'Inside this monument. If you're afraid, don't go in.'

Kha jumped down and recalled the magic words learned from tales and meant to ward off fear. He turned to his father. Ramses did not move. Kha understood that he could expect no help from Pharaoh. The only way was to go on towards the sanctuary.

A cloud hid the sun; the sky grew dark. The child advanced hesitantly, and came to a standstill halfway to his destination. In his path lay a cobra, black as ink, more than two cubits long. Its hood was spread, and it seemed about to attack him.

The terrified child dared not move. The cobra was emboldened and slithered towards him. Soon it would strike. Mumbling the ancient incantations, stumbling over the words, the little boy shut his eyes as the cobra reared up to strike.

A forked stick pinned it to the ground.

'That death was not for you,' declared Setau. 'Go back to your father, child.'

Kha looked Ramses straight in the eyes. 'The cobra didn't bite me because I recited the right words. I shall become one of the righteous, shan't I?'

Tuya was seated in a comfortable chair, enjoying the pleasant, warm winter sunshine and talking to a tall, dark woman, when Ramses arrived to visit her.

'Dolora!' cried the king, recognizing his sister.

'Don't be hard on her,' recommended Tuya. 'She has much to tell you.'

Listless, with a tired, pale face, Dolora fell at Ramses' feet. 'Forgive me, I beseech you!'

'Do you feel guilty?'

'That accursed magus bewitched me. I thought he was a good man.'

'And who is he?'

'A Libyan, an expert in witchcraft. He shut me up in a house in Memphis, forced me to follow him when he fled. If I hadn't obeyed him he would have cut my throat.'

'Why so much brutality?'

'Because . . . because . . . ' Dolora burst into tears.

Ramses helped her up and sat her in a chair. 'Explain yourself,' he said.

'The magus . . . the magus killed a servant and a young woman who acted as his medium. He got rid of them because they refused to obey him and help him.'

'Did you witness this crime?'

'No, I was shut up. But I saw the bodies when we left the house.'

'Why did this magus keep you prisoner?'

'He believed I had powers as a medium and he intended to use me against you, brother! He drugged me and asked me questions about your habits. But I couldn't answer. When he was on his way back to Libya he released me. I have been through some terrible times, Ramses. I was convinced he would kill me!'

'You have been very foolish, haven't you?'

'I am sorry for it – if you only knew how sorry I am!'

'Do not leave the court of Pi-Ramses.'

59

Ahsha was well acquainted with Benteshina, Prince of Amurru. He paid but little attention to the words of the gods, preferring gold, women and wine. He was a corrupt, venal man, concerned solely with his own welfare and pleasure.

As Amurru was called on to play a major strategic role, the head of the Egyptian diplomatic service had gone to great lengths to ensure Benteshina's active cooperation. In the first place, Ahsha had come himself in Pharaoh's name, as evidence of the esteem in which he held the prince. Also, he brought a quantity of treasures, especially luxury cloth, jars of vintage wines, alabaster vases, ceremonial weapons and furniture worthy of the royal court.

Most of the Egyptian soldiers stationed in Amurru had been recruited from the relief army, whose intervention at Kadesh had been decisive. When they returned to Egypt, they had enjoyed a long period of leave before resuming duty. Now Ahsha brought with him a detachment of fifty drill officers, responsible for training the local troops until the arrival of a thousand footsoldiers and archers from Pi-Ramses, who would make Amurru a strong military base.

Ahsha had embarked at Peluse and sailed north. Favourable winds and a calm sea had made for a pleasant voyage. The presence on board of a young Syrian woman had added to the charm of the journey.

When the Egyptian boat entered the port of Beirut, Prince Benteshina was waiting on the quay, surrounded by his courtiers. He was a jovial, well-upholstered man of fifty, sporting a shiny black moustache; he kissed Ahsha on both cheeks and poured forth a stream of praise for the fantastic victory won by Ramses the Great at Kadesh, which had radically altered the balance of the world.

'What a superb career, my dear Ahsha! So young, and minister for foreign affairs of powerful Egypt. I bow down before you.'

'That will not be necessary. I come as a friend.'

'You shall lodge in my palace; all your wishes shall be fulfilled.' Benteshina's eyes lit up. 'Would you like . . . a young virgin?'

'Who would be foolish enough to scorn the wonders of nature? Look at these modest gifts, Benteshina, and tell me if they please you.'

The sailors unloaded the cargo. Benteshina was eloquent in his expression of satisfaction. The sight of a bed of remarkably fine workmanship wrested from him a cry almost of bliss.

'You Egyptians, you know the art of living! I am impatient to try out this wonder – and not alone!'

Ahsha took advantage of the prince's excellent mood to introduce his drill officers. 'In your capacity as a loyal ally of Egypt, you must help us to build a defensive front which will protect Amurru and deter the Hittites from attacking you.'

'That is my dearest wish,' declared Benteshina. 'I am tired of wars, which damage trade. My people wish to be protected.'

'In a few weeks Ramses will send an army. Meanwhile, these instructors will train your own soldiers.'

'Excellent, excellent! Hatti has suffered a heavy defeat. Muwatallis is facing an internal struggle between his son,

Uri-Teshup, and his brother, Hattusilis.'

'Which do the warrior clans favour?'

'They seem to be divided – both men have their supporters. For the moment the emperor is maintaining an appearance of cohesion, but his overthrow cannot be ruled out. And then certain members of the Kadesh coalition regret having been dragged into a disastrous venture, so costly in men and material. Some of them may be looking for a new master, who could well be Pharaoh.'

'That's a splendid prospect.'

'And I promise you an unforgettable evening!'

The young Canaanite woman, heavy-breasted and broad-hipped, lay down on top of Ahsha and gently massaged him by moving her whole body forwards and backwards. Every scrap of her skin was scented and her blonde bush was an enchanted country.

Although he had already engaged in several successful amorous encounters, Ahsha did not remain passive. As soon as the young woman's massage had produced its expected result, he turned her on her side. He immediately found the delightful path into her secret recesses and shared with her a fresh moment of intense pleasure. It was some time since she had been a virgin, but her amatory skill made up favourably for that irreparable deficiency. Neither of them had uttered a single word.

'Leave me now,' he said, 'I'm sleepy.'

The girl rose and left the huge bedchamber, which looked out on to the garden. Ahsha forgot her immediately, thinking of what Benteshina had told him about the coalition assembled by Muwattallis, a coalition that was about to fall apart. Manoeuvring skilfully would be difficult, but exciting . . .

Which other great power could the dissidents turn to, if they lost confidence in the Emperor of Hatti? Certainly not Egypt. The land of the pharaohs was too far distant, its mentality too different from that of the small, bellicose, unstable principalities of Asia. One idea dominated the diplomat's mind, an idea so disturbing that he had to consult a map of the region without delay.

The door of the room opened and a small, puny man entered. He wore a length of multicoloured cloth which left his shoulders bare. His hair was held in a bandeau; round his neck he had a simple silver necklace and on his left elbow a bracelet.

'My name is Hattusilis, and I am the brother of Muwatallis, Emperor of Hatti.'

Ahsha lost his composure for a few moments. Was the fatigue of his journey and his lovemaking making him hallucinate?

'You are not dreaming, Ahsha. I am pleased to make the acquaintance of the head of the Egyptian diplomatic service and a close friend of Ramses the Great.'

'You, in Amurru . . . '

'You are my prisoner, Ahsha. Any attempt at escape will be in vain. My men have captured the Egyptian officers, your crew and your ship. Hatti is once again in control of Amurru. Ramses badly underestimated our ability to react. In my capacity as commander of the coalition defeated at Kadesh, I suffered an intolerable humiliation. If it had not been for Ramses' tremendous wrath and his ridiculous, insane courage, I would have wiped out the Egyptian army. That is why I had to prove my true valour as rapidly as possible and intervene effectively while you were resting on your laurels.'

'The Prince of Amurru has betrayed us again.'

'Benteshina sells himself to the highest bidder; that's only to be expected of him. This province will never again return to Egypt's fold.'

'You are forgetting Ramses' fury.'

'On the contrary, I fear it. So I shall avoid provoking it.'

'As soon as he learns that the Hittite army is occupying

Amurru he will intervene. And I am convinced that you have not had time to reform an army capable of resisting him.'

Hattusilis smiled. 'Your perspicacity is formidable, but it will be useless, for Ramses will not know the truth until it is too late.'

'My silence will be eloquent.'

'You will not be silent, Ahsha. You are going to write a reassuring letter to Ramses, explaining that your mission is progressing as anticipated and that your instructors are doing good work.'

'In other words, our armies will advance confidently towards Amurru and fall into a trap.'

'That is indeed part of my plan.'

Ahsha tried to read Hattusilis's thoughts. He was not unaware of the good and bad qualities of the people of the area, their aspirations and their grudges.

The truth dawned on him. 'Another base alliance with the Bedouin!'

'There is no better solution,' agreed Hattusilis.

'They are looters and murderers.'

'I am aware of that, but they will be useful to me to sow trouble among Egypt's allies.'

'Is it wise to confide such secrets to me?'

'Soon it will be a question not of secrets but of facts. Get dressed, Ahsha, and follow me. I have a letter to dictate to you.'

'And if I refuse to write it?'

'You will die.'

'I am ready to die.'

'No, you are not. A man who loves women as you do is not ready to renounce the pleasures of life for a cause lost in advance. You will write this letter, Ahsha, because you want to live.'

The Egyptian hesitated. 'And if I obey?'

'You will be detained in a prison that I hope will be

comfortable, and you will survive.'

'Why not do away with me?'

'In delicate negotiations, the head of the Egyptian diplomatic service will be a useful bargaining counter. That was the case at Kadesh, you remember.'

'You are asking me to betray Ramses?'

'You are acting under constraint. That is not really betrayal.'

'You will spare my life – do you expect me to believe that?'

'You have my word, before the gods of Hatti, in the name of the emperor.'

'I will write that letter. Hattusilis.'

60

The seven daughters of the priest of Midian, one of whom was the wife of Moses, were drawing water from the well to water their father's sheep from the drinking troughs, when a dozen Bedouin rode headlong into the oasis. Bearded, armed with bows and daggers, they seemed to intend no good.

The sheep scattered, the seven young women ran to hide in the tents, the old man leaned on his staff and faced the newcomers.

'Are you the chief of this community?'

'I am.'

'How many able-bodied men are there here?'

'Myself and a herdsman.'

'Canaan is going to rise up against Pharaoh with the support of the Hittites. Thanks to them we shall have the use of much land. All the tribes must help us fight the Egyptians.'

'We are not a tribe but a family which has dwelt here in peace for many generations.'

'Bring the herdsman to me.'

'He is in the mountains.'

The Bedouin consulted among themselves.

'We shall be back,' declared their spokesman. 'When we do, we shall take him with us and he will fight. Otherwise we shall fill up your well and burn down your tents.'

*

Moses returned to his tent at nightfall. His wife and father-in-law rose.

'Where have you been?' asked his wife.

'In the holy place on the mountain, where the God of our fathers appears to me. He spoke to me of the affliction of the Hebrews in Egypt, my people who are subjected to Pharaoh's authority, my brothers who lament and wish to be delivered from oppression.'

'There is a much more serious matter,' said the priest of Midian. 'Some Bedouin were here, wanting to recruit you with all the able-bodied men in the area, to take part in the revolt against Pharaoh.'

'That is madness. Ramses will crush this sedition.'

'Even if the Hittites side with the rebels?'

'But they were defeated at Kadesh.'

'That is what the caravaneers say,' admitted the priest, 'but can we trust them? You must hide, Moses.'

'Did the Bedouin threaten you?'

'If you don't fight with them, they will kill us all.'

Zipporah, Moses' wife, hung on his neck. 'You're going to leave, aren't you?'

'God has ordered me to return to Egypt.'

'You will be tried and condemned!' the old priest reminded him.

'I shall leave with you,' decided Zipporah, 'and we shall take our son.'

'The journey may be dangerous.'

'I don't care. You are my husband, I am your wife.'

The old priest sat down, in deep distress.

'Set your mind at rest. God will watch over your oasis. The Bedouin will not return,' Moses predicted.

'What does that matter, since I shall never see you again, you, my daughter and your child?'

'You speak the truth. Embrace us and bid us farewell, and let us entrust our souls to the Lord.'

*

In Pi-Ramses, preparations were under way in the temples for the midwinter festivities, in the course of which the secret energy of the universe would regenerate the statues and the objects used during the rituals. The force that animated them was exhausted, and it was the duty of the royal couple to commune with the light and to see that the offerings rose up to Ma'at, who held the universe together.

The victory at Kadesh had reassured the Egyptians. No one any longer believed the Hittite army to be invincible; everyone knew that Ramses had driven back the enemy and preserved his people's day-to-day happiness.

The capital was growing in beauty; the principal temples, those of Amon, Ptah, Ra and Set were springing up to the rhythm of the stonecutters' mallets and chisels; villas for the nobles and high officials rivalled in beauty those of Thebes and Memphis; in the port there was continuous activity; the warehouses were overflowing with wealth, and the special workshop was busy producing the blue glazed tiles that adorned the façades of the houses, giving Pi-Ramses its name of the City of Turquoise.

One of the favourite pastimes of the capital's inhabitants was to go sailing on the canals, which abounded in fish, and indulge in some angling. Munching on honey-sweet apples from one of the orchards in the rich countryside, the fishermen would drift with the current, admiring the flower gardens beside the canal, the flights of ibis, pink flamingos and pelicans, and often forgetting the fish that had taken the hook.

Plying the oars himself, Ramses had brought Meritamon and Kha, who had not failed to tell his little sister about his encounter with the cobra. The lad told his story calmly, without exaggeration. After a few hours' relaxation, Ramses intended to join Nefertari and Iset the Fair, whom the Great Royal Wife had invited to dine.

Ahmeni was waiting at the landing-stage. It took something serious to get him to leave his office.

'A letter from Ahsha.'

'Disturbing?'

'Read it yourself.'

Ramses handed the two children over to Nedjem, who always feared some accident might happen during these boat trips, and even during excursions outside the palace gardens. The minister took the children by the hand while Ramses unrolled the papyrus Ahmeni passed him.

> *To the Pharaoh of Egypt from Ahsha, the minister for foreign affairs.*
>
> *In accordance with His Majesty's orders, I met Benteshina, Prince of Amurru, who honoured me with the warmest possible welcome. Our drill officers, headed by a royal scribe, educated like you and me at the Academy in Thebes, have begun training the Amurrite army. As we assumed, the Hittites retreated further to the north, after their defeat at Kadesh. Nevertheless, we must not relax our vigilance. The local forces will not be sufficient if there is any future attempt at invasion. So it is essential to send a well-armed regiment as soon as possible, in order to set up a defensive base which will guarantee a lasting peace and the safety of our country.*
>
> *May Pharaoh continue to enjoy excellent health.*

The king rolled up the document. 'It is certainly Ahsha's handwriting.'

'I agree, but . . . '

'It was certainly Ahsha who wrote this – but under constraint.'

'That's what I think, too,' agreed Ahmeni. 'He would never have written that you and he had studied at the Academy in Thebes!'

'No, because we were at Memphis. And Ahsha has an excellent memory.'

'What can this mistake mean?'

'That he is a prisoner in Amurru.'

'Could Prince Benteshina have gone mad?'

'No, he too must be under constraint, no doubt after having traded his support.'

'Are we to understand . . . ?

'That the Hittites have made a lightning counter-attack' was Ramses' opinion. 'They have seized Amurru and laid a new trap for us. If it hadn't been for Ahsha's quick wit, Muwatallis would have had his revenge.'

'Do you think Ahsha is still alive?'

'I don't know, Ahmeni. With Serramanna's help, I shall immediately prepare an elite raiding force. If our friend is a prisoner, we shall free him.'

When Pharaoh ordered the head foreman of the foundry to resume intensive production of offensive and defensive weapons, the information spread through the capital in a few hours, and throughout the whole of Egypt in a few days.

Why hide one's head in the sand? The victory at Kadesh had not been sufficient to break the Hittites' will to conquer. The four barracks in Pi-Ramses were put in a state of alert, and the soldiers understood that it would not be long before they set out again for the north to resume the battle.

For one whole day and night, Ramses remained shut up alone in his office. At dawn he climbed up to the terrace to watch his protecting day-star being born again after the desperate battle with the dragon of darkness.

On the low wall in the eastern corner of the terrace sat Nefertari, so pure and beautiful in the rosy light of the dawn.

Ramses clasped her tightly in his arms. 'I thought that the victory at Kadesh would have opened up an era of peace, but I was over-confident. Around us prowl shadowy figures:

Muwatallis; Shaanar, who may still be alive; that Libyan sorcerer, who has eluded us; Moses, of whom I've found no trace; Ahsha, a prisoner or dead in Amurru. Will we be strong enough to resist the tempest?'

'It is your task to remain at the helm of the ship, whatever the force of the wind. You have neither the time nor the right to doubt. If the current is against you, you will tackle it – we shall tackle it.'

The sun burst forth above the horizon, its first rays falling on the Great Royal Wife and Ramses, the Son of the Light.